Migrants and Militants

PRINCETON STUDIES IN MUSLIM POLITICS

Dale F. Eickelman and James Piscatori, Editors

Migrants and Militants

FUN AND

URBAN VIOLENCE

IN PAKISTAN

Oskar Verkaaik

PRINCETON UNIVERSITY PRESS

PRINCETON AND OXFORD

Copyright © 2004 by Princeton University Press
Published by Princeton University Press, 41 William Street,
Princeton, New Jersey 08540
In the United Kingdom: Princeton University Press,
3 Market Place, Woodstock, Oxfordshire OX20 1SY

Library of Congress Cataloging-in-Publication Data

Verkaaik, Oskar.
Migrants and militants: *fun* and urban violence in Pakistan / Oskar Verkaaik.
p.   cm   —(Princeton studies in Muslim politics)
Includes bibliographical references and index.
ISBN 0-691-11708-X (cl : alk. paper)—ISBN 0-691-11709-8 (pb. : alk. paper)
1. Muhajir (Pakistani people)—Politics and government. 2. Muhajir Qaumi Movement.
3. Political violence—Pakistan. 4. Islam and politics—Pakistan. 5. Ethnicity—Pakistan.
6. Pakistan—Politics and government. I. Title. II. Series.
DS380.M83V47 2004
322.4′2′0882971—dc21   2003054716

British Library Cataloging-in-Publication Data is available.

This book has been composed in Galliard

Printed on acid-free paper. ∞

www.pupress.princeton.edu

Printed in the United States of America

10 9 8 7 6 5 4 3 2 1

Contents

Maps and Illustrations

Foreword

SINCE at least the late 1980s Pakistan has been locked in acute political turmoil. The seemingly perpetual struggle between Benazir Bhutto and Nawaz Sharif, universal charges of corruption, bitter multiparty rivalries, the fear of Talibanization, and the omnipresence of the security services and military have provided the setting in which its Muslim politics have unfolded. A marked aspect of this has been contestation over identity: what does it mean to be Pakistani a half century after the founding of the land of the pure? "Islam" provides symbolic constancy, but what form it takes depends on a constellation of factors, notably including a new ethnic assertiveness among the Muhajirs, or original migrants from India, who sense that "their" Pakistan has been taken from them.

Oskar Verkaaik has produced the first full-scale ethnography of Muhajir political mobilization and dissent. Based on fieldwork in a charged neighborhood of Hyderabad where ethnic conflict, even ethnic cleansing, has occurred, he unravels the rationale behind the rise, unexpected success, and decline of the dominant political force, the Muhajir Qaumi Movement (MQM). Established in 1984, it soon engaged in violence against Pakhtuns, Punjabis, and Sindhis but also acquired the discipline of a political party, which provided dramatic electoral victories. It drew its strength from the discontents of urban male youth and had an appeal that cut across class lines. It espoused a "modern" and at times mystical Islam that was at once different from the modernist-scripturalist Islam of official state ideology *and* self-consciously bound up with affirmations of ethnic solidarity.

Verkaaik minutely documents the evolving self-image of MQM adherents. Central to this was a sense of fun, a kind of playfulness and irreverence, which took the form of practical jokes, mockery, embarrassing opponents, and small acts of vandalism. Although others have invoked the ludic dimensions of Muslim history, whether present in festivals (such as post-Ramadan celebrations), or an Andalusian live-and-let-live spirit, "fun" is scarcely the term that jumps to mind when discussing a politically charged "Islamic" movement today. But Verkaaik explains that this became a marker of identity that separated the young men from older generations and other ethnic groups, and he carries the analysis further than others by demonstrating that fun naturally moved into violence. The two kinds of activity formed part of a continuum of provocation and transgression, both in protest against an unacceptable social position. It is thus not surprising that, at the same time as they stressed their playful aspects, MQM members argued that they embraced sacrifice and, if necessary, martyrdom. They even went so far as to appropriate the state's charge against them and to pronounce themselves "terrorists." This label, ostensibly intended to delegitimize, became an instrument of communal pride.

Nostalgia suffused the movement, with constituents investing the move from India to Pakistan in 1947 with mythic qualities. It became nothing less than an invocation of the Prophet's *hijra* (migration) from Mecca to Medina, and the seminal act of creation of the new Pakistani state. Muhajirs were thus operating simultaneously as the carriers of Islamic tradition and of nationalism. Yet they were also forward-looking. Verkaaik makes clear that this was not the story of a middle-class counter-elite movement. Rather, the MQM spoke to the lower middle classes as well as the educated professionals and sought to combat state nationalism that had developed over time by taking their issues to the street and informal neighborhood meeting points, not formal assembly halls or campuses. The old elites, whether identified with landed interests, the military, or the Islamic "establishment" as represented by the perennial Jam'iat-i Islami, were fiddling while Rome was burning. The entrenched disputes of the post-colonial elites were responsible for the fragmentation of the state, but, equally dangerously, some now opted out entirely by retreating into the safer, and more profitable, realm of business. More recently, part of the MQM constituency has revived ideas of diaspora, seeking inspiration or the better life in the Arabian Peninsula or the West. But throughout the period of its maximum impact in the 1990s, a simple, although vague, vision sustained followers—a "politics beyond politics."

Oskar Verkaaik skillfully extracts from this rich ethnography several points of larger significance to the study of Muslim politics. First, he instructively questions the conventional wisdom that radically separates the presumed universalism of Islam from the specificity of ethnicity. Pious literature may well have reinforced the assumption that "Muslim" as a category is incompatible with Pakhtun, Berber, Javenese, or indeed Arab. Yet this work points to the fluidity of borders and the ambiguities of identity. In the case of the Muhajirs with their particular worldview, ethnicity became an effective way to organize without seeming disloyal to Islam. This case study suggests that an ethnicized Islam may help to explain political dynamics more persuasively than such customary factors as kinship, language, or territory.

Second, Verkaaik develops a fresh, constructivist understanding of the state as a component of Muslim politics. Rather than accept the traditional division between state and society, he reports that the state was far from being viewed as neutral or distant. It was, by way of contrast, what social forces made of it. The Muhajirs were committed to the concept of Pakistan, but resentful that other ethnic groups had seemingly captured it. Simply put, their intention was to recreate the idea of Pakistan in their own image. If Muslim politics involves contestation over symbolic production, then the Pakistani case demonstrates that the state is both a producer of symbols, as expected, and itself constituted. The latter is often overlooked, particularly in much of the democratization literature, which often juxtaposes a rooted, vibrant civil society with a curiously deracinated state.

Third, this volume broadens the range of actors of Muslim politics. It suggests that the exuberance and disillusionment of urban young men are as relevant as the social position and attitudes of religious bureaucrats, Sufi adepts, Islamist activists, religious scholars (*ulama*), and non-traditionally educated intellectuals. The young undereducated and underemployed are found in other societies, but as the *hittistes* of Algeria demonstrate, more organized groups have often manipulated them. In the following pages, however, we find a movement centered on the young men's sense of "dangerous play"—a proprietary approach to social violence that is generational and gendered. In addition to giving agency to individuals normally invisible to the outside observer, Verkaaik has implicitly reminded us that the gender politics of Islam is far more complex than is often depicted and the question of veiling suggests.

Migrants and Militants is a multilayered and sophisticated study that provides a unique insight into a local Pakistani community that has been riven by conflict and has played a defining role on the national stage. In its nuances can also be found the political significance of what might be called a Muslim ethnicity.

James Piscatori
Dale F. Eickelman

Preface

THIS BOOK is the result of my long fascination with ethnic-religious politics in Pakistan and more in particular with a large group of migrants known as Muhajirs who after independence in 1947 left their homes in various regions of India to travel to the new Muslim state of Pakistan. Most of them now live in Karachi and Hyderabad, two large cities in the southern province of Sindh. As a group, Muhajirs initially enjoyed a favorable position and reputation in Pakistan as people who had made the sacrifice of migration in order to live in the new Muslim state. They had a large say in the Muslim League, the party led by Muhammad Ali Jinnah that had successfully worked for the establishment of Pakistan. The paradox of Pakistan was that most devoted supporters and members of the Muslim League lived in Muslim minority provinces in India, which would never be part of Pakistan, whereas the support for the Muslim League in the provinces that would become Pakistan was limited and lukewarm. The strongest supporters of the new state of Pakistan, therefore, lived outside the borders of the new state. As a result, the new Pakistani nation was initially imagined in traditions of travel, exodus, and diaspora. It was also a state founded on the basis of religion. Both of these aspects—diaspora and religion—have been extremely important in Pakistani national identity, which makes Pakistan to some extent comparable to Israel. For Muhajirs, migrants from India, they are even more important.

My interest in Muhajirs began in the late 1980s when a new political party was established that called itself the Muhajir Qaumi Movement (MQM), or Muhajir Ethnic Movement. It soon became one of the most remarkable examples of political mobilization in postcolonial South Asia. The party successfully presented itself as representative of a large segment of the population living in vast urban areas. It was especially popular among the urban youth. In that sense, it resembled several other popular religious-political movements that have arisen in the last two decades of the twentieth century, such as the Hindu nationalist movement in India or several Islamist movements in the Muslim world. Moreover, the party was involved in large-scale incidents of ethnic-religious violence and has more recently been branded as a "terrorist group." During my long engagement with the Muhajir Qaumi Movement, I have come to the conclusion that it is an exponent of and a contributor to a larger transformation of politics in South Asia, for which Thomas Blom Hansen has coined the term "democratic revolution." This includes the promotion of a new style of politics and new forms of political mobilization, responding to an urban youth culture, which profoundly differs from the state nationalism promoted by the established elite. This book will focus on three very different aspects of that urban youth culture, which I have found most remarkable and significant: violence; Islam; and a ludic, unbalancing aspect for which I use the term *fun*. This book is an ethnography of how these aspects of an emerging urban youth culture have influenced the MQM and changed the style of Pakistani politics.

I have been engaged in the study of the Muhajir Qaumi Movement since 1986, when I first visited Pakistan as a journalist. Later I studied anthropology at the University of Amsterdam, where I received much help from Henk Schulte Nordholt in my ongoing study of Muhajirs. The fulltime research for this book was made possible by grants from the Netherlands Foundation for the Advancement of Tropical Research (WOTRO) in The Hague. Between 1995 and 1999 I had the privilege to work on this research as an affiliate of the Amsterdam School for Social Science Research (ASSR). I thank the staff of the ASSR for its academically stimulating milieu. I am especially indebted to Peter van der Veer. His writings on religion and nationalism in South Asia have been a pertinent intellectual impetus for my own work. I also remain grateful to the late Jan van der Linden, whose local knowledge of Karachi and Hyderabad was gigantic, and I am fortunate that he was willing to share it with me.

I continued my studies as a fellow at the Globalization Project of the University of Chicago, where I enjoyed the inspiring company of Arjun Appadurai and Vijayanthi Rao. Most recently I have been working on this project as a researcher and lecturer at the Research Center for Religion and Society of the University of Amsterdam, where I have received much support from my colleagues Gerd Baumann, Peter van Rooden, Peter Pels, Birgit Meyer, Mattijs van de Port, Patsy Spyer, and Ingrid van den Broek.

Earlier drafts of chapters have been presented in several seminars and discussed with various scholars, including Hamza Alavi, Hamida Khuhro, Nabi Bakhsh Baloch, Ibrahim Joyo, Durreshahwar Syed, Arif Hasan, Tasneem Siddiqi, Muhammad Khalid Masud, Jan Breman, Michael Gilsenan, Pnina Werbner, Thomas Blom Hansen, Werner Schiffauer, Immanuel Siwan, Kamran Asdar Ali, Barbara Metcalf, Paul Brass, Anton Blok, Jojada Verrips, Thijl Sunier, Mahmoud Alinejad, Halleh Ghorashi, Vazira Zamindar, Shoma Munshi, Gautam Ghosh, Christophe Jaffrelot, Laurent Gayer, Muhammad Waseem, Allen Feldman, and many others. I am grateful to all of them for their comments, insights, and criticism. Petra Dekker helped me with the maps and illustrations.

I am indebted to the anonymous readers of the manuscript for their incisive comments and I am grateful to Mary Murrell and Sara Lerner of Princeton University Press and Jennifer Backer for their efficient and careful attention to the manuscript. Of course, I alone remain responsible for inconsistencies and inaccuracies.

Abbreviations

APMSF	All Pakistan Muslim Student Federation
APMSO	All Pakistan Muhajir Student Organization
IJI	Islami Jumhuri Ittehad (Islamic Democratic Alliance)
IJT	Islami Jam'iat-i Tulabah
ISI	Inter Services Intelligence
JI	Jam'iat-i Islami
JUI	Jam'iat-i 'Ulama-i Islam
JUP	Jam'iat-i 'Ulama-i Pakistan
MIT	Muhajir Ittehad Tehreek
ML	Muslim League
MPPM	Muhajir Punjabi Pakhtun Movement
MQM	Muhajir Qaumi Movement, Muttehida Qaumi Movement
MRC	Muhajir Rabita Council
MRD	Movement for the Restoration of Democracy
NWFP	Northwest Frontier Province
PML	Pakistan Muslim League
PPP	Pakistan People's Party
PSF	Pakistan Student Federation
PTV	Pakistan Television
SNA	Sindh National Alliance
STPP	Sindh Taraqqi Pasand Party (Sindh Progressive Party)

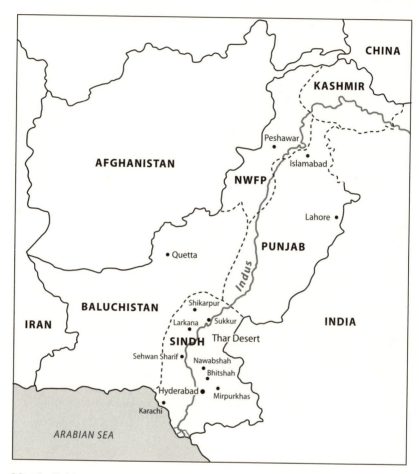

MAP 1. Pakistan

Migrants and Militants

Introduction

ON SEPTEMBER 26, 2001—fifteen days after the suicidal attacks on the Twin Towers and Pentagon—a large public gathering was held in Karachi, Pakistan, to demonstrate the city's solidarity with the thousands of victims in the United States and to offer sympathy and support for the United States-led campaign against terrorism that would soon lead to the bombing of Taliban and Al Qaeda targets in Afghanistan. In the early days after September 11, when international television networks were quick to broadcast any public articulation of anti-American or pro-Taliban feelings, this huge gathering, reportedly two hundred thousand people large, was a rare sign of public support for the pro-United States stance of the Pakistani government led by General Musharraf. A two-minute silence was observed out of respect for the victims in the United States, followed by speeches proclaiming Karachi a liberal-minded city with no place for *jihadi* groups. A resolution was issued stating that the people of Pakistan in general, and of the southern province of Sindh in particular, believe in religious harmony and condemn any kind of religious extremism.

Although this "rally against terrorism" failed to make headlines in the international press, it was remarkable for two reasons. First, it was held in Liaqatabad, an inner-city neighborhood of Karachi, which flaunts a reputation for its hard-boiled anti-state militancy. In the 1960s it had been the site of anti-government riots, playing a prominent role in the revolt against then president General Muhammad Ayub Khan. In the 1980s, when Karachi became notorious for its violence among various ethnic groups, Liaqatabad virtually became a "no-go-area" for both non-inhabitants and the police. In 1992 when the army was sent into Karachi to put an end to the so-called kalashnikov culture, which included political assassination, nepotism, blackmail, burglary, and car theft, the army's intelligence services identified Liaqatabad as a major "terrorist den" and a "hotbed of anti-state extremists." Military and paramilitary forces had a hard time fighting the armed groups of political activists from this area. And yet the largest demonstration of public support for General Musharraf during those troublesome days following the attack on New York and Washington was held in this very place.

Second, it was held by a political party called the MQM or the Muttehida Qaumi Movement (United National Movement). This party, formerly called the Muhajir Qaumi Movement (National Movement of Muhajirs), claimed to represent the Muhajir population of Pakistan, that is, the families of migrants who had traveled from India to Pakistan after independence in 1947. They were part of a mass migration of people following the partition of British India during which millions of Hindus and Sikhs traveled to India, and even more Muslims went in the opposite direction. A large portion of these migrants came from the eastern part of the Punjab and settled in the Pakistani part of that province, where they quickly assimilated and were no longer recognized as migrants. In the southern province of Sindh, however, most migrants spoke Urdu and hailed from Uttar Pradesh, Delhi, Rajasthan, Bombay, and Andhra Pradesh. Most of them settled in Karachi, as well as Hyderabad, the second largest city of Sindh. Today approximately 50 percent of the population of both cities, housing twelve million and two million people respectively, is Muhajir. For a long time the most loyal supporters of the "Islamic" parties, such as the Jam'iat-i Islami, that propagated the introduction of an Islamic Republic of Pakistan as well as the implementation of the *shari'at* or Islamic law were found among these Muhajirs of Sindh. But that was before the MQM was founded in 1984. Once established, the party embarked on what soon became one of the most remarkable examples of political mobilization in the history of Pakistan. In 1988 the young party, led by largely unknown young men from insignificant family background, swept the polls in Karachi and Hyderabad, luring the population of both cities away from the Islamic parties. Instead the party declared that Muhajirs were an "ethnic group" or *qaum*, on par with other ethnic groups like the Sindhi, Punjabi, Pakhtun, or Baluchi, and entitled to the same rights. It also proclaimed Muhajirs to be essentially urban, middle class, liberal, and broad-minded, and as such opposed to both fundamentalism and feudalism. Under the banner of this new political identity, the MQM in urban Sindh not only won several elections in a row, but also enabled groups of young party members in city areas like Liaqatabad to terrorize their neighborhoods and rule them like a state within a state. Paradoxically, the city areas that used to yield considerable support for the Islamic parties were now not only known in Karachi as places of thugs and terrorists, but they also housed the most vocal critics of religious extremism and political Islam, staging a rally against terrorism at a time when the public opinion in Pakistan as a whole showed little love or admiration for the United States and the pro-United States regime in Islamabad.

This anecdote shows how inconsistent, complex, and paradoxical politics in Pakistan can be. No clear or fixed boundaries can be drawn between the oppositional categories that are widely believed to inform Pakistani politics, such as ethnicity versus Islam, terrorist violence versus democratic politics, or modernity and liberalism versus Islamic fundamentalism. This book departs from the observation that these seemingly clear-cut oppositional pairs often conceal the internal complexities and ambiguities of

Pakistan's identity politics. Forces that are seen as dichotomous in fact often stand in a much more dynamic and complex relationship to each other. For many Muhajirs, the Islamism of the Jam'iat-i Islami, for instance, does not have to be radically opposed to, say, General Musharraf's authoritarian liberalism, as both are rooted in (albeit different) traditions of Islamic modernism and revivalism. Violence, even terrorist violence or ethnic cleansing, is only partially in opposition to democratic politics. As I will argue in later chapters, the MQM's electoral success was as much the result of the non-elitist political style of its leaders during election campaigns as of the party's involvement in ethnic riots. But perhaps most problematic of all is the dichotomy between ethnicity and religion. As these are the most crucial forces of identity politics and political mobilization in the history of Pakistan, they are also key issues in this book. Both inside and outside Pakistan, it is quite common to consider Islam and ethnicity as mutually exclusive objects of identification. Islam's claim to universalism, symbolized in the *hijra* or Islamic exodus that gave birth to the Muslim brotherhood or *'umma*, is often mentioned to argue that Islam transcends ethnic differences. In this view, Islam is considered an integrating force rather than a fragmenting one. This book, however, will show that Islam and ethnicity are often intermingled. The boundaries of ethnic groups are often drawn on the basis of particularistic trends and traditions within Islam. We will see, for instance, that Sindhis portray themselves as being inclined to mysticism and esoteric Sufism, as opposed to, say, Muhajirs, who are believed to be more orthodox. Similarly, the Pakhtun, who made up a large proportion of the pro-Taliban protesters in the public demonstrations in the fall of 2001, are typically depicted as staunch and uncompromising followers of the *shari'at* as well as tribal laws, compared to which the urban Muhajirs appear broad-minded. It was precisely this ethnic self-image of liberal moderates that the organizers and participants of the rally against terrorism wanted to show to the audience in Karachi and beyond.

This book is an ethnography of Pakistani identity politics, including ethnic and religious violence, which means that it seeks to deconstruct, defy, and go beyond the somewhat deceptive dichotomies that paint an oversimplified picture of the many paradoxes, ambiguities, and internal complexities at play. This book focuses on the MQM. This movement provides an excellent case study because it reveals the ongoing struggle with ethnicity and Islam in Pakistan. This book will also document and analyze how and why ethnic-religious identity politics can escalate into various forms of violence, such as vandalism, ethnic riots, anti-state militancy, terrorism, and state power abuse.

In 1984, during the heyday of the military regime of General Zia-ul Haq when virtually all political activities were banned, the MQM was formed by a group of former students who had earlier founded a student organization named the All Pakistan Muhajir Student Organization. It radically changed the political spectrum in urban Sindh and brought to power young politicians from the vast inner-city areas of Karachi and Hyderabad that the other political parties had mostly neglected. It was not only a revolt—and often a violent one—of the lower class and the low caste but also spearheaded by the urban youth. It helped spoil the relationship between Muhajirs and other ethnic groups in Karachi and Hyderabad, notably the "autochthonous" Sindhis as well as the Pakhtun, who arrived more recently from the northern areas of Pakistan. The MQM was the third-largest party in the national assembly of Pakistan, and it was a coalition partner in various governments in the 1990s. Its followers have, however, also been branded as "terrorists" and have been heavily persecuted by the army and the paramilitary. As a result its charismatic leader, Altaf Hussain, has been exiled in London since 1992, and it is unlikely that he will return soon.

The MQM has not only been shaped by the paradoxes of Pakistani politics, it has also added its own paradoxes, or even contradictions, to an already complex political landscape. Perhaps the most puzzling has been its combination of "fun" and militancy. As an anthropologist engaged with the Muhajir Qaumi Movement since the late 1980s, I have tried to study the MQM not just as a political party that takes part in elections, negotiates with other parties, and in doing so responds to a political culture shaped by the complementary forces of Islam and ethnicity. My ambition was also to write an ethnography of the MQM as an urban movement. One of my main concerns was why so many young Muhajirs, most of them male, joined the MQM and made it into a true mass movement. This is a question that cannot simply be answered in terms of an already existing political identity among the Muhajir youth. Although MQM supporters regularly complain about discrimination against Muhajirs (for instance in language policies or the reservation and allocation of government jobs), this is rarely their main reason for joining the movement. Similarly, it is too simple to see the MQM merely or primarily as an expression of an upcoming middle class frustrated in its effort to get access to state power and government jobs. More important, the MQM constituted for its supporters both a spectacle and a sacrifice. It was an adventure and an excellent pastime to belong to the movement and take part in its public gatherings, which were often described to me as joyful and liberating. The MQM seemed to have offered the joy of provocation and transgression. The powerful were ridiculed, social conventions were temporarily set aside, and ethnic and religious stereotypes were uprooted through role inversion and grotesque exaggeration. This ludic character of the MQM often went hand in hand with the vandalism carried out by the young male peer groups, that is, locally organized groups of friends, which played a major role in the recruitment and mobilization of new party members. All this was expressed in the term *fun*, an emic term, adopted by the young Muhajirs like many other English words. *Fun* was a boundary marker, which set the MQM apart from the established political parties, condemned for their grave, solemn, hollow, ideological language. *Fun* was even, to some extent, considered a feature of Muhajirness, part of the metropolitan, cosmopolitan Muhajir culture and a far cry from the supposedly rural dullness of other ethnic groups. Yet at the same time the MQM was also deadly serious to its followers. It evoked Islamic and nationalist traditions of martyrdom and sacrifice in the face of state persecution and tyranny. It revived a diasporic identity of Muhajirs as persecuted people throughout history in search of a homeland. Many young Muhajirs were willing to become full-time militant activists willing to kill and risk death, exile, torture, and long-term jail sentences for their political convictions.

I take this paradox of *fun* and violence as the lens through which to look at the MQM and the changing political culture in Pakistan of the past fifteen years. This enables me to focus on an important feature the MQM shares with other present-day urban political movements, such as the Hindu nationalist movement in India and possibly several Islamist movements in parts of the Muslim world—namely its ambiguous relationship to a political culture I will call postcolonial state nationalism. This is a far from monolithic way of talking about the nation, its relation to religion, the place of ethnic groups within the nation, as well as several issues that have been on the political agenda for the last decade, including corruption, terrorism, and democracy or politics (*siyasat*) itself. State nationalism is, as I will argue in the next chapter, a form of ethnonationalism, taking a perceived primordial bond of the people as the essence of the nation, and in that sense it is different from Anderson's notion of "official nationalism" that takes the state as the center from which the nation emerges (Anderson 1991: 86). As I use the term, state nationalism is a state-promoted form of ethnonationalism, taking into account that it is notoriously difficult to talk about the state as a clear-cut entity neatly separated from society, as I will argue more fully in chapter 6. The main point about state nationalism is that it was developed in the dual process of state formation and nation building after independence, although it of course fed on earlier intellectual efforts to modernize Islam and to think about the distinct place of Muslims in India. It was and continues to be produced by groups of people occupying or aspiring to occupy positions within the state apparatus. To some extent the MQM is a product of this state nationalism, and a rather radical one to boot. Its ethnic language, for instance, takes the ethnic undercurrent of the Pakistani political culture to its extreme. As an urban movement, however, the MQM is also part of a new phase of identity politics. This includes the emergence of popular movements that, although never untouched by state nationalism, are sufficiently independent of it to introduce a new style of democratic politics, plebeian, streetwise, low caste. In that sense, a new political style is introduced that is different from the postcolonial style disseminated by the main established political parties—such as the Pakistan People's Party and the Pakistan Muslim League—as well as the army. As an urban movement, the MQM operates in public spaces such as parks, bazaars, and gyms, where it contributes to what I call street nationalism or a nationalism of the neighborhood. This street nationalism of local groups of young, male MQM supporters is characterized by key values such as competitive masculinity and physicality, displacing the high cultural Islamic modernist values of state nationalism. I believe that the MQM's success can partly be explained by its ability to speak both the language of the state and the language of the street.

This intermingling of both forms of nationalism significantly changes the democratic process. It challenges the hegemony of the state in the formation of political identities and shifts the site of contentious politics from the rural areas to the cities. Contrary to the 1960s and 1970s, when regional movements with a strong rural base were the first to contest the authoritarian modernism of the postcolonial state, today's protest movements are primarily based in the underprivileged sections of large cities, where often more than half of the population is under twenty-five years old and state surveillance is often incomplete. Hence, it is important to focus on urban popular culture, particularly urban youth culture, to understand why movements such as the MQM can be so attractive to young city dwellers. There are several traditions of research that may be helpful. First there are the social historical studies on working-class culture, including the work of E. P. Thompson and Roy Rosenzweig. In both cases we see specific public spaces of leisure such as taverns and saloons, strictly separated from working spaces, become centers of "sub-political consciousness" (Thompson 1964: 55–59). This semi-public sphere of leisure could become a hotbed of an alternative popular culture (Rosenzweig 1983). Sports also offered public opportunities for performing an urban popular culture (MacClancy 1996). In a comparable argument on the construction of urban popular culture in twentieth-century North India, Nita Kumar (1988) argues that particular forms of leisure became important markers of the social boundary separating the common people from the elite. Pnina Werbner, in a study on young Pakistani immigrants in the UK, makes a similar argument about urban popular culture as implicitly subversive of elitist and state-promoted ideology:

> Unlike high cultural Islamic traditions, South Asian popular culture is "fun": it celebrates the body and bodily expressiveness or sensuality through sport, music, dance and laughter. If Islamic high culture is controlled, rule-bound and cere-

bral, South Asian popular culture is transgressive, openly alluding to uncontrollable feelings, sex and other bodily functions. It glorifies physical strength, beauty and prowess. It mobilizes satire, parody, masquerade or pastiche to comment on current affairs, to lampoon the powerful and venerable, to incorporate the foreign and the Other beyond the boundaries. (Werbner 1996: 91)

This focus on sport and leisure is instructive because, as we will see, the MQM recruited and mobilized its supporters in public spaces such as parks and gyms.

Second, in a different tradition of research on American metropolitan inner cities, which includes the work of W. F. Whyte (1940) and, more recently, Philippe Bourgois (1995), a picture of street culture emerges that is more violent, less organized, more racially and ethnically biased, and more excluded from mainstream society than early-modern working-class culture. In Bourgois's words, such a street culture is "a complex and conflictual web of beliefs, symbols, modes of interaction, values, and ideologies that have emerged in opposition to exclusion from mainstream society." It is "not a coherent, conscious universe of political opposition but, rather, a spontaneous set of rebellious practices that in the long term have emerged as an oppositional style" (Bourgois 1995: 8). As Sallie Westwood (1995) has argued in an article on racially organized inner-city areas in Leicester, such street cultures offer an alternative forum for attaining personal dignity and social prestige based on a somatic form of masculinity. Away from the permanent gaze of the state, inner-city enclaves frequently generate a masculine culture of physical strength and courage in opposition to partly condescending, partly anxious, partly jealous middle-class views on those enclaves as dangerous, chaotic, irrational, and sensual. Urban masculinity is also an important theme in Thomas Blom Hansen's work on the Hindu nationalist Shiv Sena movement in Bombay. Hansen focuses explicitly on the notion of masculinity as it is played out in the movement's rhetoric and recruitment strategies. In his view, young Hindu men seek to "recuperate" from the Muslim the image of masculinity. In Orientalist writings most Hindu groups were typically portrayed as soft and feminine, an image that reappears in postcolonial nationalist discourse. By employing an aggressively masculine rhetoric, a military style of drilling new recruits and eventually anti-Muslim violence, the movement gave young Hindu men the opportunity to liberate themselves from the feminine stigma (Hansen 1996b). This emphasis on the gendered notions of otherness is also relevant in the case of the MQM as young Muhajirs, according the ethnic stereotypes, can also be considered gentle, weak, unmanly city boys compared to the more robust rural Sindhis or Pakhtun.

A third aspect of this inner-city youth culture is its connection to global cultural trends to which young people are connected through the mass media. A growing body of work on the impact of globalization on the politics of identity shows that the homogenizing tendencies in the field of economics, international politics, and mass media do not necessarily lead to an uniformization in cultural styles and expressions. They instead intensify the production of locality and local identity in cultural terms (see, e.g., Appadurai 1996; Featherstone 1990; Meyer and Geschiere 1999). In order to emphasize the interconnectedness of local identity and cosmopolitan cultural forms, Appadurai and Breckenridge (1988) have proposed to use the term "public culture" rather than "popular culture" as an analytical concept to study urban culture, partly because the notion of popular culture is traditionally related to the notion of cultural closure and therefore inadequate for today's urban cosmopolitanism and to get away from such dichotomies as high versus low culture or mass versus elite culture. Although I agree that the term *public culture* is better able to deal with "processes of globalization within which the local operates" (Pinney 2001: 8), I prefer to use the term *popular culture*, precisely because the MQM street culture is often self-consciously and explicitly anti-elitist. Part of this street culture is that it discursively revives the distinction between the folk and the elite, or the "common people" (*am log*) and the "Westernized rich," a distinction that finds its spatial expression in the gated communities that have created recreational, cultural, and educational enclaves that are almost entirely apart from the rest of the city. Neither these "ghettos of the rich" (Hasan 1997: 188) nor the inner-city streets, however, are sites of local, in the sense of enclosed, cultures. The globalization of the mass media in particular, including satellite television, video- and audiocassettes, mobile phones, and the Internet, connects the streets to a range of cosmopolitan cultural trends. The imaginary of the MQM martyr/terrorist, for instance, is a mixture of East Asian martial art traditions, Middle Eastern styles of Muslim militancy, Hollywood cinema, and Bollywood pop music.

The MQM has managed to successfully weave this latently subversive urban youth culture, with its aspects of gender, leisure, and global youth culture, into an ethnic-religious ideology of protest and revolt, thereby contributing to a political crisis that seriously undermines the legitimacy of the state. The recent career of the state in Pakistan can be compared to that of India, where the charisma of the state as once "spectacular, mysterious and distant" has vanished and been replaced by a less grand perception of the state as an everyday nuisance (Kaviraj 1997). State corruption has become one of the primary complaints in public debate, adding to a vigorous popular condemnation of politics as such. This has a lot to do with the inability of the state to monopolize the means of violence. As the state monopoly of coercion crumbles, "competing myths of authority and fear cluster around the real perpetrators of violence" (Hansen 2001: 63).

These "real perpetrators of violence" are most often local groups of strong-arm boys and their leaders. Obviously, the distrust of the state within inner-city areas grows with every story of state power abuse, human rights violation, extra-judicial persecution, and the omnipresence of secret intelligence services. However, this widespread suspicion of state forces and state officials does not necessarily indicate a popular rejection of state power as such. On the contrary, popular talk of corruption and state power not only indicates that state officials and politicians increasingly violate the rules of transparent and bureaucratic conduct but points to a growing public awareness of these very notions of transparency and impartiality that the modern state stands for (compare Gupta 1995; Parry 2000; Varma 1999). A growing line of work, indebted to Philip Abrams's distinction between the "state-idea" and the "state-system" (Abrams 1988), focuses on how the notion of bureaucratic state power can be used to legitimate as well as discredit the works of the state apparatus (Bourdieu 1999; Fuller and Harriss 2001; Hansen and Stepputat 2001; Mitchell 1991, 1999). Following this argument, it can be said that the crisis of governability in Pakistan is to a large extent due to a growing discrepancy between the rhetoric of accountability on the one hand and rampant corruption on the other. The public cynicism regarding politicians and state forces prevalent in the inner-city areas that make up the backbone of popular movements like the MQM, however, does not result in anarchy nor a renewed longing for authoritarianism. Rather, the public imagines itself increasingly in opposition to a state captured by corrupt politicians. This opposition between a fragmenting, corrupt state and the nation calling for the rule of law helps explain the public support for a "politics beyond politics," be it in the form of ethnic purity, an Islamic revolution, or even, insofar as the military has successfully portrayed itself as the only institution capable of discipline and integrity, a military takeover. All these options promise an alternative to the fussiness and fragmentation of democratic politics, but only the latter has actually been implemented, most recently in 1999.

The emphasis on urban youth culture in relation to present-day protest movements has several ramifications for ongoing debates on political—ethnic or religious—violence. It is primarily to this theoretical debate in anthropology and beyond that this book makes a contribution. In the 1990s a perspective on processes of othering and purification became the dominant approach in the anthropological study of political violence. This approach focuses on instances of ethnic and religious violence in times when both the state and the modern ideology of identity seem to be in crisis. Zygmunt Bauman, for instance, links ethnic or religious violence to the anxiety caused by a postmodern blurring of boundaries. Drawing on Mary Douglas's work on purity and danger (1966), Bauman argues that the progressive postmodern frustration of the modern project for clear-cut social categories results in an obstinate desire to purify the social world from the in-between (Bauman 1997). We find similar arguments on modernity and social purity in a range of recent studies on group violence. Liisa Malkki (1995), for instance, introduces the discrepancy between social classification and social displacement or exile to interpret ethnic violence in East Africa. E. Valentine Daniel argues that the violence between the Tamil and the Singalese in Sri Lanka signifies a growing feeling of uncertainty about the boundaries of ethnic-religious identities. "A people's willingness to fight for, kill for, and die for a reality is not a sign of their certainty of that reality but indicates that the reality in question has been brought under the crisis of radical doubt" (Daniel 1996: 67). Arjun Appadurai borrows from Baudrillard the term "implosion" to make a similar argument. For Baudrillard, "implosion" denotes the disappearance of the modern distinction between reality and its representation. According to Appadurai, ethnocide can be called an implosion of modern ideology insofar as it enables one to replace everyday ambiguity by the imagination of strict categorization. In the act of killing the other, his or her identity is restored and fixed once and for all. "In ethnocidal violence, what is sought is just that somatic stabilization that globalization—in a variety of ways—inherently makes impossible" (Appadurai 1999: 322). In all these cases, the crisis of modernity, and the modern state as the main promoter of ethnic and religious categories, is taken as a critical explanatory factor for ethnocide, genocide, or religious violence.

This approach is primarily concerned with the distorted relationship between violent groups and their "others." An older anthropological approach to political violence, however, focuses on social and cultural processes within groups of perpetrators of violence. This approach can be seen as an ongoing critical engagement with crowd theory as it was developed by Gustave Le Bon (1897), Emile Durkheim (1995), and Sigmund Freud (1923). Whereas Freud and Le Bon were pessimistic about the impact of the crowd on the behavior of the individual as they thought that participation in crowd activities damaged the rationality and morality of the conscious mind and brought to the surface uncontrolled instincts, Durkheim had a much more positive view on the crowd as potentially generating the notion of the sacred that makes social solidarity possible. Yet, Marcel Mauss already acknowledged that the crowd's euphoria could as well be aroused by collective violence as by other more positive collective actions. Mauss applied Durkheim's notions of collective effervescence and ritual communion to the Nazi celebrations of power and solidarity and recognized how these violent rituals produced collective emotions and representations of identity (in Lukas 1973: 338).[1] In other words, this approach opens the possibility to study collective violence as constitutive of social identity, in contrast to the above-mentioned postmodern perspective that explains political violence from the anxiety of failing social identities. The focus shifts from processes of othering and purification to processes of group identification through collective aggression. This includes studies by social historians like E. P. Thompson (1973), Natalie Zemon Davis (1973), and Charles Tilly (1978) on the moral economy of violence and the work of Stallybrass and White (1986) and others working in the spirit of Bakhtin (1984) on collective transgression. I would also like to add more recent works such as David Apter's study of militant organizations as "discourse communities" (Apter 1997) and Martha Crenshaw's analysis of terrorist groups as communities accommodating a variety of individual needs such as social status and recognition, excitement, and material benefits (Crenshaw 1988). Recent ethnographies of militant organizations such as Allen Feldman's book on the IRA (1991) and Joseba Zulaika's work on the ETA (1988) pay attention to the disciplining into an aggressive masculinity, the competition for status and prestige, as well as the aestheticization of violence and death.

Although these two sets of approaches are usually separated in recent studies on political violence, they can easily and fruitfully be combined. Both can be used to overcome the weak points of the other. The former approach can be criticized for assuming the omnipresence of a modern ideology of identity, while not dealing with how, under which circumstances, and in which social groups these identities become so politicized, polarized, and pressing as to lead people into radical violent action. The former approach typically focuses on the national, ethnic, or religious identity of the perpetrators and victims of political violence but does not answer questions about other features of identity, such as generation, gender, or class. It often fails to recognize that the perpetrator of violence has a relationship not only with his victim but also with his fellow perpetrators. The latter approach is therefore better equipped to highlight the dynamics within violent groups. However, we also need to engage the processes of radical othering within the groups that are involved in collective violence. These groups are, after all, not cultural enclaves but are constantly under the influence of various and competing articulations of ethnic, national, and religious social identities.

This book, then, tries to give a detailed account of how groups of perpetrators of ethnic or religious violence relate to dominant discourses on ethnic and religious nationalism. Very often these groups are bound together by a "street culture" in which key values such as masculinity, physicality, and a lack of respect for these dominant discourses are expressed in explicitly plebeian, transgressive, and ludic practices. The *fun* of these practices is often self-consciously contrasted to the seriousness of state nationalism. We therefore cannot simply expect these groups to abide by dominant discourses on nationalism, ethnicity, and religion, and yet they are often in the forefront of ethnic and religious violence. This is the puzzle of *fun* and violence: how can we explain that groups of people who express their profoundly ambiguous feelings about official nationalist discourse in collective ludic practices of transgression are also willing to sacrifice themselves for the ethnic-religious cause? I will try to solve this puzzle by presenting an analysis of political violence as a process that gives due attention to the peer-group dynamics of militant activities, the effervescence of collective violence, and their political aspirations in opposition to the state and other ethnic groups.

THE ARGUMENT AND THE PRESENTATION OF THE DATA

My analysis of the Muhajir nationalist movement differs from most studies about this phenomenon. Even though Pakistan—urban Sindh in particular—cannot be called an over-researched part of the world, there is recent scholarship on the MQM and Muhajir nationalism. But apart from two master's theses (A. A. Khan 1991; Verkaaik 1994), there are no studies based on anthropological fieldwork in Muhajir communities from which the movement originates. The bulk of the work done thus far looks at the rise of Muhajir nationalism from a national-level perspective. These studies interpret the MQM as a movement of an upcoming would-be middle class that tries to get access to state institutions and opposes economic discrimination by the state. The argument has been most elaborately developed by Hamza Alavi (1988, 1989, 1991), who uses the term "salariat" to denote a societal group of white-collar workers or those who aspire to such a position. The new nationalist movement is said to be a salariat-led movement. For others, the MQM is primarily the reactionary revolt of an urban middle and lower-middle class that is modernist in culture (F. Ahmed 1998; I. Malik 1997: 223–56; Zaidi 1992). The question of why a class struggle takes the form of ethnic polarization is answered by reference to the ethnic and linguistic policies of the state (Rahman 1996; J. Rehman 1994).

In my view, however, the Muhajir nationalist movement cannot so easily be reduced to a distorted class struggle, just as, say, the Hindu nationalist movement does not simply reflect the dynamics of caste politics in India (Hansen 1999: 17). Present-day nationalist movements certainly do empower groups that were previously marginalized, but these groups do not neatly coincide with classes or castes. For one thing, almost everyone in urban areas in South Asia now claims to belong to the middle or lower-middle class, but neither the MQM nor the Hindu nationalist movement represents everybody—despite the MQM's claim that it speaks for 98 percent of the Pakistani population. Furthermore, present-day nationalist movements attract followers and supporters from a wide social spectrum.

It is true that the MQM is poorly represented in the overly rich and the overly poor sections of Karachi and Hyderabad, but it is also clear that the movement is home to both university students and low-status artisans such as shoemakers. Socially upward as well as downward mobility is an aspect of the nationalist movements of the 1980s and 1990s, but it is not their only or single most important aspect. In the case of the MQM, I will show that there are many other factors at play, such as gender, generation, kinship, education, place of origin in India, place of present residence, and possibly several others. The multitude of such aspects blurs the picture and makes it impossible to locate the movement's following in straight sociological terms.

I rather propose to take the Muhajir nationalist movement as primarily a popular movement that is "street nationalist." Although the MQM originated in a student organization established on university and college campuses, it soon left—or rather was forced to leave (see chapter 3)—educational institutions and began to campaign in the streets of the densely populated neighborhoods of Karachi and Hyderabad. Rather than mimic and strive for a middle-class modernist lifestyle, it mocked and ridiculed high cultural and Islamic modernist values. In this sense, it marked a new phase of democratic politics throughout South Asia.

To make these claims I will be most concerned with the "streets." That does not mean that the broader picture will be left out; in fact, chapter 1 will examine the relevant political and cultural developments that have taken place on a national and provincial level. This chapter discusses processes of state formation and nation building and analyzes them in relation to the simultaneous emergence of Sindhi nationalism. It also examines the response of various segments of the Muhajir population to this dual process of nation building and ethnicization. Chapter 2 describes the rise, heyday, and imminent decline of the Muhajir Qaumi Movement within the broader framework of national and provincial politics.

I will then focus more explicitly on the "street aspects" of the movement, starting with a general introduction of the neighborhood where I did fieldwork. This inner-city area in the city of Hyderabad, named Pakka Qila, has a peculiar spatial setting, as it is located within the fortifications of the former palace of the Sindhi kings. After the British conquest of Sindh in 1843, the royal palace became a military camp of the British colonial army and was off-limits to civilians. As a result it was largely an empty spot when Pakistan became independent in 1947 and large numbers of Muslim refugees and migrants began to pour in from India. Located in the vicinity of the railway station where most migrants arrived, it was turned into a refugee camp and later became a permanent settlement with a population of about forty thousand people, virtually all of them Muhajir. Most inhabitants are self-employed artisans with a large number of shoemakers originating from Agra. Although Sindhi nationalists claimed the citadel as a symbol of Sindhi history and autonomy and demanded that the Muhajir settlers be relocated, Pakka Qila became one of the most well-known and devoted strongholds of the MQM and in 1990 played a major role in the most gruesome case of ethnic violence in the history of Pakistan, leading to cases of ethnic cleansing that subsequently subdivided the city of Hyderabad in Muhajir and Sindhi areas. Chapter 3 will introduce this area to the reader.

The remaining chapters aim to describe and analyze the interrelations between violence and nationalist ideology from a processual perspective. Chapter 4 discusses street humor and competitive masculinity as means of mobilization. I will analyze violent group action in its ritual and effervescent aspects and offer some ethnographic descriptions of how the ludic may lead to violent acts such as looting, arson, and rioting. I will argue that youthful group aggression helped spoil social and ethnic relations within a wider context of fierce and often violent political competition. It led to equally violent reactions from militant organizations of rival ethnic groups and increasingly also from the state, which was party to the ethnic tension. When aggression was answered with aggression, the neighborhoods associated with Muhajir militant nationalism came under siege, as happened during the summer of 1990. Chapter 5 is devoted to an analysis of these large-scale violent events with special focus on to the dynamics between violence and the interpretation of violence by young MQM supporters transforming themselves into full-time militants, martyrs, and "terrorists." Chapter 6, finally, looks at similar issues in more recent years. Having discussed young male peer-group violence in chapter 4 and large-scale ethnic violence in chapter 5, I will examine a third, more recent and more routinized form of violent conflict including state persecution and anti-state militancy. This chapter also discusses the discourse of terrorism employed by state forces to justify extrajudicial methods of persecution and maintaining law and order. It also focuses on how MQM activists reversed the terrorist stigma and turned it into a matter of pride and identity. Discussing public perceptions of the state, this chapter also deals with how this atmosphere of ongoing violence has generated an increasingly nostalgic and diasporic collective identity among Muhajirs.

Taken together, chapters 4 to 6 argue that the history of the Muhajir nationalist movement can be described in terms of changing forms or phases of violence: "playful riots," ethnocide, and anti-state militancy or "terrorism." It is not my intention to argue that these different forms are separated or that the one follows neatly after the other. Forms of violence different in mood, scope, and direction often overlap, but it is nevertheless possible to distinguish different phases in which any one of the three mentioned forms of violence dominates. These different phases also generate changes in rhetoric, discourse, and collective fantasies. If youthful aggression goes together with physical symbols of masculine might, the confusing and life-threatening incidents of large-scale violence evoke images of martyrdom, suffering, and purity. In more recent years, there is clearly a relation between violent state persecution by the military and an emergent culture of war, militancy, and terrorism among full-time MQM activists. By highlighting these changes in the dynamics of violence and the imagination, I hope to show the processual and interrelated character of both.

ABOUT THE RESEARCH

To end this introductory chapter I want to say a few words about the circumstances under which the research was conducted and about people who have significantly influenced the research. As the volume titled *Fieldwork under Fire* (Nordstrom and Robben 1995) illustrates, anthropological fieldwork on political violence has various difficulties. In a society reigned by fear, mistrust, and violence, it is often nearly impossible to establish rapport with key informants. Moreover, several MQM activists from the neighborhood of Pakka Qila were in jail where I could not visit them. Others lived in exile or were in hiding, and in order not to damage the delicate trust I had built up, I had to refrain from making inquiries as to their whereabouts. I could of course hang out in places where men, especially young men, gathered. On the other hand, I did not have to make a living in one of the neighborhood's workshops nor did I have to maintain a family there. With some exceptions I did not have access to the seclusion of private homes. I know very little about the women of Pakka Qila. Above all, Pakka Qila was not a place one could just go to and rent a place to live. Most houses were simply too small to accommodate a guest for an extended period of time.

So I lived elsewhere. I rented rooms from a family I had come to know during my earlier visits. The house was located in the suburb of Latifabad, a part of Hyderabad that had been built in the 1960s. Since the ethnic riots of 1990, practically the only non-Muhajirs who lived there were small communities of Sindhi goatherds. Initially I thought that not living in the area of study was a disadvantage. Later I began to appreciate the advantages of staying elsewhere. It enabled me to draw comparisons between Latifabad and Pakka Qila. Social control and neighborhood solidarity in the latter, for instance, appeared to be stronger than in Latifabad. The part of Latifabad where I lived was home to shopkeepers, schoolteachers, low-ranking bureaucrats, and others who would be categorized as lower-middle class in Pakistan, and they hailed from various regions in India, whereas the population of Pakka Qila was more homogeneous in terms of occupation and place of origin. Kinship ties tended to be more prevalent. There were many other differences that gave me a comparative perspective I would not have had if I had lived in Pakka Qila.

For similar reasons I decided to do fieldwork in Hyderabad. I had worked in Karachi for three months in 1993 and again for three months in the spring of 1996 when I consulted newspaper archives on the MQM and Pakistani politics. I found that Muhajir nationalism in Karachi had a different meaning than it had in Hyderabad. In Hyderabad the term *Muhajir* connoted ethnic exclusion much earlier than it did in Karachi. Studies on Muhajirs and the MQM have thus far focused on Karachi only. These studies tend to deny the differences in position of several regional branches of the MQM and fail to see the many local variations that Muhajir nationalism may take.

But of course staying outside made it more difficult to find my way into Pakka Qila. Fortunately I received the help of two men who have played an important role during my fieldwork. First there was Aqeel, with whom I had worked in Karachi in 1993. He had a Muhajir background himself. His late father had been born in Allahabad, India. Having arrived in Pakistan, his father preferred Hyderabad to Karachi as a place to settle because he did not like the humidity of the seaside. He opened a dairy shop, keeping buffalos for milk just outside the town. Aqeel, the second of five sons, was considered the brightest and was granted the privilege of going to college. He later studied sociology at Sindh University. The family wanted to have one son working in the civil service while the others would run the shop. Originally not rich, the brothers did reasonably well financially.

The violence of May 1990 that had started in Pakka Qila had considerably changed Aqeel's life. Anticipating that they would one day have to leave Hyderabad because of ongoing ethnic violence, the family decided to buy a house in Karachi and establish a branch of the family business there. Having just completed his studies, Aqeel was singled out for this task. When I met him in 1993, he and his young wife lived in a house that was far too big for them. He did not find it easy to start a business in a city where he had few friends and relatives. Helping me was a welcome side job, which he performed with great skill and energy.

In 1994 and 1995 the violence shifted from Hyderabad to Karachi; 1995 was an especially bad year for Karachi. More than two thousand people were killed in ambushes, bomb blasts, and shootings among state forces, the MQM proper, and the breakaway MQM-Haqiqi. Meanwhile Hyderabad became much safer, and the brothers decided to leave Karachi. Aqeel went back to Hyderabad and opened a new dairy shop in the center of the city, but this was not without difficulties either. In addition to regular armed robberies, there was the nuisance of strikes. Almost weekly the MQM called for a shutdown of the market to protest the killing of its activists in Karachi. It was a major loss of revenue for dairy shops, butchers, and others who make a living selling perishable goods. One day, when a rival Sindhi nationalist party had called for a strike, Aqeel ignored the call and a grenade was promptly thrown through his window, seriously injuring two of his employees.

When I met him again in September 1996, he was busy, working ten hours a day, seven days a week, but he nevertheless found the time to discuss plans and strategies with me. In the evening he would often come up to Pakka Qila to help me. His introductions were invaluable. He and his wife also welcomed me as a brother in their home. And thanks to Aqeel I had a major breakthrough after three months of fieldwork.

Next to the Qila Gate, which is the main access to the fort, is a police station. Since the patroling policemen never stopped me to ask what my business was as a foreigner, a rumor spread that I was sent by the government. There was a reason for this. When I started fieldwork, Benazir Bhutto, who was deeply distrusted by the inhabitants of Pakka Qila, was the prime minister. Her party, the Pakistan People's Party (PPP), ruled in Sindh and the provincial government was involved in a major effort to crack down on the MQM. A few months before I arrived, a film crew from Britain had obtained permission to interview MQM activists in the Central Jail in Hyderabad and then made a film that was highly critical of the MQM. In Pakka Qila this was considered a state-sponsored piece of propaganda. If Bhutto had not been behind it, then how had the film crew managed to get permission to film inside the prison? Perceiving that sending foreigners was a new trick of the PPP government to spread anti–MQM propaganda, one man bluntly asked me how much Benazir paid me.

After some months, however, I had a stroke of luck, although it did not immediately appear that way. A printing press owner with whom Aqeel and I had spent an evening talking turned out to be an informer from one of the intelligence agencies operating in Hyderabad. For some time men identifying themselves as intelligence agents came to Aqeel's shop for information. At the same time my request for a visa extension was refused, but I never knew whether there was a connection with the printing press owner. Thanks to a member of one of the leading families of Hyderabad, who apparently knew the way to the higher authorities of the agency, the issue was resolved. I did have to leave the country to have my visa extended, however.

While I was abroad, Aqeel told the customers of his shop that I had been forced to leave because we had had an argument with the printing press owner, whom Aqeel knew was generally considered a hypocrite (*munafiq*). We had been told that the local MQM had left the man untouched because influential men of the PPP protected him. The day the PPP lost the provincial elections in February 1997, the man cleared out his workshop and disappeared. Aqeel's handling of this matter caused people to be much more cooperative after my return. Sharing an enemy proved to be a fertile ground for trust. As a word of welcome someone said to me: "So now you are a terrorist, too."

A second episode, however, was even more important in establishing a workable relationship with the men of Pakka Qila. It happened shortly after the affair with the printing press owner. During the two weeks I was out of the country I quit smoking cigarettes. I did this because I thought not smoking was healthier than smoking, but almost immediately after I quit, I developed an extremely violent cough. A friend from Holland came over for Christmas and gave me some pills, which did not help. I bought an ayurvedic syrup (a medicine made according to the traditional Hindu system of medicine) from a local doctor, but it did not help either. It may be a throat infection, I thought, and took amoxicillin—an antibiotic. Halfway through the course I had such a coughing fit that I strained the muscles connecting my ribs. Now even breathing was painful. I got up from chairs stiff as an old man. Finally I went to see a regular doctor. She said, "Try Augmentin," a different antibiotic. But I remembered what a Sindhi singer-poet had once told me: "Prayers are like antibiotics. If you take them too often, they no longer work." I thought it wiser to start smoking again.

The problem was that by now Ramzaan, the month of fasting, had begun. As a Christian I of course did not have to fast, but smoking in front of a group of people who are collectively longing for a cigarette but cannot have one in public is a rather uncomfortable situation if one does not have an excuse other than Christianity. So I spent my time in the communal garden of Pakka Qila, which had a reputation for being a place where you could do anything you liked without recrimination. In the shade of the Mosque of the Date Palm Tree you could have anything you fancied in the month of Ramzaan: tea, marijuana, hashish, cigarettes, etc.—generally speaking, anything that is "drinkable" (in Urdu, the verb for drinking also covers smoking). The consumption of solid food, however, was discouraged.

The man who was in charge of this little garden, which also featured the seven graves of the May 1990 victims, was Pir Sahibzada Syed Mazhar Hussain Moini. I was reading *Anna Karenina* then and did not understand what the author meant by men with moustaches—in plural—until I met this Mazhar Sahib. He was a seventy-year-old widower with several white moustaches and had been an influential man in the neighborhood till the younger generation had deprived him of his power base. He was very proud of his titles and genealogy (*shajra*), which he had, after many requests, recently received in writing from relatives in Ajmer, India. During one of our first meetings he took me to his house to show me the document. Under his name was written in pencil "gone to Pakistan," which to me appeared not unlike the "expired" written under the names of those who had died without heirs. But it did not bother Mazhar Sahib. What mattered to him was the written proof that he had a respectable background.

For weeks Mazhar Sahib had watched me blundering in my first efforts to do fieldwork, but he had a great sense of compassion and an even greater sense of humor. I explained my problem to him and asked him if he would employ me as the caretaker of the park and its graves and allow me to smoke on the grounds during Ramzaan. Apart from the seven martyrs of May 1990, there were two more graves: one of a Sufi saint belonging to the Chishti order who had died in Hyderabad in 1992; and the other of Nawab Muzaffar Hussain Khan, a member of the provincial assembly in the early 1970s who was buried there in the early 1980s. "No problem," Mazhar Sahib replied. "Start looking for diamonds." He meant removing the litter people had left behind. I felt stiff at first, but the exercise did me good.

Although this was not fieldwork in the strict sense, now that I had become Mazhar Sahib's employee, the regular visitors of the park began to see me as his protégé. The graves and the Mosque of the Date Palm Tree formed an appropriate setting for all sorts of discussions. Moreover, most of these conversations were supervised by Mazhar Sahib, who felt himself old and respectable enough to cut short anyone he thought was talking nonsense. Not that he was successful; it only resulted in more and hotter discussions. Aqeel was also often present during these meetings, translating and explaining concepts I did not understand, and together he and Mazhar Sahib often led the conversation and brought up new topics. Although I never participated in the social life of the area, I did at times manage to be in a situation where my presence became nearly irrelevant. With a break of two months in spring I continued research in and around this little park until August 1997.

CHAPTER ONE

Ethnicizing Islam

THIS CHAPTER discusses the story of state nationalism in Pakistan, which is an ongoing and complex project rather than a completed and unilinear achievement. The relationship between Islam and ethnicity is probably the most problematic and paradoxical aspect of this process of nation building. Pakistan is a peculiar case of "ethnonationalism" (Tambiah 1996: 11–12). Rather than in the state, the Pakistani nation is rooted in refashioned primordial attachments or, in the words of Clifford Geertz (1993: 259), "assumed givens" of social existence. Yet these assumed givens are not congruities of blood, speech, or custom, but primarily of religion. Insofar as Pakistan is seen as the land of the pure—*pak* meaning "pure"—the purity of its people lies in Islam. At the same time, however, the notion of Islam as a primordial attachment translated into nationalism has always been problematic. Islam claims universal relevance transcending ethnic and territorial attachments and drawing boundaries within the universal community of Muslims can be condemned as a form of civil war (*fitna*). For this reason Islam has been considered incompatible with ethnic solidarity from the first days of Pakistan's existence onward. The day after independence, Pakistan's first prime minister, Liaqat Ali Khan, publicly stated that "with the coming of Pakistan, a great deal of misapprehension seems to have been aroused in the hearts of many living in Pakistan. They seem to think in terms of Sindh for Sindhis and Bengal for Bengalis, [but] Pakistan is the very opposite of provincialism and racialism."[1] As we will see in this chapter, the *hijra* or Islamic exodus from Mecca to Medina was often referred to as signifying the birth of the Islamic brotherhood that transcends ethnic differences. Lacking a territorial, linguistic, or dynastic basis for the new nation that could overcome regional differences, the new rulers—initially organized in the Muslim League—took to Islam to bring the various regions and social groups together. However, this was never an unambiguous project. The famous address of the leader of the Muslim League, Muhammad Ali Jinnah, to the Pakistan Constituent Assembly on 11 August 1947 called for the equality of citizenship rights irrespective of religion, which indicates the "secular outlook of the Muslim League [that] lay beneath the temporary millenarian enthusiasm of the closing stages of the Pakistan movement" (Talbot 1998: 5). The postcolonial political elite never intended to create an Islamic state on the basis of the

Islamic law or *shari'at* let alone a *mullahocracy* that would bring to power the *'ulama* or clerics. After many intellectual and political debates and discussions, a notion of the Pakistani nation came to dominate based on a liberal interpretation of the works of Muhammad Iqbal, compatible with the discourse of progress and modernization and fostered by the military. Yet the close and problematic linkage between the nation and Islam explained the intensified public debates on the meaning of Islam as well as efforts to "purify" Islam from the heretic and the superstitious. It also meant that Islam largely set the limits of public debate. Although it is possible to support a wide range of positions on the interpretation of Islam—from orthodox to heterodox, liberal to Marxist, and secular to Islamist—one can hardly speak out against Islam as such lest one be accused of both heresy and unpatriotic loyalties. Hence, regional groups resisting the authoritarian regime in Islamabad legitimized the regional basis of their protest by articulating an ethnicized Islam of their own, particularly in the 1960s during the regime of General Ayub Khan. In this way, they tried to form ethnic organizations without being accused of anti-Islamic and anti-patriotic activities. This was especially the case in Sindh among Sindhi groups, who formulated a Sindhi tradition of mysticism with reference to the many shrines (*dargah*) of local holy men in the Sindhi countryside. This had huge ramifications for the migrant population, in particular when the national government in the 1970s to some extent endorsed this ethnicization of Islam by searching for a politicized Islam distinct from both Iqbalian modernism as promoted by the military and from the Islamism of the Jam'iat-i Islami and other such parties. It is against this background of ethnicizing Islam that the turn to ethnic-religious politics by young Muhajirs in the late 1970s and early 1980s has to be understood.

My understanding of nationalism and ethnicity in Pakistan largely follows Peter van der Veer's conceptualization of religious nationalism in South Asia as a discourse on both the religious community and the nation. In other words, it rejects the "Great Divide" between the "cold" and traditional non-West, steeped in mythical notions of time and space, and the "hot" and modernized West, governed by history, which in an evolutionary fashion becomes a model for nationalism elsewhere. Contrary to what theorists like Anderson (1991) and Gellner (1983) argue, the modern nation does not replace the traditional religious community; rather, the nation is imagined on the basis of notions of the religious community rethought and reinvented in reaction to global processes such as colonialism and Orientalism (Van der Veer 1994: ch. 1). Ethnicity in Pakistan is the outcome of a related process of contesting the nation on the basis of a similar linkage between the people and the religious community. In other words, ethnic groups in Pakistan are not fruitfully understood in terms of a primordial origin, such as kinship or language,[2] nor are they first and foremost symbolically imagined communities that reproduce a sense of togetherness and shared destiny on the basis of largely reinvented traditions.[3] In my view, ethnic groups in Pakistan are best understood as discursively produced categories of both governance and contentious politics. These categories are inextricably linked to the nation and as a consequence to Islam, and have therefore also become confused with various interpretations of Islam. In the popular perception, the emotionally most sensitive and discursively most evocative boundary separating ethnic groups lies in recently ethnicized traditions of Islam rather than in language, kinship, territory, or custom. This is of course not to deny that these differences can always be contested and rejected with reference to a discourse of Muslim brotherhood and Islamic nationalism.

This chapter examines this dual process of nation building and the ethnicization of Islam. Although this is a national process, I will focus mainly on the way it took shape in the province of Sindh, discussing the contributions and responses of both Sindhis and Muhajirs to this process. This chapter also gives a first indication of how the public (self-)image of Muhajirs has changed with the advent of the MQM. Before the rise of the MQM, the stereotypical image of Muhajirs was shaped by the cultural and political migrant elite, which had a large say in the Pakistani bureaucracy and saw itself (and by implication the group of migrants as a whole) as educated, modern, rational, and closest to the progressive Islamic revivalism in the tradition of Aligarh University. In addition to this, Islamist movements such as the Jamʿiat-i Islami put forth a different image of Muhajirs as devout and religiously disciplined Sunni Muslims in the Deobandi tradition. However incompatible and sometimes hostile to each other these two ethnicized images might be, they both reject religious practices that are commonly considered to belong to a traditional or popular culture. Whether liberal or "fundamentalist," Muhajirs were believed to be modern and educated city dwellers compared to, for instance, the Sindhis or the Pakhtun. The MQM, however, brought to the fore a different picture of Muhajirs. Less devout and less disciplined, the new image of Muhajirs relates to more mystical and ecstatic religious practices. Without completely throwing earlier ethnic stereotypes overboard, the MQM created a public platform on which young Muhajirs can present themselves as more passionate than the public image of the Muhajir of the earlier generation allowed for. To critics, however, this is a picture of illiteracy, superstition, and backward tradition.

This chapter, then, starts with a brief discussion on postcolonial nation building with a special interest in the legacy of Muhammad Iqbal and the place his writings have within postcolonial state nationalism. It illustrates the ethnicization of Islam by focusing on the Sindhi revolt against Islamabad in the 1960s and 1970s. The chapter ends with an exploration of popular conceptualization of the nation and Islam in terms of sacrifice, migration, territory, discipline, and education.

MODERNIZATION AND AUTHORITARIANISM

As Ayesha Jalal (1995) has shown, remarkable comparisons can be made between the postcolonial history of Pakistan and India. Although both countries have often taken different routes in managing civil politics, leading to decades of military dictatorship in Pakistan while India proudly came to be called "the largest democracy of the world," India and Pakistan share not only a colonial past but also a postcolonial history as well as an interrelated present and future. The recent and simultaneous advent of highly successful, largely urban-based political mass movements such as the MQM in Pakistan and the Hindu nationalist movement in India is therefore hardly accidental.

The interconnectedness between nationalism and religion is probably the single most outstanding feature the countries share. Drawing on Orientalist notions of the spiritual East, the forerunners of Indian nationalism translated modern notions such as national autonomy in a reinvented religious tradition (Breckenridge and Van der Veer 1993; Chatterjee 1993; Cohn 1987; Inden 1986). Religious nationalism became the lens through which local conflicts were looked at (Freitag 1989; Pandey 1990) and was also of crucial importance for anti-colonial mass mobilization (Chatterjee 1986; Gilmartin 1989; Nandy 1983; Talbot 1996). The Muslim League developed the two nations theory according to which Hindus and Muslims constituted not just different religious communities but also distinct nations, each entitled to the right of self-determination. Partition formally established the link between religion and nationalism as it gave South Asian Muslims—at least some of them—their own state.

In India the Congress Party under the leadership of Jawaharlal Nehru established a governmental style that Jalal has termed "structural authoritarianism." Thanks "to the momentum of the nationalist movement, the Congress' organizational structure and the similarity in the social background of the top leadership" (1995: 39), the Congress Party managed to dominate in an essentially multiparty system of parliamentary democracy. The Muslim League, in contrast, was weakly organized in the areas that became part of Pakistan, and it did not inherit a preexisting colonial state apparatus, as did the Congress Party. Local landlords and spiritual leaders filled the vacuum caused by the virtual absence of state power, and they had a poor and sometimes hostile working relationship with the Muslim League and the central bureaucracy, both of which were dominated by the urban migrant population. The center therefore had difficulty establishing authority over the provinces. In addition to this, military disputes with India over Kashmir threatened the center from without. Under these circumstances, the military—mainly dominated by Punjabis and to a lesser extent Pakhtun—managed to gain the upper hand over the political leadership that was largely Muhajir (ibid. 48–63).

Both the military regime of General Ayub Khan and the Congress Party under Nehru embarked on a process of state-led modernization. The rhetoric on the necessity of social reform went hand in hand with a condescending notion of the masses as "backward" and "uneducated." Ayub Khan, for instance, concluded that the population of Pakistan was not yet ready for a parliamentary system, opting instead for a form of "controlled democracy" that placed the pseudo-democratic process directly under the supervision of the army. Underlying this authoritarianism was the notion of the state as a benevolent parent disciplining the people and enlightening them into cultural modernity through formal education and the purification of popular Islamic practices from what was perceived as superstition and "Hindu perversions" or "innovations."

Authoritarianism was first challenged in the form of regionalism and ruralism. Stanley Tambiah had elaborately analyzed this process for Sri Lanka, where modernization had already come under attack in the 1950s. The British era had not only fostered the development of an urban elite but also empowered a rural elite that claimed to "speak on behalf of the village fold from whose ranks they had sprung" (Tambiah 1986: 69). In Pakistan, too, regional movements emerged in all provinces except the Punjab. In East Bengal in particular (Roy 1983) but also elsewhere in Pakistan, a rural tradition of syncretism was formulated in reaction to the state's authoritarian modernization.

The center responded to such protest movements with "aristocratic populism" (Bose and Jalal 1998: 223). In the 1970s Zulfiqar Ali Bhutto in Pakistan, like Indira Gandhi in India, recruited locally influential landlords and peasant leaders as local party representatives. The alliance with regional leaders destabilized the center, which increasingly relied on the charisma of government leaders for authority. Ultimately the process of fragmentation resulted in a second period of military rule after the installation of martial law in 1977. Under General Zia-ul Haq, the military sought to control society by a renewed state-promoted religious nationalism called "islamization," which shared some similarities with the renewed emphasis on caste or "the communalization of politics" in India (Jaffrelot 1996: 369–71).

I want to look at these developments more closely by first examining the discourse of Islamic modernism that legitimized the leading role of the state in nation building and social reform, and then focusing on popular reactions against this authoritarian statism.

The Legacy of Muhammad Iqbal

Up to the 1970s, nation building was primarily a political project of the Muslim League and, more important, the bureaucracy and the military (Jalal 1995: 50–51). These small but influential segments of society were dominated by an urban elite influenced by the modernist tradition of the Aligarh school (Lelyveld 1978: 321–27, Metcalf 1982: 327–34).[4] The man primarily associated with the reconstruction of Islamic thought that critically shaped Pakistani nationalism is the philosopher-poet Muhammad Iqbal. Slightly provocatively, Iqbal may be called the patron saint of the Pakistani elite. He lies buried near the Pakistan Minar or Independence Monument, at the feet of the Badshahi mosque in Lahore, a supreme monument of the Moghul legacy of Pakistan. A university has been named after him and he has been called the national philosopher. The early national ideology of Pakistan cannot be understood without a brief glance at his work.

Iqbal's philosophy drew from three main sources: classical Sufism, German idealism, and early Indian Islamic reformists such as Shah Waliullah (1703–62) and Syed Ahmad Khan (1817–98). Iqbal borrowed mysticism from early Islamic thinkers like Jalaluddin Rumi and Al-Ghazzali, including the Quranic notion that God is closer to a man than his jugular vein and the notion that the sublimation of the self has to be achieved in one's worldly life. However, he rejected passive meditation and world-renouncing asceticism like Indian reformists had done before him. He felt akin to Nietzsche, whom he called a *majzub* or a restless seeker of God (Chaudri 1994: 165–67). He was attracted by the ideal of a man of will, capable of heroic living (Stepanyants 1971: 30). He probably admired Nietzsche's style of writing. Like Nietzsche's work, Iqbal's philosophy is subject to different interpretations. In very general terms, his philosophy can be summarized as follows.

Iqbal defined God (*khuda*) as the "Absolute Ego" (*khudi*) or "the whole of Reality" (Iqbal 1954: 59). The term *khudi* had an evil connotation in Islamic literature, but Iqbal made it one of his central themes (Hakim 1991: 125). It is man's task to liberate himself from the temporal and material aspects of reality and establish a complete unification with God. This self-sublimation is achieved by means of a rationally directed creative will (Iqbal 1954: 108). Iqbal, for instance, interprets the legend of the fall from paradise as a positive act of disobedience, the first act of free choice enabling man to "rise from a primitive state of instinctive appetite to the conscious possession of a free self" (ibid. 85). Will and free reasoning (*ijtihad*) are therefore the typically human attributes with which man may achieve personal liberation. For Iqbal, as for Gandhi, nationalism was not merely a political liberation from colonialism but primarily a personal emancipation from the mental decay and passivity that he sensed had pervaded Indian culture. These two aspects of nationalism had to be taken together; one would fail without the other. Iqbal, in other words, not only opposed the fundamentalist belief that new interpretations of the religious sources are perversions but also urged Muslims to free themselves from the rule of spiritual leaders and clerics. He, for instance, defended the fall of the caliphate in Turkey as he considered it a symbol of stagnation (Masud 2002).

In Pakistan today, Iqbal's philosophy reverberates most clearly in the importance given to education and literacy. Of course, Iqbal was not the only Islamic modernist who stressed the importance of education as a cultivator of character. It has been a more widespread theme (Lelyveld 1978: 117), and it is now common practice in Pakistan to consider the emphasis on education as one of the central themes of Islam. Education is seen as the means through which to achieve the mental purification Iqbal deemed necessary. In effect, illiteracy serves as an explanation for many unwanted national phenomena, including the sorry state the Pakistani nation finds itself in today. Since the creation of Pakistan was, according to Iqbal, not so much the apotheosis of Muslim liberation but rather the first step toward it, education is seen as a prerequisite for the three principles—faith (*iman*), unity (*ittehad*), and discipline (*nazm*)—with which the ideal of Pakistan has to be achieved. The nation failed because of a lack of these principles, which in turn is blamed on high illiteracy rates—not as a parameter of how many people are able to read and write but as a more elusive indication of the mental development of the nation.

The link between formal education and religious mentality made it possible to conceive seemingly more traditional forms of Islamic practices as "backward" and "superstitious." To some extent, education offered a new way of distinguishing pure Muslims from impure Muslims. The paramount position of holy men or *pirs* as spiritual leaders and healers increasingly came under attack as a form of folk and traditional Islam perverted by un-Islamic influences (Ewing 1983: 259; J. Malik 1998). Popular religion, seen as a tradition untouched by education, was seen as unbefitting the modern nation of Pakistan.

Moreover, popular religion became linked with ethnicity. Durreshahwar Syed, daughter of the late G. M. Syed, the Sindhi nationalist leader, told me how she had formed a women's organization to establish schools in the countryside. She asked a minister—a Punjabi residing in Karachi—to preside over the inauguration. In his speech he said: "I totally agree with the objectives of the organization. Education is of the utmost importance for Sindh. We have to educate the Sindhis and make them into good Muslims." A daughter of a *syed* (descendant of the Prophet) herself, Durreshahwar was stunned and insulted.

The reputation of Sindh as a backward country steeped in traditional and mystical mentalities reinforced similar images that existed prior to independence. In Sir Richard Burton's early accounts, for instance, Sindh appears as a country stuck in backwardness to the point of mental debility. In his first book on Sindh, Burton wrote that "the dark complexion of the Sindhi points him out as an instance of arrested development. . . . He is idle and apathetic, unclean in his person, and addicted to intoxication; notoriously cowardly in times of danger, and proportionally insolent when he has nothing to fear; he has no idea of truth or probity, and only wants more talent to be a model of treachery" (1988: 283–84). He was fair enough, though, to make an exception for Sindh's women. In a later work, which includes a chapter titled "The Sindi Man—His Character, and Especially What He Drinks," he describes the Sindhi woman's attitude as "not ungraceful, she carries herself well, she never stoops and, observe, she has high but not round shoulders" (1993: 328). Her eyes, "large and full of fire, black and white as an onyx-stone, of almond shape, with long drooping lashes," he labels "undeniably beautiful" (321). In the eyes of E. B. Eastwick, another early British traveler, Sindh was almost a tabula rasa, a "young Egypt" that lay waiting to be developed economically and culturally by the colonizers (Eastwick 1849). Half a century later, after a period of rebellion (Ansari 1992: 57–76), the tone became less optimistic. A colonial officer reported that, "even native artisans, servants and other immigrants from the Punjáb, Cutch and Bombay, loathed the country, not because of the heat or the distance, but because it was an 'uncivilized, unimproved place, difficult to get at and difficult to get away from' " (Aitken 1986: 146). Still later, in the twentieth century, Sindh became a place to study Sufism. In the work of Ernest Trumpp, H. T. Sorley (1940), and after 1947 Annemarie Schimmel (1981, 1986), Sindh emerges as the cradle of esoteric Islam, a "mystical land of love and tolerance." Today these are phrases no politician working in Sindh can ignore and from which a whole industry of folklore, history books, and music concerts is drawn. If Sindh were not such a violent place, its reputation as a land of peaceful mysticism would have great potential for tourism.

Sufism is the most recent label in the process of ethnically categorizing a subject people. It is interesting to see that such categorization produces remarkably similar stereotypes cross-culturally. In what is nearly the opposite part of the globe, the Mapuche of Chile have been categorized as brave and fearless warriors, bloodthirsty bandits, lazy drunkards, the white man's burden, and, finally, gentle savages gracefully lacking education (Stuchlik in Jenkins 1997: 62). Add promiscuity and you have all the stereotypical images of the Sindhi. As Jenkins reminds us, the categories tell us more about the identity of the categorizers than of the categorized. In Pakistan after 1947, the categorizers did not only have an evolutionist concept of time and tradition, they also located the modern in the traditions of Indian Muslim revivalism and found tradition in the popular and the periphery. Identified as tradition, Sufism was either pushed into the domain of the private and the esoteric (Ewing 1997: 253) or, as a public practice, deemed passive and impure. Thus Sufism was considered as either world-renouncing, apolitical mysticism or a popular, superstitious belief in amulets (*tawiz*) and the healing powers of a saint, the blind loyalty to rural spiritual leaders, the worship of shrines, and the use of hallucinogenic drugs. The government of Ayub Khan actively tried to undermine these practices by establishing alternative, state-run centers of healing and education in the vicinity of shrines (Ewing 1983: 261).

That Sufism became the main characteristic of the Sindhi—rather than, for instance, drunkenness or the image of the fanatical "Mad Sindh"— reflects the patronizing modernist attitude toward the peripheries, which was benevolent rather than overtly hostile. Seen from the center, the spread of modernist Islam was a valuable and liberating gift that would be happily accepted once the receiver began to appreciate its value. It is also important to see that this state nationalism was not quite a state-produced discourse, consciously designed for the justification of a policy of nation building. The idea that Sindh had to be freed from tradition also pervaded the Sindhi cultural elite. The Sindhi nationalist movement of the 1950s and 1960s, for instance, was led by social reformers and schoolteachers whose first ambition was to liberate the Sindhi peasant (*hari*) from his ignorance. In the writings of Ibrahim Joyo, a leading intellectual of the Sindhi nationalist movement, the romanticization of the peasants as the righteous owners of the earth goes hand in hand with lamentations about their life as unfortunate, uneducated, wild men who tyrannize their womenfolk, abuse their children, fight each other, and touch the feet of fake saints and landlords. "Their thatched houses built of sticks and straws are as good or as bad as the nests of birds or the holes and dens of wild animals," the social reformer writes, continuing:

> The only advantages in life they know are plenty of sunshine and Nature's pure air. Their only pleasure in life is to seek recompensation for their own miseries in tyrannizing over their hard-worked and emaciated women-folk, during the day, and have them by their side, during the night, and in brutalizing and exhausting their children by dinning into their sensitive ears abundant words of choicest abuses, or prematurely yoking them in to hardest possible labor. . . . The only duty they know is to work like bullocks for their landlords and moneylenders, to touch the feet of their Zamindar-Masters [landlords] and Pirs [spiri-

tual leaders], and worship them literally as living gods, and lastly to instruct their children to do like-wise. . . . They in relation to their masters stand in the same position as their own bullocks stand in relation to them. . . . Man is said to be the most marvelous handiwork of God; but when one looks at these forsaken human creatures living under the most suffocating slavery of body, mind and soul, one simply shudders at the thought: "So, this is what man has made out of man!" (Joyo 1947: 103–4)

This dual nature of the essentially good but ignorant peasant (*hari*) is a deep-running theme in Sindhi nationalism. The discourse of an educated and modernist center versus a traditional and uneducated periphery, however, was not only applied to Sindh, but similar ideas on cultural inferiority were attributed to the Bengalis, which also contained more hostile racist stereotypes (F. Ahmed 1998: 27–28), probably because Bengalis had already been shown to be ungrateful for the gift of Pakistani nationalism.

Although the national ideology of Islamic modernization cannot be explained as a consciously designed legitimization of concrete policies of state building, it did give a certain logic to particular government decisions. For instance, the choice of Urdu as the national language resonated with the *ashrafization* of Urdu, that is, a long-term process of making Urdu the language of cosmopolitanism and distinction, compared to which Sindhi, Bengali, or other "regional" languages were inferior. The form of "controlled democracy" designed by Ayub Khan and known as the "One Unit Scheme," also did not contradict Pakistani modernism. In this scheme, provincial boundaries were abolished in West Pakistan, creating the two "units" of West and East Pakistan. This was to a large extent meant to control the Bengalis of East Pakistan, the largest ethnic group, larger even than the Punjabis, who would therefore have a dominant say in democratic politics even in West Pakistan. In his autobiography, Ayub Khan justifies this move by stating that the East Bengalis "belong to the very original Indian races," "have been and still are under considerable Hindu cultural and linguistic influence," and "have not yet found it possible to adjust psychologically to the requirements of the newborn freedom" (1967: 187). Eventually President Ayub Khan justified the decision to postpone elections and then hold them in the state-monitored format that prevented the holding of truly free elections by saying that "our people are mostly uneducated" and "easily misled," "especially nowadays when Communism from within and without is so quick to make use of [democracy's] weaknesses" (188). The reference to "Communism," capitalized, suggests a link between Pakistani modernism legitimizing army-led authoritarianism and the modernization theory that underlined U.S. foreign policy in that period.

As a reaction against such measures and discourses, a new Sindhi nation-alism arose alongside a reorientation of Sufism. The 1960s were the high tide of not only Ayubian authoritarianism and Iqbalian modernism but also a seemingly contradictory boom of shrine pilgrimage. A major aspect of this development were the pilgrimages to rural sanctuaries by left-wing and mainly urban-based intellectuals, artists, students, school-teachers, and writers who visited the shrines of saints for a night of ecstatic music and mystical poetry. These shrines had hitherto been mainly of local, rural, or otherwise limited significance, but their reputation and impor-tance rapidly spread over a much wider area. Two of these holy places lie in Sindh: the shrine of Lal Shahbaz Qalandar in Sehwan Sharif on the west bank of the Indus and the shrine of Shah Abdul Latif in Bhitshah on the east bank. They would both become centers of Sindhi nationalism and anti-government resistance.

The Sufi Saints of Sindhi Nationalism

Sindhi nationalism had existed before the regime of General Ayub Khan introduced authoritarian modernization policies. It had in fact begun prior to 1947. It was initially a project of a group of young modernists from landlord families, a small network of men mostly educated in En-glish-language high schools in Karachi (H. Khuhro 1981: 171–74). They demanded that Sindh be allowed to separate from the administrative unit known as Bombay Presidency that linked Sindh to Bombay since 1847. They wanted Sindh to be a province of its own. Sindhi members of the Indian National Congress first raised the issue of Sindh's autonomy in 1913 (Pirzada 1995: 41). Both the Congress Party and the Muslim League supported this demand (H. Khuhro 1982: xxv). In the 1920s, however, following the Khilafat Movement and the outbreak of communal riots along the Indus (Pirzada 1995: 45), the movement gradually became a Muslim affair only, bestowing an Islamic dimension on Sindhi national-ism. The question of separation now became the project of a young group of Muslim politicians under the leadership of Muhammad Ayub Khuhro and Ghulam Murtaza Syed.[5]

In 1930 M. A. Khuhro, son of a landowning family in Larkana, pub-lished a pamphlet called *A Story of the Sufferings of Sind*, which gives an impression of the cultural arguments put forth by this young generation of politicians. Drawing on Arabic historical sources in which Sindh, or the Indus Valley, is identified as a separate country between Persia and "Hind" (India), the author distinguishes "Sindhians" from "Indians" (M. A. Khuhro 1982: 196–97). Another piece of evidence for the thesis of Sindh's historically determined separate identity was the discovery four years earlier of Mohenjo-daro, an archaeological site where the five-thousand-year-old remains of the Indus Valley civilization were under excavation (ibid.: 203). Khuhro furthermore mentions the specific climate and economic features of the land around "the great river Indus" (204). Sindhi Muslim nationalism therefore contained a strong historical-territorial element, contrary to the two nations theory later adopted by the Muslim League in other parts of India, according to which Indian Muslims were essentially a foreign and diasporic nation with no special attachment to India's territory. In the 1950s and 1960s, the Sindhi love for the homeland, and the life-giving river Indus (Sindhu) in particular, was most profoundly articulated in the poetry of Hyder Bakhsh Jatoi, a social reformer and poet who wrote long ecstatic verses in praise of the "River King" (Jatoi 1995: 70–76).

Apart from the Indus, the peasant or *hari* was the second important persona in early Muslim nationalism in Sindh. The *hari* figure enabled Sindhi nationalists to discriminate between a predominantly Hindu urban population, increasingly seen as exploiters with divided loyalties, and the truly Sindhi population of downtrodden Muslim peasants. In 1930 G. M. Syed founded the Sindhi Hari Committee, depicting the Sindhi *hari* in a similar fashion as Gandhi had portrayed the untouchable *harijan*. After 1947 Hyder Bakhsh Jatoi became the president of the committee. In his pamphlets Jatoi replaced the exploitive persona of the Hindu moneylender (*bania*) with a range of equally wicked figures, such as the landlord (*zamindar*) who came from the Punjab and illegitimately appropriated the Sindhi soil; the immigrant or Muhajir who took the possessions of the Hindus who had left for India, even though these Hindu properties had originally been stolen from the Sindhi peasants; and the Sindhi village headman (*wadera*) who had worked himself up to the status of landlord while exploiting the peasants from whose ranks he himself had come (Jatoi 1995: 112). Today the *wadera* serves as the stereotypical crook, the evil genius in television soap operas and Urdu movies, who exploits his landless laborers, rapes their women and sons, drinks whiskey, and drives around his vast sugarcane fields and cotton plantations in a four-wheel-drive Pajero jeep with tinted windows.

Sindh was declared a province in 1935. Three years later, most Sindhi Muslim leaders allied themselves with the Muslim League (Pirzada 1995: 84–85). Yet many a Sindhi Muslim leader saw the Pakistan Movement as a continuation of their earlier struggle for Sindh's separation. G. M. Syed, who had become the leader of the Muslim League in Sindh, said in 1943:

> By Sindhu I mean that part of the Asian continent which is situated on the borders of the River Indus and its tributaries. In past ages, Sind and Hind have been considered separate entities; and Sind included Kashmir, the NWFP

[Northwest Frontier Province], the Punjab, Baluchistan and the present province of Sind. But as time went on, the name began to connote a smaller and smaller area until now it is assigned only to that part of the land which is watered by the tail end of the great river. Today again, fully aware of this fact, we are moving to weld together those different parts into one harmonious whole, and the proposed name, Pakistan, connotes the same old Sindhu land. (R. Ahmad 1987: 442–43)

The quote is a very early attempt to find a historical-territorial legitimization for Pakistan as the land of the River Indus. In the 1970, this view became much more popular and widespread and was to some extent even endorsed by the national government. But before that happened, the notion of restoring a historical Greater Sindh, not uncommon among early Sindhi members of the Muslim League, became one of the pillars under a more radically separatist form of Sindhi nationalism as it was developed by the same G. M. Syed in the 1960s and 1970s. In his post-independence writings, G. M. Syed linked the river as a symbol of the distinctiveness of Sindh to an understanding of Islamic mystical traditions that enabled him to argue against the authoritarian modernization efforts from Islamabad.

G. M. Syed's Reformation of Sufism

Born in 1904, G. M. Syed was a descendant (*sajjada nishin*) of a saint buried in his native village of Sann. He became one of the most controversial and paradoxical public figures of Pakistan. As a syed, claiming direct descent from the Prophet's genealogy, he felt the need to be a spiritual guide to others. His first political move was to found a syed committee to urge his fellow-syeds to lead a respectable pious life and take their leadership responsibilities seriously. After founding the Sindh Hari Committee, he became an active Muslim leader during the 1939 communal riots in Sukkur (Soomro 1988), for which he would later, during a visit to India in the 1980s, make apologies. He organized the Muslim League in Sindh but parted with Jinnah before independence. Branded a traitor for the first time, he retreated from politics.

He began to publish a large number of books on mysticism. As his daughter Durreshahwar Syed told me, he "experimented with religion." He wore black clothes, then changed to white clothes, prayed and meditated for days on end, did not pray at all for a long period of time, became a staunch vegetarian for several months, etc. He joined the Theosophical Society in Karachi and founded the Sufi Society of Sindh (*bazm-e-sufia-e-sindh*) in 1966. He formulated his interpretation of Sufism in several books, beginning with *Paigham-i Latif* (The Message of Latif), published in 1952, in which he rejects Iqbal's philosophy as a form of oppositional "deism" that stands in the way of a more holistic and tolerant "pantheism" (G. M. Syed 1996: 133–35). A more controversial book appeared in 1967 under the title *Religion and Reality*. In addition to being called a traitor, he was now also declared a heretic in several fatwas. This did not stop him from regularly fulminating against what he considered the one-dimensional orthodoxy of the mullahs and the ʿ*ulama*.

In *Religion and Reality*, Syed presents an evolutionary theory of religion in which the revelations disclosed to the Prophet Muhammad are not so much the last stage but rather a major step forward. Despite the revelations several residues of a more primitive religion live on in Islam, such as the circumbulation of the Kaʿaba in Mecca, animal sacrifice, and circumcision (G. M. Syed 1986: 110–27). Other stages in the evolution of religion are Hinduism, Buddhism, Christianity, and "Science" (109). The final stage in the evolution of religion is mysticism (*tasawwuf*) or "natural religion" that acknowledges the oneness of the divine (*wahdat ul wujud*). In G. M. Syed's interpretation, mysticism is a completely deritualized pantheism and the rejection of the notion of an anthropomorphic God. In effect religion, by which is meant ritual and dogma, creates false communities. Syed does, however, recognize the loyalty to one's family, nation, and homeland as genuine stages toward a superior love for God. Mysticism initiates one in genuine feelings of solidarity with the whole of humanity, but it does account for more exclusive forms of solidarity based on the "natural" boundaries of kinship, language, and territory.

G. M. Syed took his inspiration from a range of men he considered prophets of mysticism, including Buddha, Christ, Muhammad, Gandhi, the twelfth-century philosopher Ibn Arabi, the thirteenth-century mystic and poet Rumi, the ninth-century Mansur Al-Hallaj who was executed for his famous theopathic cry, "I am God/Truth" (*Anaʿl-Haq*), and several mystical Sindhi poets. Within the latter category Shah Abdul Latif is by far the most important. G. M. Syed is in fact one of the main persons who turned this eighteenth-century poet, buried near the Sindhi village of Bhitshah, into the national poet of Sindh. Shah Latif's grave in Bhitshah, geographically at the center of the province, attracts musicians from all over the province who come to sing his verses, and it would probably come as a shock to many Sindhis to find that their national poet needs an introduction. Several Sindhis told me they took Shah Latif's collection of verses (*risalo*) as the Sindhi interpretation of the Qurʿan, which probably hints at the notion of Jalaluddin Rumi's *Masnawi* as the translation of the Qurʿan in Persian. They also compared the status of Shah Abdul Latif as the national poet of Sindh with the place of Shakespeare in the English national culture.

Like G. M. Syed himself, Shah Abdul Latif was a descendant of the Prophet through the lineage of his grandson Imam Hussain. After an unfortunate love affair, he became a wandering ascetic, carrying with him three books: the holy Qur'an, the *Masnawi* of Jalaluddin Rumi, and the Sindhi verses of his great-grandfather Shah Karim. His own verses, which he soon started to compose, were a combination of those three. He took the folklore of his great-grandfather's verses, imbibed them with Rumi's mysticism, and linked the new product to the Word of God. He recited his verses in Sindhi, an extraordinary move in a time when poets wrote in Persian. When he returned to his ancestral village of Hala, he had already become a famous poet who had won the admiration of the king, Ghulam Shah Kalhora. After his death he became a role model for other Sindhi poets, like the more ecstatic Sachal Sarmast and the Hindu poet Sami (Ajwani 1991: 109).

Popular love stories inspired him. Such stories were told in a vast geographical area, including the Indus Valley, the Punjab, Rajasthan, and Gujerat. Although their origin is obscure, they must have been several centuries old (Aitken 1986: 484; D. Syed 1988). Latif's favorite story was the one of Sassi and Punhu. Of the thirty-odd chapters or books (*surs*) he left behind, five are about Sassi, his favorite heroine. Although various versions of the story exist, the main story line runs as follows.

A daughter is born to a Brahmin and his wife who live in Thatta, the former capital of Sindh, south of Hyderabad. She is a lovely child, but the astrologers declare that her fate is to become a Muslim. Determined not to let the family be disgraced, the parents place the child in a coffer and let it drift away on the Indus. Downstream in Bambhore, a childless laundryman rescues the child and adopts her as his daughter. She becomes a very pretty girl. One day Punhu, the handsome son of the Baluchi chief of Kach, passes by, setting Sassi's heart on fire. Punhu, too, is fatally attracted to Sassi. He forgets his family duties, stays to live in her foster parents' house, and manages to persuade the foster father to let her marry him. Meanwhile, news of the affair reaches the proud old Baluchi chief in Kach, Punhu's father. Furious, he sends a dozen of his sons to get the fugitive home. In Bambhore the brothers enjoy Sassi's hospitality, eat her food, and make Punhu drunk on wine. In the dead of night, they take him away upon the back of a dromedary. In the morning Sassi notices her husband's absence and immediately sets out to find him.

Most of this is not mentioned in Shah Abdul Latif's verses, which focus primarily on Sassi's dramatic, desperate, barefooted quest through the hot and barren wilderness of the dreadful desert. Finally she meets a goatherd, to whom she pleads for a draft of milk. Unfortunately the man has just had a dream in which he was told he would soon meet his bride, so he starts to make advances. To preserve her honor, Sassi prays to be rescued and is promptly swallowed by the sand. Having recovered from the shock of what has just happened to Sassi, the goatherd starts to pile up a mound of stones to construct a grave to atone for his bad deed, and while he is busy Punhu, who has meanwhile escaped from his brothers, arrives. Spotting the grave he understands what has happened. Overcome by grief he collapses and is also swallowed up by the sand, where he is finally and eternally united with his beloved.

Shah Abdul Latif's verses on Sassi have been interpreted in several ways. For Durreshahwar Syed (1988: 59–107) they express the poet's feminism. Other interpretations hold that Sassi's quest represents man's search for a mystical unification with the divine. Ultimately one can only be united with the beloved in death but not just any death—it has to be a self-sacrifice inspired by love. This is also the reading of G. M. Syed, who spends a great many pages on the interpretation of Shah Abdul Latif's verses on Sassi's trials. However, he gives the story a profound political twist. He interprets the verses as a description of Sindhi mentality. Through Sassi and other folk heroines, "Shah Latif observed in the people of Sindh . . . courage, bravery and a spirit of self-sacrifice" (1996: 83). Further, "Sassi stands for the oppressed people" (197). The self-sacrifice through which one finds redemption is translated into a national inclination to fight unconditionally against tyranny. The verses of Shah Abdul Latif become a patriotic cry to join the Sindhi struggle against despotism.

G. M. Syed's writings, then, gave a boost to the popularity of the story of Sassi and Punhu. However, Sassi's popularity and commodification in more recent years—many products such as soap, sweets, and jewelry are named after her—have also been enhanced by other forces, including the national government under the leadership of the Pakistan People's Party, which incorporated the heroine into a new form of state nationalism.

The Pakistan People's Party: Sassi Becomes Respectable

The Sindhi protest movement against the authoritarian modernization policy began to gain momentum in the second half of the 1960s. The resistance brought together different groups of Sindhis. G. M. Syed was from the pre-1947 generation of Sindhi political leaders with an aristocratic background. A second group consisted of left-wing writers and activists such as Hyder Bakhsh Jatoi, Ibrahim Joyo, and Rasul Bakhsh Palijo: village boys who had gotten the rare opportunity to study in Karachi, Junagadh in Gujerat, Bombay, or Aligarh. The third and most numerous group consisted of young students: sons of artisans, doctors, shopkeepers, small local landlords, and other members of an emerging middle class that benefited from the introduction of roads, irrigation schemes, and a cash economy into the Sindhi countryside (Zaidi 1992: 98). Apart from G. M. Syed's reformed Sufism and the socialism of men like Jatoi, Joyo, and the student leader Jam Saqi—the latter wrote a book on the eighteenth-century saint Shah Inayat of Jhok under the somewhat anachronistic title *A Socialist Sufi*—a third major rallying point of the movement was the Sindhi language. In fact, in the early 1970s a major controversy over the question whether Sindhi or Urdu should be the official language of Sindh would lead to the first large-scale incidents of violence between Sindhi and Urdu speakers in Hyderabad and Karachi (Rahman 1996: 115–17). I will come back to this episode in the next chapter. For now it is important to note that the Sindhi movement became one of the most vocal components of the social uprising that brought down the military regime of Ayub Khan in 1968 (Jalal 1995: 61; Wolpert 1993: 129–30). As a result, the first democratic elections in Pakistan's history were held in 1970.

Two parties won the elections: the Awami League in East Pakistan and the Pakistan People's Party in West Pakistan. When neither the Pakistan People's Party nor the army was willing to transfer power to the East Pakistanis, a revolt broke out in and around Dhaka, leading to civil war, the disintegration of Pakistan, and the independence of Bangladesh. In West Pakistan, the Pakistan People's Party (PPP) under the leadership of Zulfiqar Ali Bhutto came into power. This resulted a considerable transformation in political culture and state nationalism. The rearrangement of power led to the empowerment of new regional elites as the PPP became an awkward coalition of peasants, artisans, and factory workers on the one hand and the rural elites of landlords and *pirs* on the other. In ideological terms, the Bhutto years meant a break with Iqbalian modernism.

Bhutto himself was not as straightforward a modernist as Ayub Khan. His training at the universities in Berkeley and Oxford awakened in him a deep attachment to his youth in Larkana in Upper-Sindh. He matured into a complex character appreciating Western decadence while romanticizing the life of the Pakistani poor. He was familiar with rural conduct and speech and was willing to employ them himself. His style of campaigning in Sindh resembled the popular festivals (*melas*) held at the shrines of holy men. His public performances were colorful, lively, and full of humor, songs, banners, portraits (A. Syed 1992: 69–70). He spoke the local dialect and wore the peasant's dress known as *salwar kamiz*. He asserted that "social justice" (*musawat*) was the real ideal of Pakistan and that he would be a *mujahid* (soldier) for its cause (76). He called himself the "leader of the people" (*qaʿid-i awam*). Promising to provide food, clothing, and shelter (*roti, kapre aur makan*) for everybody, he was one of the first national politicians who sat down with peasants and laborers to talk with them from a position of mutual respect. He became a truly charismatic figure for hundreds of thousands of Pakistanis.

Bhutto soon ran into trouble with the rapidly radicalizing Sindhi separatist movement of G. M. Syed and appropriated their symbolism for his own purposes. He promoted the public veneration of Shah Abdul Latif but tried to make him into a Pakistani national poet rather than a Sindhi national one. In January 1974 he inaugurated the government-sponsored Bhitshah Cultural Complex, with exhibition rooms and guest houses surrounding the shrine of the poet, saying that "Latif is not the poet of Sindh alone."[6] A permanent cultural exhibition was modeled after similar phenomena in Stratford-upon-Avon and Shantineketan, the birthplaces of Shakespeare and Tagore, respectively. Shortly before his fall in 1977, Bhutto declared 1978 the year of Shah Abdul Latif.

The patronage of the PPP turned Shah Abdul Latif into a respected national figure. In March 1984 Zia-ul Haq, the general who cannot be accused of Sindhi separatist sentiments, inaugurated the Shah Abdul Latif Chair at Karachi University. In 1996 the poet's favorite heroine, Sassi, became an ambassador of Pakistan when she was the paramount figure in a cultural program held during the World Cup Cricket. To give foreign guests "glimpses of the culture of the Indus Valley which is Pakistan today"[7] a ballet about Sassi was broadcast on the national PTV (Pakistan television). Despite protests from conservative circles condemning Prime Minister Benazir Bhutto for promoting vulgarity (*fuhashi*) on public television, the show could hardly be called scandalous or revolutionary. Sassi had become very different from the determined Sindhi patriotic rebel of the late 1960s. She no longer fought generals and mullahs. She had become respectable, a desperate victim, looking for the protection of her lost husband. This time poor Sassi died a mere submissive beauty.

Zulfiqar Ali Bhutto and Lal Shahbaz Qalandar

Although Bhutto adopted G. M. Syed's admiration for Shah Abdul Latif, the two men were very different politicians. Always wearing white clothes in his later years, Syed portrayed himself as a living symbol of serene, cool, world-renouncing devotion to the divine (*'ishq*). He took part in politics while denying its relevance by way of his public identity as a descendant of the Prophet (*syed*). To deny him his claim of detached superiority, the tactic used most often was to feminize his spirituality, that is, to denigrate his serene and self-effacing devotion by calling this "feminine." For many members of the MQM, for instance, Syed, with his Sassi, was a sissy. He was commonly believed to lack the energy and potency to rule. He was at best a comical figure, unserious and harmless. The Bhuttos, in contrast, were much more respected. They were feared as physically strong and dangerous. They openly dared not to be good. Mumtaz Ali Bhutto, Zulfiqar's cousin and his chief minister of Sindh in the early 1970s, called himself a traditional wrestler (*mahl*) and a wild boar hunter, and he often referred to his political opponents as weak members of the "third sex" (Mujtaba 1996: 75). Zulfiqar Ali Bhutto also cultivated an image of a robust man who knew how to drink and wrestle and who had little patience for moral meddlers from the mosque. When, after a visit of state to Turkey, a journalist accused him of having drunk a glass of wine in Istanbul, Bhutto cried, "Slander! I had many more than just one."

The Bhuttos revived another long-existing image of the Sindhi, namely that of an unruly lot inclined to wrestling, cockfights, drinking and "hot" passion. This image of the Mad Sindh correlates with historical armed uprisings of bands of fakirs led by spiritual leaders. One example is Shah Inayat of Jhok, who in the early eighteenth century formed a self-supporting society of fakirs independent of the ruling landlords and spiritual leaders and subsequently ran into trouble with the Moghul governor of Sindh when he refused to pay taxes. His community was besieged. Shah Inayat was betrayed, taken prisoner, and beheaded. As he praised his executioner for freeing him from the fetters of worldly existence, poets saw in him a martyr (Lari 1994: 153–55). The brotherhood of the Hur in Upper-Sindh is another example. This brotherhood, led by their spiritual head, Pir Pagara, rose against the British in the 1890s and again in the 1940s (Ansari 1992). The passion of these warrior fakirs is said to be as self-effacing as G. M. Syed's mysticism but far more energetic and violent. There was no place for the vicious quality of religious passion in Syed's reading of Sufism—a phenomenon perhaps comparable to the evolution of the *sadhu* from an aggressive band member into a peaceful world renouncer (Pinch 1996)—but Bhutto's image management drew heavy on the hot passion of the intoxicated fakir.

The geographical center of Bhutto's political spirituality was the shrine of Lal Shahbaz Qalandar in Sehwan Sharif on the west bank of the Indus, not far from his hometown of Larkana. The saint, one of the most famous along the Indus for centuries (Rizvi 1975: 306), was known as a *majzub*, or restless ecstatic who deemed God's love more important than His law. His love for the divine gave him the ability to fly, for which he was named Lal Baz or Red Falcon. In the 1960s the song associated with the saint, with the rhythmic, recurring line *dam-a-dam mast qalandar*, became the party song of the PPP. *Dam-a-dam* can refer to running blood or hot breath. *Mast* describes the hot ecstatic unification with the divine intoxification. *Qalandar* is the name of an order that specializes in expressive ecstasy as well as a group of nomads who make a living as dancers, actors, transvestites, bear tamers, and other taboo breakers (Berland 1982). Taken together *dam-a-dam mast qalandar* sounds like a cry to war with plenty of pent-up rage. It is accompanied by a rhythmic beating on large drums (*dhamal*) and a whirling style of dance (Sakata 1997). Other dancers carry a stick or a ram's horn on their shoulders while performing what was once described to me as the Mandela shuffle: a *sur place* jumping up and down. At public meetings of the PPP the audience often burst into the song, clapping and dancing to its fast beat (A. Ahmed 1988: 82). Upon hearing it, party members would automatically begin to shake their head vigorously, preferably with their eyes closed. Singers of international fame like Nusrat Fateh Ali Khan and Abida Parveen introduced the song abroad. After Bhutto's downfall Sehwan continued to be a hotbed of PPP resistance against the military regime of Zia-ul Haq. In the 1990s supporters would greet their new leader, Bhutto's daughter Benazir, shouting "Benazir Bhutto Mast Qalandar." Posters and calendars are now for sale that show the portraits of the Bhuttos floating in thin air around the dome of Lal Shahbaz Qalandar's shrine. It is said that Bhutto, "martyred" on the gallows in 1979, regularly circumambulates the shrine in a shiny white limousine, wearing a spotless white peasant dress that reflects the moonlight.

The tradition of Lal Shahbaz Qalandar was not the only spiritual power or passion Bhutto tried to absorb. He sometimes also styled himself on the model of the Shiʿa *matamdar*, that is, the person who performs physical acts of mourning in devotion to Imam Hussain, the most important martyr in the Shiʿa tradition. I will discuss the importance of the *matamdar* in Pakistani politics in a later chapter. For now, it is important to know that the *matamdar* can be a symbol of self-sacrificing resistance against tyranny. Black clothes—the color of Shiʿa protest and penance—were in fashion among young PPP supporters. Together with the red falcon saint, the *matamdar*'s spirit of self-sacrificing resistance produced the PPP's *jiyala*—a somewhat reckless but tough party activist, driven by the passion of unconditional commitment.

In the 1960s and 1970s then, in reaction to an authoritarian and patronizing state nationalism emphasizing the importance of formal education and personal discipline, a public identity of the Sindhi came into existence that centered around the shrines of the two local holy men, Shah Abdul Latif and Lal Shahbaz Qalandar, as well as the passions for which they became the personification. Their present-day patrons, G. M. Syed and Z. A. Bhutto, soon became each other's worst enemy. Whereas Bhutto tried to refashion Pakistani nationalism by adding to it the geographical notion of "the land of the Indus," Syed on the basis of his theosophical reading of Sufism completely rejected Muslim nationalism and the two nations theory on which it was founded, opting instead for the separation of Sindh as an independent nation. After founding the separatist Jeay Sindh Movement in 1973, Syed was held under house arrest till his death in 1995.

Nationality Theory

What, then, was Bhutto's vision of "the land of the Indus"? Clearly a territorial concept, it was employed to restyle the project of nation building that had hitherto failed to suppress regional identities. We find a clear example of this territorial notion of Pakistani nationhood in *The Indus Saga and the Making of Pakistan* by Aitzaz Ahsan, a lawyer and prominent PPP leader. The book tries to answer Nehru's *Discovery of India* and his thesis of a culturally and historically united subcontinent, as well as refute the two nations theory. Ahsan presents a historical-territorial argument according to which the territory of present-day Pakistan has been a political and cultural unity since the time of the Indus Valley civilization, five thousand years ago. It has produced a mentality, an "Indus person," basically a "family man with a liberal outlook," "a brave soldier and a bad administrator" (Ahsan 1996: 339–50). In 1975 the famous Sindhi philosopher A. K. Brohi had described Pakistan as the "cultural cross-breeding" of the "Father-Principle" of Islam with the "Mother Indus" (Brohi 1981: 21).

The thesis of a territorial identity gained popularity in the 1970s. It was an alternative to the ideal of Muslim nationalism that lay scattered after the partition of 1971. A Pakistani had always had a double identity. As a Muslim he belonged to the ʿ*umma* or universal brotherhood of Muslims. As a Pakistani he belonged to the *millat*—a term that traditionally stands for religious community but in the modern Muslim world is sometimes used as a synonym for nation. Whereas the ʿ*umma* explained Pakistan's eastern border with India, the *millat* did so for the western borders with other Muslim countries. Bhutto now added a third community, the *qaum*, to which a Pakistani was supposed to belong. He took *qaum*, or people, as an ethnic-territorial unit, identifying four *qaum* in Pakistan, which coincided with the four provinces: the Punjab, Sindh, Northwest Frontier Province, and Baluchistan. Being a Punjabi, Sindhi, Pakhtun, or Baluchi was no longer considered to be in opposition to a Pakistani national identity. Analogous to the two nations theory, one could coin this ideology the threefold identity theory as it brings together the attachment to the three communities of ʿ*umma, millat,* and *qaum* into one national identity. In its abbreviated form it captures the emotions of primordial protection and nurture it tried to incorporate in Pakistani identity.

A more commonly used term for the same phenomenon was "nationality theory," which became an issue of hot debate in the 1970s (F. Ahmed 1998: 1–11). It was energetically defended by Marxist theorists who applied Stalin's definition of the nation as an "historically evolved, stable community of language, territory, economic life and psychological make-up" to the Pakistani context, arguing that the place of the provinces in Pakistan was similar to the "nationalities" in the Soviet Union (ibid.: 229–31). For Feroz Ahmed, one of the most prominent Sindhi leftist intellectuals, the confrontation was "between an abstract concept of Pakistan, nurtured jealously for twenty-five years by certain vested interests, and the concrete reality of Pakistan, rooted in the thousands of years of the history of its regions" (ibid.: 42).

But the matter was more than an academic discussion based on a primordial conception of ethnicity and nationhood. The nationality theory also enabled one to see Muhajirs as a flawed and in-between category, a people with neither history nor a sense of territorial attachment, urban, on the move, and unreliable. One finds an example of this idea of the uprooted Muhajir in Benazir Bhutto's autobiography. When confronted with a marriage proposal from the family of Asif Zardari, the son of a Sindhi landlord, she ponders over his credentials, listing as one of his positive points that "He is from Sindh, so he knows our customs and courtesies. He's not a rootless phenomenon like the urban professional people who can pack their bags and go anywhere. He's a rural, with commitments to his family and tribe" (Bhutto 1988: 354). Although not mentioned explicitly by name in this quote, the "rootless phenomenon" without a sense of loyalty is, of course, the Muhajir, the urban migrant. Here we see crystallized in a crude ethnicized form the stereotypical notion of the migrant as a detached and untrustworthy person who must be kept out of the family.

The new state ideology was put into practice in several ways, such as the introduction of Sindhi as the provincial language. A "quota system," regulating access to government jobs and educational institutions on the basis of ethnicity, was implemented. In Sindh, this reservation program distinguished between rural and urban areas, which in effect meant a distinction between Sindhis and Muhajirs (Verkaaik 1994: 43–44). Moreover, Muhajirs—like other groups who did not identify as Punjabis, Sindhis, Pakhtun, or Baluchis—were asked to assimilate. They were expected to learn the Sindhi language. They were asked to call themselves New Sindhis and prove their loyalty to Sindh—its language, culture, and history. This of course opened the way for Muhajirs to question the PPP's commitment to the Pakistani ideal of Muslim fraternity and to argue that Muhajirs had made sacrifices for Pakistan, not Sindh, and that they had come to Pakistan to live in dignity as first-class citizens and never to bow for a despot again, be it a Brahman or a Sindhi landlord. Yet the reaction, culminating in the emergence of the MQM, was much more complex than a plain rejection of the nationality theory. To a large extent the MQM made the new policy of ethnicity its own and adopted the "Sindhi" passions with which it was associated.

Before addressing the question of how the MQM appropriated these various strands of state nationalism and turned them to its advantage, however, I will first look at how state nationalism has been internalized. What are the popular perceptions of concepts such as the nation, the ethnic group, territory, migration, and sacrifice? This is of course a notoriously difficult question to answer because beliefs and convictions cannot be packaged into systems. No sense of culture, identity, community, or place is ever self-evident or fixed because all these concepts are products of symbolic communication, and the meaning of symbols is by definition "polysemic" and subject to change (Geertz 1993: ch. 1; Turner 1967: 50–51). It is nonetheless possible to descry general, or generalized, patterns and trends. I will start with a discussion of Richard Kurin's work, in particular what he calls "the culture of ethnicity," which includes ethnically distinct notions of personhood and the self in relation to the natural and the supernatural. I will continue with my own observations on sacrifice and passion, as well as on migration and territory, and how these notions shape popular conceptualizations of the nation.

The Culture of Ethnicity

In the early 1980s, prior to the unprecedented and unexpected success of the MQM and its ethnicization of Muhajir identity, Richard Kurin tried to relate latent forms of ethnic othering between rural Punjabis and urban Muhajirs to a larger ontological framework, which includes various notions of the self (*shakhs*) and its relation to natural and supernatural powers.[8] Comparing the ontology of Punjabi villagers and Muhajir city dwellers, he focused on two sets of concepts in particular: the related concepts of *nafs*, *ʿaql*, and *ruh*, and the notion of "hot" (*jalal, garam*) and "cool" (*jamal, thanda*) powers. As Kurin explains, *nafs* covers the bio-psychological powers of man: physical strength, sexual desire, carnal appetite. *Ruh* is bodyless spirit: light, angels, jinns. *ʿAql* is a human quality that can be understood as the instrument with which to strive for the spiritual (*ruhani*) world and combat the animal instincts of *nafs*. In the theology of the influential twelfth-century thinker Al-Ghazzali, *ʿaql* is the human capacity through which to achieve the sublimation of self (Lapidus 1984: 46–52). In nineteenth-century India, *ʿaql* came to be seen as the source of reason, justice, and normative order (Metcalf 1984: 189). It enables man to speak in intelligible language (Kurin 1988: 223–26). For culturally dominant, often urban social groups, *ʿaql* was the source of personal discipline with which they could set themselves apart from the rural, the wild, the peripheral, the female, and the childlike, all of whom were believed to be governed by unbridled *nafs*. As Kurin argues, the underprivileged and the rural meanwhile thought of *nafs* much more positively as the indispensable source of life. From this perspective, too much *ʿaql* makes a man artificial (*naqli*), unpassionate, a scheming smooth talker (*chalak*). *Nafs* represents the uncomplicated purity of nature, territory (*desh*), the mother figure, and milk (228–34). In Hyderabad, a dairy shop's advertisement for pure *desi ghee* (local clarified butter) brought these different associations of *nafs* together.

Things, however, become more complicated with the introduction of the opposites hot and cool. These are moods and qualities, poles on a scale on which potentially all phenomena can be ranked. All food, for instance, can be characterized by its hot or cool properties. Almonds are hot, like most meat, mangoes, alcohol, clarified butter, ice cream, etc. By eating them you become inflicted by their hotness. Again, hotness is associated with life, virility, physicality, creation, and destruction (Kurin 1984: 209). But it does not completely overlap with *nafs*, because the spiritual world can also be hot. God Himself has a hot (*jalal*) as well as a cool (*rahman*) quality. There are hot, intoxicated forms of love and passion (*mast*) as well as cool and serene forms (*'ishq*). Colors can also be classified as hot or cool. Red and black are the hot colors of anger and martyrdom, while white and green are the cool colors of death and mercy.

The importance of Kurin's work lies in his observation that these different concepts constitute a "culture of ethnicity." Reviving older ways of thinking about differences between the city and the countryside as well as the court and its subjects, rural Punjabis and urban Muhajirs use these concepts to think about their differences. These are important concepts of self-identification and othering. Moreover, despite differences, both groups share this "culture." Both groups share the opinion that Punjabi villagers are more *nafs*-oriented and "hotter" than the comparatively "cool" and *'aql*-minded city-dwelling Muhajirs.

In my own work in Hyderabad, I found that similar ideas comprise relationships between Muhajirs and Sindhis. To many Muhajirs hailing from the former heartlands of the Moghul Empire, Sindh was a peripheral backwater of the subcontinent, a culturally barren outskirt, rural and tribal wilderness. Today, the rural-urban divide is at the root of many crude stereotypes ascribed to the Sindhi such as laziness, submissiveness, or intellectual slowness, which can all be explained by a lack of education and, as a result, *'aql*. On the other hand, a Sindhi's "hotness" makes him potentially violent like a wild man and intoxicated like a fakir. Sindhis, too, can take the same concepts to reach an antipodal moral evaluation of the rural-urban divide. For them, to feel the earth (*khak*) under your feet makes you humble (*khaksar*) and pure (*pak*), compared to the one-sided focus on disciplining one's instincts, displayed by urban Muhajirs.

However useful, Kurin's work is not entirely unproblematic. The main difficulty lies in the fact that it is hardly situational and ignores historical change. Kurin does not explain why concepts are defined in a seemingly fixed and mostly oppositional manner. It is my impression that outside the scope of ethnic categorization, the concepts are used in a more fluid and less antagonistic manner. These concepts are all too complex to fit into a clear-cut oppositional scheme. The dichotomization of these concepts relates to an evolutionist notion of time, which assumes that the transition from tradition to modernity, or ethnicity to nationhood, is an irreversible passage. In Pakistani state nationalism, the privileged vehicles for this personal passage to a modern mentality are formal education and migration.

Education

During my fieldwork I found that education was an important aspect in self-identification and othering. The terms *illiterate* and *uneducated* were both used in the vernacular to explain the perceived difference between the other and the self. As such, both terms stood for a lot more than the inability to read and write; it rather connoted to a "backward" mentality. I have heard *illiteracy* used as an explanation for a range of unwanted forms of behavior and phenomena such as reckless driving, the use of drugs, strong commitment to spiritual leaders, the prevalence of kinship loyalty over national solidarity, and a stagnant economy. Even a passion for kite flying was sometimes explained to me with reference to *illiteracy* because although kite flying is a widespread pastime in Pakistan, some condemn it as a Hindu practice and therefore not suitable for an educated Muslim.

To some extent, the distinction between the *educated* and the *uneducated* revives an older divide between the high caste of pure Muslim descent (*ashraf*) and the low caste of indigenous converts (*ajlaf*). The *ashraf*—plural of *sharif*, meaning cultured, noble, soft-spoken—were the groups occupying high positions in the Moghul Empire. They included subcastes or *zat* like the Syed, Siddiqi, Qureshi, or Sheikh, who claim a foreign and fully Muslim genealogy. In contrast, the *ajlaf*—plural of *jilf*, meaning vulgar, rude, low—belong to occupational groups such as cobblers (*mochi*) or butchers (*qasai*). Although the academic debate about caste among South Asian Muslims has somewhat dampened over the past few years, it is still a hot topic in Pakistan.[9] Caste is said to be a Hindu influence that has infiltrated Muslim thinking and divided the Muslim community in India. It is also believed to be an expression of social inequality that is hostile to Islam as it distinguishes between social groups on the basis of birth. To suggest, therefore, that someone is from an *ajlaf* family background is considered disrespectful. It is only done in gossip to insult or as a joke. Similarly, to flaunt an *ashraf* ancestry is condemned as a misplaced effort to claim a state of ritual purity on the basis of birth. All the same, migration—from India to Pakistan as well as from rural areas to the city—has given many families the opportunity to leave behind the low-caste stigma and claim a high-caste, foreign, pure Muslim family background. In other words, although the caste idiom has almost entirely disappeared, the anxieties and aspirations surrounding it still exist and have to some extent been revived by the distinction between the *educated* and the *illiterate*. Not only do these qualities to some extent resonate with such concepts as "cool" and "hot" or ʿaql and nafs, they have also been attributed to ethnic groups as a whole, as pointed out above.

This process can be called the ashrafization, or even ʿaqlization, of the Pakistani nation, which was linked to a similar process of ajlafizing, or nafsization, of ethnic groups like the Sindhis, the Pakhtun, or the Baluchi. Ethnic protest movements in the 1960s reversed the stigma by making the folk the basis of their political identity. Similarly, it can be said that the nationality theory as it was developed during the 1970s aimed at reconciling these two connected but opposing discourses by incorporating the latter into the former, thereby making a more favorable evaluation of nafs and "hotness" part of the national identity.

Migration

Whereas the discourse of education, modernity, and the nation to some extent overlaps with a discredited caste idiom, the imagination of the nation in terms of migration and homeland derives from the tradition of Islamic exodus (hijra) as well as the paramount emotional importance given to graves. In order to introduce the oscillating manner in which many Pakistanis (Muhajirs in particular) relate to these traditions, I will quote from a novel by Intizar Hussain, originally published in Urdu under the title Basti. A resident of Lahore, Intizar Hussain himself was born just over the border. The book's title does not merely mean "place" or "land" but also expresses an emotional attachment to it. The main character of the novel is a young professor of history, born in a town called Rupnagar in Uttar Pradesh. The novel describes his doubts and memories during the last months of 1971, just before the parting of Bangladesh:

> When Pakistan was still all new, when the sky of Pakistan was fresh like the sky of Rupnagar, and the earth was not yet soiled. In those days how the caravans arrived from their long, long journeys! Every day caravans entered the city and dispersed among the streets and neighbourhoods. . . . The refugees told whole long epics about how much suffering they had endured on the journey, and how many difficulties they had overcome in order to reach the city. They told about those whom they had left behind. Then the refuge-givers and the refugees together remembered those who had clung to the earth, refusing to leave their homes and their ancestors' graves. (I. Hussain 1995: 90)

In a further passage, those who stayed behind appear again in his thoughts:

> These old men who stayed on alone were not held back by the thought of their property, but by the thought of their graves. There was no problem about property: people could go to Pakistan and enter a claim, and by entering false claims they could even get a larger property in return for a smaller one. But no one can

enter a claim for a grave. . . . Yar [friend], you Muslims are wonderful! You're always looking toward the deserts of Arabia, but for your graves you prefer the shade of India. (139)

These passages articulate two different notions of sacred territory. The first passage evokes the tradition of the *hijra*, during which the Muslims fled from hostile Mecca and were received by the local population of Medina with great hospitality. The second passage, in contrast, mentions the emotional attachment to the graves of ancestors and saints in one's place of birth.

There has been, and still is, extensive attention paid to the importance of graves, especially the graves of holy men or *pirs*, for community, identity, and political mobilization in anthropological literature on Pakistan (Ansari 1992; Ewing 1983, 1997; Gilmartin 1988; Sherani 1991; Werbner and Basu 1998). Surprisingly, given the crucial place of travel and migration in public debates and state nationalism, less work has been done on the tradition of the *hijra* in Pakistan. An exception is an article by Khalid Masud, in which he argues that traditionally the dominant interpretation of the *hijra* doctrine in South Asia was the one offered by the Hanafi school of Islamic law. According to this formulation, the exodus to Medina did not deny the importance of blood ties among different groups of *muhajirin* (those who took part in the *hijra*), nor did it create inheritance relations between the *muhajirin* and the *ansar* (the residents of Medina). The issue of the interpretation of the *hijra* doctrine was revived in colonial times along with the issue of whether colonial India was enemy territory (*dar al-harb*) from which one was obliged to migrate. In the twentieth century a new type of intellectual, not trained in traditional legal thought, sought interpretations of the *hijra* that justified nationalist action. The *hijra* came to be seen as a denial of the importance of blood ties and an emotional territorial attachment. The *hijra* doctrine is thus no longer merely a theological concept but a topic of public debate (Masud 1990).

Crucial in this debate is the idea of Islam as foreign to India, an idea fostered by nineteenth-century Muslim poets and intellectuals, as well as a nineteenth-century Orientalist understanding of Islam as first and foremost a Middle Eastern religion. As Ayesha Jalal (1997) has described, this self-imposed foreignness fed upon a sense of nostalgia for a lost Muslim civilization in India. This so-called Andalusia syndrome, which links the loss of India to the earlier loss of Muslim Spain to the Christians in 1492, typically portrayed *ashraf* Muslim culture as superior but decaying (S. Khan 1973: 79–109; Metcalf 1982: 238–58; Sharar 1975). It turned Muslims into a diasporic nation, a nation without a homeland, for surely returning to one's perceived place of origin—Arabia, Persia, Central Asia—was not an option. With the formulation of the Pakistan Demand in the 1930s (Aziz 1987), nostalgia was turned into a political program that would end the nation's diasporic status.

The link between migration to Pakistan and the *hijra* was made soon after independence. As early as September 1947, the term *muhajir* (one who takes part in the *hijra*) was used when Pir Illahi Bakhsh, education minister of Sindh, was reported to have "revived the good old Arab memory of the brotherhood between the muhajireen and the ansar . . . when he took a family of Muslim refugees from Amritsar from the railway station to his house as guests."[10] Initially the use of *muhajir* was used to overcome differences among social, linguistic, regional, or sectarian groups. The term had several positive connotations. It ascribed a degree of agency to the migrants that other possible terms like *panahgir* (refugee) lacked. It regained a sense of dignity for those who had been forced to flee their homes. It also contained the element of sacrifice as it suggested that one had come for a greater cause than merely personal benefit. Apparently there was initially little opposition to the use of the term. Only in the 1950s did several Sindhi politicians introduce the term "New Sindhis" as a more appropriate term for the migrant population. Generally speaking, however, the term *muhajir* initially spoke of solidarity and a religiously inspired optimism to overcome social differences.

During my own field research in the late 1990s, I found that migration to Pakistan was still compared to the *hijra*, but the emphasis had shifted from the solidarity upon arrival between the migrants and the hospitable local population to the uniqueness of the migrant experience. The local population lacked that experience. Migration was often compared to a second birth, a rite de passage into a new mentality that combined cosmopolitanism, modernity, and a sense of patriotism. It was also seen as a sacrifice of primordial attachments that proved one's will power (*hosla*) and love for the nation. It was often stressed that Muhajirs, unlike the local population, had actually made a conscious choice for Pakistan. Yet this very aspect of choice could also be used to argue that Muhajirs were also capable of making a choice *against* Pakistan, whereas the local population, attached to the nation by destiny and birth, could not. The migration experience, in other words, now divided migrants from non-migrants, whereas it had formerly brought the two categories together as refugees (*muhajirin*) and hosts (*ansar*) in the tradition of the *hijra*.

The Barelwi "Cult of Graves"

Education and migration, then, are important markers of Muhajir identity. Both are presented as evidence of the successful initiation into modernity and Islamic nationalism. Yet Muhajir identity is far from one-dimensional and unambiguous. The so-called Barelwi cult of graves provides an important counterpoint to the discourse of migration and modernity. Although I will introduce the neighborhood that provided the data for this study more fully in chapter 3, I will briefly discuss the religious debates that were going on among the inhabitants of this area to show that notwithstanding ethnic stereotyping, not all Muhajirs are staunch Islamic modernists rejecting tradition as a sign of illiteracy or unpatriotic primordial sentiments. In fact, several traditions of the custom-laden Barelwi interpretation of Islam were self-consciously defended as the proper form of Islamic conduct despite the condemnation of these practices as improper "innovations" (*bid̄at*) by reform movements.

The Barelwi tradition was one of the last Indian reform movement of the nineteenth century. The Barelwi ʿ*ulama* are often seen as representing the South Asian Islamic tradition prior to modernity as they rejected other reformists for their modernist interpretation of Islam.[11] The Barelwi ʿ*ulama* defended "the mediational, custom-laden Islam, closely tied to the intercession of the *pirs* of the shrines" as the true form of Islam. "Like the other ʿ*ulama*, they opted to turn inward, cherishing religion as an ever-more important component of their identity. But in a period widely held to be threatening to their culture, they blamed not only the colonial ruler but—perhaps even more—the reformist Muslims. They wanted to preserve Islam unchanged: not Islam as it was idealized in texts or the historical past, but Islam as it had evolved to the present" (Metcalf 1982: 296). In the context of reform, the Barelwi ʿ*ulama* defended the importance of genealogy (*shajra*), shrines (*dargah*), and the sacred authority of the spiritual leader (*pir*).

The debate among nineteenth-century reform movements continued in the area of this study, where most people considered themselves Barelwi Sunni Muslims. Four out of the five mosques within the neighborhood were said to be Barelwi mosques, the fifth a Shiʿa mosque. A large mosque of the Ahl-i Hadis—a radical purist form of reformist Islam—stood just outside the citadel, impressing the nearby inhabitants with a muezzin whose Arabic pronunciation was said to sound like the real thing. The mosque was recently built—not, however, with money raised by local donations but, I was told, with gifts from abroad, mainly Saudi Arabia. Whether true or not, the message was that the Ahl-i Hadis were a foreign phenomenon. Although impressively elegant, the mosque attracted few believers. Within the neighborhood it had the unfavorable reputation of being "fundamentalist," "Taliban," or "Wahabi"—the latter meaning "foreign" in popular idiom. Of all reform movements, the ultra-orthodox Ahl-i Hadis were seen as the most erroneous. But Deobandi tradition, a widespread reformist movement locally associated with the Jamʿiat-i Islami, was also condemned for its attacks on spiritual music, shrine visits, and the use of amulets (*tawiz*) issued by saints. The elitist Aligarh tradition, finally, was associated with the bureaucracy, the English-speaking elite, and what was seen as their mimicry of the immoral West.

The Barelwi view is particularly critical of the notion that the dead and the divine are transcendental (*ghair-hazir*) and mediated only through light (*nur*). In this view, the only exception to the divine's transcendental existence is the revelation of the Qur'an, which accounts for the Qur'an's miraculous uniqueness (*ijaz*). While the uniqueness of the Qur'an is of course acknowledged, the Barelwi view also holds that the dead—the saints and the ancestors—intervene in the life of the living through messages mediated through dreams and states of trance. For this reason, various religious practices take place around graves. This includes visiting the tombs of saints or their successors within the same order (*silsilah*). Some of them are famous and attract huge numbers of visitors, while others are small and looked after by only a few people, including the successor of the saint (*sajjada nishin*) and the majordomo of the shrine (*khalifa*). Similarly, an important date in the Barelwi calendar is the feast of *shab-i-barat* on the fourteenth of the month Sha'ban, when one visits the graves of the ancestors and prays for their well-being in the hereafter.

Despite migration and the impact of Islamic reform movements these practices continue. The importance of graves does not seem to be on the wane. The graves of ancestors and saints left behind across the border often instill people with a sense of nostalgia, which is a counterpoint to the future-oriented reading of migration as a turn toward liberation and progress. A growing number of migrants from the older generation have been on pilgrimages to their ancestors' graves in India over the past ten to twenty years. Such trips are grounds on which the Pakistani government grants permission to travel and issues passports. These visits reestablish a link with the past that perhaps seemed unimportant earlier. The continuing emotional attachment to the graves of saints and ancestors contributes significantly to the incompleteness and ambiguousness of the stereotypical image of the Muhajir as a modernist who has left tradition behind in the act of migration.

SACRIFICE AND PASSION

In what I have called the ethnicization of Islam, a state-promoted discourse on the relation between national identity and Islamic reform has led to a differentiation in mentality between the predominantly rural Sindhis and the predominantly urban Muhajirs in which the tropes of education and migration, as signifiers of modernity, play important roles. Whereas Sindhis have formed a distinct Sindhi form of Muslim nationalism based on refashioned local traditions of saint worship and mysticism,

Muhajirs are primarily associated with the legacy of late nineteenth- and early twentieth-century reform. These stereotypes are, however, only partly rooted in everyday life. Moreover, the MQM response to this has been a complex one. An important strategy has been to transgress these ethnic boundaries, thereby appropriating the Sindhi tradition of revolt and passion. To end this chapter, then, I will briefly discuss notions of sacrifice and passion related to the nation. How do various forms of passion relate to different understandings of the nation?

Sacrifice

It is fair to say that nationalism is often conceptualized as a form of sacrifice in Pakistan. It is typically considered a self-effacing turn away from one's own interest or the interest of one's family or close neighbors in favor of the interest of a larger community. Various historical figures are held up as role models. Liaqat Ali Khan, first prime minister of Pakistan, for instance, was born a rich landlord, but after a life dedicated to the Pakistani cause he was reported to have only two hundred rupees in his bank account. However, such sincere nationalists are considered rare. More often nationalist discourse is distrusted and often condemned as hollow, concealing the compromising business of politics (*siyasat*). In its true form, however, nationalism in popular perception stands opposed to the particularistic interests of politics and as such is comparable to, albeit not quite the same as, religious sacrifice.

In this respect the most often used term for sacrifice is *qurbani*. Literally the term refers to the gift of an animal on the occasion of *baqr' id*, the day commemorating Ibrahim's sacrifice of his son. Part of the meat is distributed to the poor while the remaining parts are shared with family, friends, and neighbors. But the expression can also be used for any sort of work or gift for which one is not immediately rewarded in cash or kind. The spirit of nonreciprocity is crucial. To make a sacrifice (*qurbani dena*) is one of the most popular expressions in political discourse. Because of this, it hardly has a religious connotation any longer. Sometimes a distinction is made between a religious sacrifice (*din ki qurbani*) and a political or worldly sacrifice (*dunya ki qurbani*).

The term *khidmat* is also popular. Regularly translated as "social work" and regarded as a religious duty, it is highly valued. In this respect it is sometimes quoted from the *hadis*, or sayings of the Prophet, that there is no greater prayer than providing aid to fellow human beings. The MQM has run a *khidmat-e-khalq* committee for social work since 1978 collecting money and other donations in the name of this committee. During aid-donating or *imdadi* programs, the committee distributes *zakat* and "charity" (*khairat*) during the fasting month of Ramzaan. Widows, the disabled, families of "martyrs" (*shuhada*) and students from poor families are entitled to gifts. The organization has also arranged dowries for orphan girls and provided free medical treatment and ambulance services. In 1989 it held a "free market" (*muft bazaar*) in Karachi to distribute free clothing and groceries. *Khidmat* purifies the party from the corruption of politics and proves its true nationalist motives.

As Pnina Werbner has argued, sacrifice in Muslim South Asia is a symbolic language of hierarchical social relationships. Gifts to God are either given downward to the poor in the form of alms (*sadaqa*) or upward to saints in the form of *nazrana* (Werbner 1990: 151–71, 227–58). Werbner also acknowledges that "alternatively, offerings are made to communal causes such as the building of a mosque" (1998: 103). Although giving to the mosque is also indexical insofar as it offers large donors the opportunity to stand out as men of honor and wealth, the egalitarian spirit of this form of religious gift giving is immanent. Moreover, it is a matter of pride that mosques are, almost without exception, community mosques, built with money raised through local collections. This collection is in fact a never-ending process. A mosque always needs redecoration, a new fan, an addition, etc. By making these donations, no matter how small, one enters an ideally egalitarian community of people who can all call the mosque their own. This egalitarianism of the mosque is a popular model for the egalitarian notion of the nation.

The hierarchical language of sacrifice, however, is also an important model for sacrificing for the nation. In this case, the sacrifice is made in the name of a charismatic leader who epitomizes the nation. The comparison with *nazrana*, or a gift as a mark of respect to a spiritual leader, would be appropriate here, but as a model it features less often in political discourse. One occasion described to me as a form of *nazrana* giving included an incident in the 1980s when MQM leader Altaf Hussain was seated behind a desk on the public street to personally collect from his followers their gifts to the party. Crowds queued up before their leader, who bureaucratically wrote down each and every gift in a notebook as a sign of transparency. More commonly, however, the application of the term *nazrana* to this event was rejected because it was felt to wrongly elevate Altaf Hussain to the status of a spiritual leader. The term *nazrana* was also said to be inappropriate because it expresses an unequal relationship.

Passion

A true sacrifice is perceived as a matter of passion. A pure sacrifice is never made because of ulterior motives, such as social pressure or personal gain, but as an expression of passion. Passion is believed to be capable of turning the tables on existing power relations. It also provides an alternative to a dominant moral code of honor that underlines hierarchical social relations, gender roles, and rules for moral behavior. Passion is an expression of the spiritual power to fight opponents who are physically or socially stronger and defeat them against all odds. By renouncing the gendered, hierarchical world, one surrenders to a greater power and through the medium of devotional love absorbs part of it. Closest to home, passion in the form of romantic love is considered a beautiful feeling as well as a dangerous threat to the family hierarchy. Other forms of passion can be even more disturbing.

One such form is known as *'ishq*. An "intense and compelling possessive love" (Kurin 1984: 215), *'ishq* can denote sexual desire between two people and, in its eternal or *haqiqi* form, connote a man's desire to be wholly possessed by God—directly, or indirectly through his *pir*. *'Ishq* is a form of passion in which the effemination of the believer in the face of a greater power takes place most clearly, as it has produced an extensive symbolism of spiritual marriage in which the believer plays the part of the bride (216). In contrast, the *majzub* and the *mastan*, or those drunk on divine love, represent a passion that is much more constructive/destructive. They are rebels and madmen, associated with boiling blood and hot breath. In these cases, mystical unification does not lead to an ascetic, contemplative, or world-renouncing attitude but to a whirling, rhythmic, sometimes violent state of ecstasy.

One finds similar contrasting moods in the primarily Shi'a practices of *majlis* and *matam*. The former is primarily contemplative, the latter more ecstatic. A mourning congregation or *majlis* is a gathering in which the passion play of Imam Hussain's martyrdom at the battlefield of Karbala is narrated. The recitations are often interrupted with expressions of mourning, repentance, and love for the Prophet and His family. *Matam*, or self-flagellation, which comes in four types (Schubel 1993: 145–57), is more physical. However, even the more radical forms, such as walking on fire and cutting one's back with knives, are reported to be physically painless (146). The act is seen as an expression of faith, which makes one indifferent to physical pain.

Finally, *hosla* (will power) is also seen as a passion that gives a man great strength. Although perhaps not as radical as the other forms of religious passion, *hosla* also requires the effacement of aspects of the self. Although it does not carry as strongly a religious connotation as the other passions, it is nevertheless commonly believed to originate in true faith.

If religious passion may lead to renouncing the world and withdrawal, world renouncing can also be the source of rebellion. Several national politicians have styled their appearances, conduct, and speeches on the traditions of religious passion in order to challenge the status quo.

Whereas General Ayub Khan, with his erect posture, moustache, and army uniform, was unmistakably a straightforward manly figure who symbolized the status quo, many of his colleagues were less unambiguous. Consider for instance three different types of nationalist leaders. G. M. Syed, the leader of the Sindhi nationalist movement, presented himself as a descendant of the Prophet (*syed*), dressed in white clothes and deeply absorbed in a painful mystical search for truth and love. Zulfiqar Ali Bhutto regularly styled himself on the model of the Shiʿa *matamdar* or the intoxicated *mastan*. The frail Jinnah, finally, is widely remembered an icon of disciplined *hosla*.

The Sindhi nationalist turn to Sufism described above also included the incorporation of the power embodied in the passions of the mystic. In particular the transgressive and drunken "madness" of the *majzub* and the *mastan* has become part of the Sindhi revolt against the center. As figures typically portrayed as being outside or beyond the reach of the law, the *majzub* and *mastan* constituted models for rebellion against the orthodox and the cerebral, which were widely embraced especially by the youth who took part in the Sindhi movement and the Pakistan People's Party under Zulfiqar Ali Bhutto. To a lesser extent, this is also true for the passion of loyalty and the strength to endure physical pain embodied by the Shiʿa *matamdar*.

All of this was part of an ethnic revolt against the authoritarian modernization of the state leading to a reformulation of the Pakistani nation no longer opposed to ethnic loyalty. This was unfavorable to Muhajirs, who were not recognized as a separate ethnic group on par with Punjabis, Sindhis, Pakhtun, and Baluchis. In reaction to this, however, the newly formed MQM did not oppose this new definition of the nation but adopted it by proclaiming Muhajirs an ethnic group of its own. Moreover, it did so by appropriating the Sindhi nationalist passions of rebellion against the center. This constituted a remarkable blurring of ethnic categories and a break with the public image of Muhajirs as educated modernists and migrants.

Appropriating the Sindhi Passion of Revolt

This chapter, then, has set the stage for a more detailed examination of the MQM's response to a process of nation building in which Muhajirs, as a group, were first seen as the vanguard of modernity and nationhood but then became the largest group of people not recognized as an ethnic group in a reformulated state nationalism taking ethnicity as an integral part of national identity. This response was a remarkable one, shocking to many in Pakistan, and I will try to do justice to the complexity of the rise of the MQM in the following chapters. I will end this chapter by briefly indicating how the MQM took over, at least temporarily, the Sindhi model of revolt and the Sindhi nationalist language of religious passion. Two examples must suffice to illustrate what I have in mind. Both have to do with the way MQM supporters address their leader and founder of the party, Altaf Hussain.

In the heyday of the MQM, one of the most popular party slogans was Mast Qalandar Altaf Hussain. One could regularly come across groups of young men driving around town on their motorcycles, the party flag tied to their vehicle, shouting this cry. It was a double-edged sword. On the one hand it was a parody of the custom of their rivals in the Pakistan People's Party, supported in Sindh mainly by Sindhis, who would shout "Mast Qalandar Benazir Bhutto" on *their* rides or marches, comparing the power of their loyalty to their party leader Benazir Bhutto to the drunken passion of the saint Lal Shahbaz Qalandar, buried in Upper-Sindh. On the other hand, it was not merely a provocative joke. The slogan could also be taken seriously as an expression of one's self-effacing commitment to the leader of the movement, a confirmation of a passion as absorbing as the mad passion of the *mastan*.

One finds a similar ambiguity in Altaf Hussain's title of Pir Sahib (Mister Holy Man). People commonly address their spiritual leaders as Pir Sahib. In national politics, the title is particularly associated with the Pir Pagara, the spiritual and political leader of the already mentioned brotherhood of the Hur in Upper-Sindh and an influential politician in Sindh and Pakistan as a whole. From the perspective of the Muhajir city dweller, the Hur represent perhaps the most typical example of rural Sindhi tradition. Hailing mostly from districts adjacent to the Thar Desert that separates Sindh from Rajasthan in India, the Hur are in many ways the antithesis of urban Islamic modernism. According to a possibly apocryphal story, one day Altaf Hussain arrived at a place of conference in Karachi with the Pir Pagara to discuss provincial politics. Supporters of both leaders gathered outside and when the Pir's followers spotted their leader, they began to welcome him by the name of Pir Sahib. Promptly, the much more numerous MQM supporters began to do the same. It was primarily experienced as a joke to address a Muhajir leader from a humble urban background in the same way as the revered and turbaned leader of a Sindhi brotherhood is addressed. It was funny in an absurd way as it mixed up and transgressed ethnic-religious categories. Subsequently the title became popular and prevailed as an accepted way of addressing the party leader. Still later, when ethnic violence rendered many people homeless, Altaf Hussain made himself a living icon of their suffering, and as a consequence the title of Pir Sahib gained a different meaning. It became the proper way to address a man many Muhajirs saw as their only possible savior.

These two anecdotes indicate the far from one-dimensional ways in which the MQM positioned itself within the field of ethnic-religious stereotypical categories. As I have argued in this chapter, these ethnic categories were partly the result of a state-promoted nationalism, which endorsed Islamic modernist, high-caste (*ashraf*), Urdu-mediated values as more Islamic and more patriotic than regional folk customs, languages, and religious practices. The ethnic categorization was also partly promoted by ethnic movements such as the Sindhi nationalist movement that protested state nationalism by adopting its categorization while reversing its moral evaluation, turning "low" and "backward" into "authentic," and "modern" and "educated" into "uprooted" and "detached." This reversed, ethnic form of nationalism was to some extent taken up and incorporated into state nationalism by the government led by the Pakistan People's Party in the 1970s. The "culture of ethnicity" included Islam, separating so-called folk and traditional Islamic practices from high culture, modernist Islam, and dividing these categories along ethnic lines. As indicated by the two examples above, the MQM's response to this was an ambiguous one, sometimes disrespectfully mixing up categories, sometimes embracing them. I will start analyzing this process in the next chapter by presenting a history of the MQM: its rise, its heyday, and its imminent decline.

CHAPTER TWO

The Muhajir Qaumi Movement

THE MQM has many faces and can be described in many ways. Many social scientists, for instance, see the party as a remarkable phenomenon of mass mobilization. From this perspective, an interesting aspect of the MQM is the sudden reformulation of Muhajir identity from one derived from the notions of Muslim brotherhood and Pakistani nationhood to one based on the exclusiveness of ethnicity. Foreshadowed by the founding of the All Pakistan Muhajir Student Organization (APMSO) in 1978, the MQM was established in 1984 by a group of friends who had met in educational institutions in Karachi. They declared Muhajirs a separate cultural group of people that despite their migration to Pakistan had "not signed a contract to uphold Pakistan and Islam" ("hamne pakistan aur islam ka theka nahi liya hai"). Harking back to the tradition of the *hijra* or Islamic exodus, they portrayed their migration as the founding crisis of a new Muhajir "ethnic group" (*qaum*).

To many of its members and supporters, the MQM is primarily a revolutionary party fighting for the rights of the underprivileged strata of the urban population. It is celebrated as a party of the "poor people" (*gharib log*), or "common people" (*am log*), promoting social equality (*musawat*). They see the MQM as a revolution against a ruling elite of landlords, bureaucrats, and the military and stress the humble, lower-middle-class background of their leaders. For them, the party is also a source of hope, pride, joy, and liberation. In 1988 and 1990 large numbers of supporters took to the streets to celebrate "as a cultural liberation" the party's unexpected election victories in a way that "was reminiscent of the days when Pakistan was created."[1]

Those less sympathetic to the party primarily associate the MQM with violence. They stress that the party has been involved in numerous riots against several enemies, starting in 1985 when it was accused of fueling and exploiting animosity between the Pakhtun migrant population of northwest Pakistan and the so-called Biharis (double migrants who traveled from North India to East Pakistan after 1947 and from Bangladesh to Pakistan after 1971). Since then the MQM has been involved in various incidents of ethnic violence. According to its opponents, the MQM has significantly contributed to a so-called kalashnikov culture of theft, blackmail, political assassination, and intimidation, which has made the cities and towns of Sindh unsafe since the mid-1980s. It is further argued that as soon as the MQM rose to power after the 1988 elections, it became involved in gross nepotism to accommodate its activists and supporters. The party is now blamed for the widespread practice of *bhatta*, or "tax" collection by private parties, as well as for the steep increase of burglaries and car thefts. The party, it is said, constantly needs money to supply its activists with firearms and to secure a luxurious lifestyle for its leaders.

The MQM's self-image, meanwhile, has been changing. Speeches and interviews by its leaders initially depicted the MQM as a rebellious, anti-establishment party that borrowed much of its rhetoric from Sindhi sepa-ratists and the populist Pakistan People's Party (PPP). As the previous chapter has shown, the opposition against the military regime of the 1960s identified with peasants and the rural areas, generating a tradition of revolt and political romanticism built on aspects of a refashioned popular religion. After the restoration of democracy in 1988, the MQM joined hands with the PPP led by Benazir Bhutto in a coalition that was felt to be a Sindhi-Muhajir agreement against the common enemy of the army. In addition to this, both the PPP and the MQM loathed the dominance of the Punjab, by far the most populous province of Sindh. Within a few years, however, the ethnic and rebellious rhetoric of the MQM gave way to a more mainstream Islamic vocabulary of justice and righteousness in the face of oppression and tyranny. The MQM began to present itself as a party for all oppressed people (*mazlum*) constituting, it claimed, 98 per-cent of the Pakistani population, exploited by a tiny elite of feudal land-lords (*wadera*) or the twenty-two families who rule Pakistan as if it was their landed property (*jagir*). The MQM accused the PPP of being hi-jacked by Sindhi "feudals" and left the coalition.

The turn toward a discourse of class and justice rather than ethnicity and revolt was, however, a slow and incomplete process. For years the MQM was in limbo in terms of whether to continue as an ethnic, Muhajir movement or to become a more mainstream party representing the urban "middle class"—a social category that in the MQM's definition of the term includes practically everyone who is not overly rich. The party leader-ship regularly announced that the name of the MQM would be changed from Muhajir Qaumi Movement to Muttehida Qaumi Movement, mean-ing the movement of the united nation rather than the Muhajir nation. In 1997 the new name was finally adopted. Despite the name change, however, the Muttehida Qaumi Movement has remained primarily a party of the underprivileged segments of the Muhajir population.

The MQM has also experienced more severe divisiveness. In the summer of 1991, the breakaway MQM-Haqiqi was formed—*haqiqi* means true or righteous. Those loyal to the original MQM and its leader, Altaf Hus-sain—now known as the Haq Parast Group,[2] MQM-Altaf, or, most recently, the Muttehida Qaumi Movement—immediately accused them of being the stooges of the military's secret intelligence agency, the ISI, hired to eliminate Altaf Hussain and damage the party. Not surprisingly, given that divided militant movements are usually the most violent (Crenshaw 1988: 22), the result of the split has been a sharp increase in militant action. Infighting between activists of both factions has replaced the violence that used to take place between MQM militants and members of other ethnic, mainly Sindhi organizations. Since the launching in 1992 of so-called Operation Clean-up, an army operation against both the MQM militancy in the cities and the widespread phenomenon of banditry in rural Sindh, state forces have been a third party to the disruption of social life in Karachi and Hyderabad. In the mid-1990s Karachi became virtually a city of war. Semi-autonomous gangs of militants ambushed each other and state forces in an effort to control small patches of the city. Dozens of MQM activists died in what were euphemistically called "police encounters," violent clashes between the police and the MQM for which the pleonastic term "extrajudicial killings" was used. In 1995 more than two thousand people were killed in ambushes, bomb blasts, and shootings among state forces, the Haq Parast Group, and the breakaway MQM-Haqiqi.

The split of the party as well as the army operation significantly curbed the power of the MQM. Most of its leaders fled the country to escape imprisonment. As early as 1992, paramount leader Altaf Hussain left Karachi for London, officially for medical reasons, and has not returned. The army operation has eliminated the local leadership, the so-called sector-in-charge, who were crucial executors of party discipline in the various neighborhoods of Karachi and Hyderabad. Because of the strict hierarchical organization of the party, this has seriously weakened the grip of the party on the population of both cities. All the same, the mercilessness of the state forces has revived among the Muhajir population the notion of a besieged, diasporic nation, suffering under the tyranny (*zulm*) of a hostile state. This continues to drive many Muhajirs into the fold of the MQM.

This chapter examines these various phases in the turbulent and short history of the movement. The first section analyzes the early MQM's conflict with the traditional Muhajir parties, notably the Islamist Jamʿiat-i Islami (JI), as well as the Jamʿiat-i ʿUlama-i Pakistan (JUP) led by Barelwi ʿulama. Taking advantage of several incidents of ethnic violence in the mid-1980s, the MQM offered a much more powerful alternative to the lukewarm support the JI and the JUP gave to the attacked Muhajir population. For years these parties virtually vanished from the political scene in urban Sindh. The second section focuses on the heyday of the movement in the late 1980s and early 1990s. By examining the aspects of revolutionary change, transgression, and provocative action, I will try to explain what made the movement so attractive to many young Muhajirs. The third and fourth sections look at the movement's decline: the emerging animosity with Sindhi-dominated parties, in particular the PPP; state persecution; the internal split of the party; and the response of the party to these threats.

In my discussion on the MQM I will mainly make use of newspaper articles, information gathered through interviews, and oral sources including speeches made by MQM leaders, some of which are recorded on video and audiotape. In my experience, these oral sources have a larger impact on MQM supporters than written sources, including those published by the MQM, as most MQM supporters tend to listen to speeches and take part in public manifestations rather than read books and brochures. Nonetheless, some important MQM brochures are used.[3]

RISE IN VIOLENCE

To understand the sudden rise of the MQM, it is necessary to know the political preferences of the Muhajir population prior to the MQM. It is very often said that the MQM brought Muhajirs together on one platform. Certainly the Muhajir vote was scattered over various political parties before the MQM attracted the support of most Muhajir voters. In the early years of Pakistan, the Muhajir elite would generally support and to some extent dominate the Muslim League. Among the poorer segments of the Muhajir population, there were many who voted for one of the *jam'iats*, parties like the JI and the JUP, locally known as "Islamic" parties. In Karachi the JI, founded by Maulana Mawdudi and considered one of the first modern Muslim organizations proclaiming the "Islamic Revolution," attracted considerable support. In Hyderabad the JUP was more popular. The latter was a strange coalition of two groups with very different backgrounds. On the one hand the party included the Urdu-speaking *pirs* and *'ulama* in the Barelwi tradition (M. Ahmad 1993: 41–44; Nasr 1994: 127; Sherani 1991: 233–34). On the other hand, the party became a platform for young and radical Muhajir students who had become politically active in the late 1960s. Many of them had been members of the All Pakistan Muslim Students Federation (APMSF), an almost solely Muhajir and Hyderabad-based organization, that to some extent foreshadowed the founding a decade later of the All Pakistan Muhajir Students Organization (APMSO)—the forerunner of the MQM. These students had opposed both the military regime of General Ayub Khan and the Sindhi student movement that had become a powerful force at Sindh University in Hyderabad. Jointly these two groups managed to win the JUP seven seats in the provincial assembly in the elections of 1970. The JI, in contrast, was more popular in Karachi and would become one of the more vocal opposition parties in the 1977 elections. Like the JUP, the JI was an anti-establishment party and opposed the PPP's endorsement of refashioned popular Sufism as well as Islamic modernism à la Muhammad Iqbal, preaching the sovereignty of the Islamic law (*sharīʿat*) instead (Nasr 1994: 77–78).

However, the "Islamic" parties never won the Muhajir vote so decisively as the MQM managed to later. Many Muhajirs used to support other parties. Because of the PPP's links to trade unions, a large number of Muhajir workers and artisans supported Bhutto in the 1970 election. There were also various local parties attracting the Muhajir vote. Apart from the JUP, for instance, Hyderabad produced still another party, the Muhajir Punjabi Pakhtun Movement (MPPM). Led mainly by Muhajir bureaucrats and businessmen, this party tried to unite all migrants, including Punjabis and Pakhtun, who had come to Sindh after independence in order to counter the growing Sindhi nationalist movement. Although the party won only one seat in the provincial elections of 1970, its powerful chairman, Nawab Muzaffar Khan, became the de facto spokesman of the Urdu-speaking population, in particular during the language crisis in 1972 when Sindhi and Muhajir groups clashed violently over a dispute on the new status of Sindhi as the provincial language. This man posthumously played a role during my field research as he lay buried in the little park within the neighborhood of fieldwork. His grave was the largest among nine other graves, including those of the victims of ethnic violence in the 1990s, and a little shrine of a local *pir*, a recently expired holy man belonging to the Chishtiyya order.[4]

In sum, although it would be wrong to say that Muhajirs prior to the MQM overwhelmingly supported the "Islamic" parties, many Muhajirs did vote for them. Today, however, many Muhajirs distrust both parties, typically condemning them for "promising us a place in heaven but failing to get us one in Pakistan." The "Islamic" parties are often dismissed as weak and ineffective, as well as hypocritical in their Islamic rhetoric. This harsh judgment signifies a remarkable change of opinion among Muhajirs. To understand this change, we have to go back to the early history of the MQM.

The APMSO and Early Years of the MQM

Largely the same group of young men who would establish the MQM on 18 March 1984 founded the All Pakistan Muhajir Student Organization (APMSO) on 11 June 1978. The group had met in the pharmacy department of Karachi University in 1974. Because of a shift toward a semester system, a group of twenty-seven students had not been registered on time and failed to gain admission. They raised an Intermediate Student Action Committee to demand midterm admission. The president of this committee was twenty-one-year-old Altaf Hussain who even at that early stage made quite an impression on his fellow students as he wore a revolutionary cap and shockingly tight trousers (S. Hussain 1991). Under his leadership the committee was successful. The students were admitted and the university vice-chancellor resigned.

After this first success in student politics, Altaf Hussain disappeared from the scene for several years. His place was taken over by Azim Ahmad Tariq, born in Karachi in 1948. Together with twenty of his friends and independently of any other student organization, Ahmad Tariq organized a group of *madadgars* (helpers) to assist new students in study-related matters. Initiated by the Pakistan Student Federation (PSF)—the student organization of the PPP—student politics had rapidly gained momentum in the 1970s. Student organizations held important instruments of power, most crucial of which was the allotment of rooms in student dormitories. At Karachi University, the Islami Jam'iat-i Tulabah (IJT)—the student wing of the JI—was by far the most influential of all organizations (Nasr 1992a: 72), facing opposition mainly from the PSF. Ahmad Tariq and his friends were influenced by the rebellious spirit of the mid-1970s and rejected the "Islamic" parties that opposed Bhutto's references to socialism and Sufism. But they did not feel at home in the PSF either. Most other parties and their student organizations were based on ethnic affiliations, such as the Jeay Sindh Students Federation, the Pakhtun Student Federation, and the Punjabi Students Association. Ahmad Tariq's little group decided to form its own organization.

Altaf Hussain, meanwhile, initially calculated that the JI was a better horse to bet on. During the 1977 election campaign he toured the city with JI candidates who led the opposition against Bhutto. Disappointed that his efforts were not rewarded, Altaf returned to Ahmad Tariq to raise the APMSO in 1978. He immediately became the spokesman of the group. "The refugee students have been suffering for the last several years," he said during the APMSO's inauguration, demanding the abolishment of the "quota system," which allotted places in educational organizations on the basis of ethnic background.[5]

Fellow students recall how at first the APMSO made a pathetic impression and was considered "a bunch of silly boys." In the first four years the organization was ridiculed and constantly harassed, said Tariq Javeed, one of its founding members.[6] Other organizations also complained about the violent and arrogant attitude (*goondaism*) of the IJT. The latter's so-called *danda (stick) force* used to drive opponents out of the dormitories (Anwar 1997: 91). From 1972 onward, violence, humiliation, and threats had been on the rise on campuses (Nasr 1994: 179). In February 1981 the

APMSO set up stalls to welcome new students and register them as new members. Students of the IJT destroyed the stalls, took the money, and beat the APMSO members out of the campus.

For several years the APMSO lived almost invisibly. It started an obscure magazine called *Al-Muhajir* in May 1982. Together with left-wing and ethnically based student groups it took part in the United Students Movement that opposed the IJT. Its leaders, however, could no longer return to the campus. The IJT had warned Ahmad Tariq, Altaf Hussain, and others to stay away. In the words of Altaf they were forced to leave student politics and start a popular movement:

> In other institutions, too, our workers were forced to stop working for APMSO. We all sat down to think if we could continue despite the armed opposition. But my companions insisted on carrying on, whatever the conditions may be. I went to visit Karachi's significant personalities to make them understand that they were Muhajirs and ask for their help because we were working for Muhajir rights, but no one lent an ear to us. Therefore I called a meeting of all my partners in a small Federal B. Area [typical Muhajir-dominated area in Karachi] house and told them that the situation was worse than ever. I told them that we had to postpone our struggles because of lack of resources. I will never forget that sorrow I saw on their faces after my announcement. They were so depressed that the tears were rolling down their faces. They said that they would work for the Muhajir cause at any cost. So I said that since we could not enter Karachi University or any other educational institution, we would preach our message in every street of every town and city. (quoted in Munir Ahmad 1996: 21–23)[7]

According to this quote, the humiliation experienced at the campus was a blessing in disguise since it forced the young rebels to expand beyond the narrow circle of students and the elite—"Karachi's significant personalities"—and disseminate their message among the "people" (*awam*). Years of hard work, dedication, and learning in the wilderness of the city followed. These years produced the heroic image of Altaf Hussain and his associates driving around the city on their small Honda 50cc motorbikes, spreading the MQM's message door to door—almost like modern, urban, wandering Sufi preachers. "Initially," says an MQM brochure, "there were meetings in the living rooms of people's houses, from there it progressed to the roofs of the houses, and then it was the locality grounds and streets where the meetings were held."

This door-to-door mobilization campaign was given a tremendous boost by the outbreak of ethnic clashes in 1985. These incidents spread the MQM's message far beyond the sphere of student and neighborhood politics. The MQM was the first to interpret the violence as an attack on Muhajirs. Although initially not involved in riots, the new party took up the plight of the victims with a Muhajir background and portrayed the atrocities as part of a much longer history of anti-migrant sentiments and policies in Pakistan. This was the kind of process for which Stanley Tambiah has used the phrase "transvaluation of violence."

The Transvaluation of Violence

Transvaluation—not in the Nietzschean sense but the way it is used by Tambiah—is a process of interpreting violence preceded by another process that Tambiah calls "focalization." Focalization is "the process of progressive denudation of local incidents and disputes of their particulars of context and their aggregation." Transvaluation is defined as "the parallel process of assimilating particulars to a larger, collective, more enduring, and therefore less context-bound, cause or interest" (Tambiah 1996: 192). For instance, complex riots in which many local parties are involved are reduced to an instance of animosity between ethnic or religious groups. Tambiah applies these concepts to the riots that took place in Karachi in April 1985 and preceded the rise of the MQM. The processes of focalization and transvaluation indicate that the riots did not start as supralocal fights between ethnic communities turning prejudice into violence. They started as an expression of a more concrete kind of social frustration.

In fact, the trouble started with a traffic accident that took place in a part of Karachi known as Liaqatabad. A bus ran over a student named Bushra Zaidi and killed her. This happened during a period of time when many people complained about the dangerous driving habits of bus drivers. Recent Pakhtun settlers from northwest Pakistan and Afghanistan had taken over public transportation. Competition between various private companies was so tough that drivers were forced to overload buses and drive recklessly (Shaheed 1990: 204). The buses, admired by foreigners for their colorful decorations, were locally known as "yellow devils." When one of them ran over Bushra Zaidi, her fellow students took to the streets to protest the incident. It was a time of military rule when political activities and public demonstrations were banned, which might explain why the police reacted in a violent manner. This provoked male students, many of whom allegedly belonged to the IJT, to fight the police and later to avenge Bushra's death by setting the property of Pakhtun settlers in the city on fire. The next day Pakhtun bus drivers living in Orangi Township, a city suburb miles away from Liaqatabad, attacked a bus loaded with students who were on their way to attend the funeral prayers for Bushra. They subsequently destroyed the property of Bihari migrants living in the same area. These migrants from Bangladesh competed with the Pakhtun migrants for land to build new houses. Rumors and newspaper reports encouraged an interpretation of these events as ethnic animosity. In this way, a complex dispute involving several parties was reduced to an articulation of ethnic strife (Tambiah 1996: 185–91).

Although I largely agree with Tambiah's analysis, I would like to make some additional observations. First, the escalation after Bushra's death was probably not simply a spontaneous outburst of widespread public frustration with the reckless driving habits of Pakhtun migrants. Although I have insufficient evidence for this, it appears that the episode should also be seen in the light of an ongoing competition between different groups of smugglers. In the mid-1980s Karachi had become a major market for drugs and weapons, mainly because of its position as a transit port for the war economy in Afghanistan. One of the complaints often heard in Karachi against Afghan refugees and recent Pakhtun migrants stemmed from their alleged involvement in smuggling. However, gangs of Muhajirs were also active in the business. In March 1984, for instance, a police squad arrested a group of Muhajirs from the neighborhood of Liaqatabad on the charge of smuggling, which led to public unrest in the following days.[8] Criminal organizations regularly fought the police (A. Hussain 1990: 189) and may have acted as "fire-tenders" who "convert a moment of tension into a grander, riotous event" (Brass 1997: 15–7). They probably possessed the firearms used in the riots.

Criminal organizations were clearly involved in the second set of large-scale ethnic clashes, which occurred in the fall of 1986. In October bus-loads full of MQM supporters from Karachi were on their way to a public party meeting in Hyderabad when they stopped at Sohrab Goth, a Pakhtun-dominated area on the outskirts of Karachi along the northbound highway. Sohrab Goth had a reputation as a smugglers' den. There was an exchange of insults, then shooting. An infamous MQM supporter, who happened to be a champion in martial arts, died. This led to acts of retaliation in Karachi and Hyderabad, during which Pakhtun property was destroyed on a large scale. Hundreds of MQM supporters were arrested, including Altaf Hussain. Six weeks later the police raided Pakhtun settlements in both Sohrab Goth and Orangi Township in search of drugs and arms. Armed with sophisticated weapons, Pakhtun criminals later attacked Bihari areas in a part of Orangi Township known as Aligarh Colony (A. Hussain 1990: 187).

Second, political parties and their student organizations also interfered with the riots, particularly in their aftermath. The MQM was one of the most active and radical parties in this process and played an active role in the rehabilitation of Bihari victims in Orangi Township (Ismail and Rahman n.d.: 2–3). The still relatively young and small MQM unconditionally took up the cause of the Biharis, who, as double migrants who had come from India to Pakistan by way of East Pakistan or Bangladesh, exemplified the diasporic identity of Muhajirs even more than ordinary migrants. In contrast, the "state had nothing to offer," as most aid came from nongovernmental organizations (Shaheed 1990: 208). The response of other political parties was equally disappointing. The MQM thus emerged as the only party willing to offer support, defense, and retaliation. In their speeches, Altaf Hussain and other MQM leaders drew a straight line from the present riots back to the partitions of 1971 and 1947, declaring that the MQM was ready to defend the dignity of everyone who had been or would be the victims of such partitions. Moreover, the MQM annually renewed that message by commemorating the massacres in large public meetings. On one of those occasions, MQM chairman Azim Ahmad Tariq said: "Two million Muhajirs have given their lives for the sake of Pakistan, a country which was achieved in the name of Allah. We left our homes and hearths for Pakistan, our entire cities were destroyed, but we are being killed for it." Another speaker said: "Urdu-speaking people are being persecuted for making Pakistan. About five million of us have been killed since the partition in India, Bangladesh and Pakistan itself."[9]

Moreover, these riots offered an excellent opportunity to challenge the "Islamic" parties. The JI in particular found itself in an awkward position when the fighting started between Pakhtun groups on the one hand and Urdu-speaking Biharis and other Muhajirs on the other. The party, fully in support of General Zia-ul Haq's military regime till 1984 (Nasr 1994: 195), had earlier played a critical role in mobilizing public opinion in favor of the Afghan resistance (*mujahidin*) against the Soviet occupation of Afghanistan. It had a rapidly increasing number of Pakhtun supporters in the Northwest Frontier Province (66–67). But it also relied on its Muhajir following in Karachi. Reluctant to choose sides, the JI decided to keep silent over the riots, inviting a prompt reaction from the MQM. "Where have your Islam, Pakistan and army gone when innocent Muhajirs were being butchered?" asked Shahbir Hashmi, an MQM leader from Hyderabad.[10] Altaf Hussain himself sneered at the bearded "fundamentalists" for being "traders in Quranic verses"—the idea being that the JI leaders were opportunists selling Quranic verses like merchants rather than being truly devoted Muslims. "I also participated wholeheartedly in the sin [*gunah*] of supporting the Jam'iat-i Islami," he publicly confessed. "I am also a sinner [*gunahgar*] like so many of us who were blindfolded."[11]

These vigorous attacks against the JI continued throughout the mobilization campaign of the early MQM. They went hand in hand with regular clashes between MQM militants and members of the IJT. They continued until the elections of 1988, which the MQM won by astonishingly large margins, convincingly defeating the JI as well as other parties that had once enjoyed a portion of the Muhajir vote.

The Thrill of Power

The mid-1980s were a period of transition from the military regime led by General Zia-ul Haq to the restoration of democracy in 1988. This was a turbulent period as several parties competed for power not only by means of the democratic process but also through violent clashes in streets and on campuses. Apart from several outbursts of ethnic violence—in April 1985, October/December 1986, and again, as we shall see, in September 1988 and May 1990—political violence became an almost daily occurrence in Karachi and Hyderabad. Meanwhile, various parties held public meeting in an attempt to mobilize the people to bring down the military regime. It was through one such public meeting that the MQM emerged as a party to reckon with. In August 1986, a few days before Pakistan's Independence Day, the first MQM public meeting was held on a playground in central Karachi within a stone's throw of Jinnah's grave (*mazar*), a national monument and an important landmark in Karachi. Nature was benevolent that day. While Altaf Hussain made his first public speech before an audience of tens of thousands, proclaiming Muhajirs a separate ethnic community (*qaum*), a tropical shower of rain blessed him. He stoically continued his speech, making an impression on the crowd and turning the meeting into an enormous success. Altaf's speech attracted a larger audience in opposition to the military government than that of any other political party in Karachi.

In 1987, the new party proved capable of winning elections when it defeated the established parties during the municipal elections in many neighborhoods of Karachi. Twenty-eight-year-old Farooq Sattar became the mayor of Karachi. But the big test came in the fall of 1988 when national elections were held. The party's campaign was directed against the various parties associated with the military regime, notably the Islami Jumhuri Ittehad (Islamic Democratic Alliance) that consisted of the JI, the Pakistan Muslim League, and other parties considered the heirs of Zia-ul Haq. The MQM argued for an alliance of both Muhajirs and Sindhis, maintaining that the whole province of Sindh was being treated unfairly by the federal center in the Punjab. The MQM argued that Muhajirs had become part of the autochthonous population, genuinely loyal to the province, unlike more recent settlers from the Punjab and the Frontier Province. "Sindh is not another Dubai for us," one MQM slogan said, meaning that Muhajirs had come to Sindh for more lofty reasons than just earning money like Pakistani labor migrants in the Gulf. They had come to stay, to live, and to die in the province and therefore belonged to the province, whereas Punjabis and Patkhun could return to their places of origin up north (Alavi 1991: 179–81). "The conditions prevailing in Sindh," said Altaf Hussain in a public statement, "have proved that the Sindhis will never tolerate any move against their cultural and national status," adding that Sindh consists of "two nationalities having exclusive rights to the resources of the province."[12]

The MQM made overtures to various Sindhi parties. Altaf paid a visit to G. M. Syed, the Sindhi separatist leader who was putting together a Sindhi national alliance of several Sindhi nationalist parties. Negotiations were also held with the Sindhi-dominated PPP. While both Muhajir and Sindhi political leaders made speeches against the Punjabi-dominated federal state, including the army, bands of Muhajir and Sindhi youth threatened and attacked Punjabi settlers who had lived in small Sindhi towns like Nawabshah and Mirpurkhas for more than half a century.[13]

The election campaign was successful. While Sindhis massively voted for the PPP, the MQM secured practically all seats from the urban areas in Sindh. Supporters of both parties jointly took to the streets of Karachi to celebrate the electoral defeat of the Islami Jumhuri Ittehad. The red, green, and white bangles of the MQM were regularly exchanged with the red, green, and black ones of the PPP. To participators and observers alike, the sudden Muhajir-Sindhi fraternity (*Muhajir Sindhi bhai bhai*) came as an unprecedented surprise. At the street level, the new love of the Muhajir youth for the Sindhis was perhaps most profoundly expressed by the wearing of the *ajrak*. This batik shawl, a confirmed attribute of the Sindhi peasant—the Sindh Museum near Hyderabad devotes a complete room to the many local variations—suddenly became highly fashionable in Karachi and Hyderabad.

There were different aspects to the MQM's approach to the Sindhis. It was to a certain extent motivated by the strategic considerations of the party leadership, who realized that it had to join a coalition to gain power, rightly anticipating a victory for the PPP in the national elections of 1988. On a popular level, it had the quality of flirtations: a playful and semi-serious case of making advances to a Sindhi rural culture that was portrayed as exotic and authentic rather than dangerous or backward. These flirtations had an element of provocation, challenging the high cultural Islamic modernist values of the Muhajir elite. This made it difficult to pinpoint exactly where the MQM fit into the scheme of ethnic categories. MQM supporters and sympathizers often mentioned this provocative public behavior as one of the main attractions of the MQM, recalling that they felt a sense of liberation, togetherness, power, and joy while taking part in party activities. Provocation was also part of two practices that emerged during the heyday of the MQM: the personality cult of the leader and the ritual of taking the oath. They astonished and often shocked out-siders and were for this reason greatly enjoyed by MQM supporters.

The MQM's Personality-Cult

Altaf Hussain was born in Karachi on 17 September 1953. His parents had come to Pakistan from Agra. He grew up in a modest family house in the equally modest neighborhood of Azizabad in a large family of eleven children. He became involved in politics as a student and was one of the founders of the APMSO in 1978. In 1979 he was sentenced to nine months in jail and five lashes of the whip for having burnt the Pakistani flag in an APMSO demonstration on Independence Day. He disappeared from the scene of student politics for several years. He left Pakistan in 1984 and became a taxi driver in Chicago. It appears that he returned to Pakistan in December 1985, possibly after the formal abolition of military rule earlier that year. However, this part of his biography is a matter of controversy as it is usually denied or downplayed by MQM supporters, because it would mean that Altaf was not present on the occasion of the party's official foundation in March 1984, an unacceptable thought for many of his followers. Almost everything that has been said or written about Altaf Hussain's life prior to August 1986 is shrouded in a mist of uncertainty.

The first public meeting of the MQM in August 1986 made Altaf a public figure. He soon became the undisputed leader of the movement. His style as a leader was often dramatic. In public speeches he regularly burst into tears when narrating the plight of the besieged Muhajirs, thus making himself an icon of their suffering. The habit is nicely captured on the cover of an MQM audiocassette depicting him as a colossus of King Kong's proportion towering over the urban dwellings of his people (see fig. 1). While the tiny and faceless creatures below him bury their dead, huge tears fall on them from the giant's eyes like a blessing from the skies. Accompanied by the text, "Martyrs and prisoners of the MQM, my songs are for you" ("MQM ke shaheed o aseero mere naqme tumhare liye hai"), the picture shows Altaf's solidarity with the Muhajr victims.

But he is not only the nation's sufferer. He is also a king who on the occasion of his birthday in 1991 was honored with a crowning ritual (*taj poshi*) of the kind usually reserved for a *pir*, a king, or a master (*ustad*). With a golden sword he cut a gigantic birthday cake. Some believe he possesses miraculous powers (*barakat*), and because of this he is asked to kiss babies. Once in Karachi, it is said, his face miraculously appeared on a leaf of a peepal tree. I have often heard supporters declare that they owe him everything they have and all that they are. Moreover, the leader is

FIGURE 1. Cover of an audiocassette of MQM songs, showing Altaf Hussain looking down on his followers and crying over the MQM wounded and dead.

FIGURE 2. Billboards in a shopping street in Hyderabad, showing pictures of MQM party leader Altaf Hussain and the party symbol of a rectangular kite.

everywhere as huge pictures of him can be seen in the streets of Muhajir-dominated areas alongside party symbols such as the rectangular kite in green, red, and white (see fig. 2).

And yet he is still one of them. The most often told story about him in my fieldwork area was refreshingly anticlimactic. When the leader arrived for a visit to the neighborhood, big words were anticipated, but the first thing he said was, "As a child I had a very good *rabri* here." *Rabri* is a milky sweet with a rubbery texture. "Does the shop still exist?" The shop happened to be the most popular sweet shop in the vicinity.

Furthermore, it is often said that he works hard. He sacrifices his health and comfort for the nation. He is said to have ruined his eyes by reading history and writing speeches at night when everybody else is asleep, which is why he always wears sunglasses. When, after listening to his speech, the audience once asked him when he was going to get married, he smiled and answered: "There is a time for everything, and when it comes, along with the right person, I will send you a card. For the time being I am married to the MQM."[14] When he did get married in Dubai to a Pakistani bride in 2000 and brought her back with him to his residence in London, it caused a stir among his followers. Some of them were deeply disappointed and feared they had permanently lost their leader to a comfortable life in England.

All these examples and more were given to me when I asked, "What constitutes Altaf's charisma?" How does one interpret all these different examples? According to Clifford Geertz (1983), charisma is a sign of involvement with the animating centers of a society, an involvement expressed through the many symbols of power that surround the charismatic person. The charismatic figure takes his charisma from the symbols of power he is associated with. This is to some extent true in the case of Altaf Hussain, but more important, I think, he derives his charisma from the fact that he transforms himself into a living symbol of the Muhajir nation. He presents himself as an ordinary man, almost without character traits of his own. This enables one to project one's own notion of Muhajirness onto the leader. More than merely expressing meaning, as Geertz argued, Altaf, as a charismatic person, absorbs the various shades of meaning of Muhajirness ascribed to him by his followers. In this way he can be a semi-saint or a reincarnation of a Moghul king wearing a crown, but also a "brother" (*bhai*), a modern cosmopolitan wearing fashionable sunglasses, a sincere hardworking man, a straightforward fellow who appreciates a good *rabri*, a green-card holder who returned from the United States, or a sufferer among sufferers. His charisma seems to grow with every image of hope, power, suffering, and justice his followers invest in him.

The element of provocation lies in the fact that some of these images are clearly grotesque and meant to be funny. To be sure some are not, and others that are funny to some are taken seriously by others. We already saw the example of Pir Sahib: the notion of Altaf as a spiritual leader and a savior, which was initially a joke but had significance for the victims of violence. Similarly, the crowning of Altaf as a Moghul king was widely remembered as a show of parody, funny because it was known that Altaf was a man from a modest background residing in one of the overpopulated city areas. It was, perhaps, a comment on the pomp of certain politicians who like to carry themselves in what they think was the fashion of the Moghul Empire. It was probably an effort to transgress the boundary separating the "big people" (*bare log*) from the "common people" (*am log*) by applying attributes of nobility to a commoner. Most important, those who spoke of Altaf as their *pir* or supreme "leader of the movement" (*qaʿid-i tehreek*) were aware that such statements were shocking to other people. The notion of Altaf as a spiritual leader or *pir* in particular was likely to be condemned as an adoption of a backward folk tradition and, because it concerned a secular leader, a mistaken one to boot. In other words, while some may sincerely have considered Altaf as their savior, others did so merely tongue-in-cheek, collectively enjoying the moral outrage this caused outside their own circles.

The Oath

The ritual of taking the oath to the MQM had a similar double quality. In the 1980s and early 1990s, the taking of the oath was a rather insignificant and unimportant initiation rite new recruits underwent in order to be accepted as full party members. It was, apparently, a rather dull ceremonial affair. In order to become an MQM member one had to fill out a form that asked for one's name, father's name, address, etc., repeat the oath a senior party member would read aloud, and finally take part in several classes on party discipline and ideology. These classes contained lessons in the MQM's historiography of the Pakistan Movement as well as the position of Muhajirs in Pakistan (Verkaaik 1994) and taught new recruits the importance of loyalty and obedience to one's superiors in the party hierarchy. The text of the oath also stressed this form of discipline. Parts of the oath, as translated from the work of Munir Ahmad (1996: 86–89), ran as follows:

> I, . . . believing that Allah is here and watching over me, swearing by His book and my mother, take oath that I shall remain loyal to the MQM and Altaf Hussain for my whole life. I will not take part in any conspiracy, planning or action against MQM or Altaf Hussain and I will not maintain any link with anyone who is involved in any of the acts mentioned above. I swear by my mother that if any conspiracy against MQM or Altaf Hussain or any act harmful to them come into my knowledge, I shall immediately inform Altaf Hussain or other main leaders, even if the conspirator be my brother, sister, mother, father, any relative or friend. . . . I swear that I will keep every secret of my party and regard it more precious than my life. I swear that I shall accept Altaf Hussain's decision as final in any matter and obey all his decisions. If I disobey any of his decisions, I must be regarded as a traitor. I swear that I have and I will have blind trust in party leader Altaf Hussain. . . . May God help me to remain firm and loyal to the MQM.

The text fascinatingly combines God and the Holy Qur'an as supreme authorities with the emotional strength of family ties, especially the mother. It also combines the format and the language of a judicial declaration with elements of a prayer. It was initially meant as an instrument to discipline new party members. Although its language was sometimes evocative, the oath was hardly a rite de passage in the classical anthropological sense. Nothing was done to bring about the liminal phase necessary for a sudden and radical change in status and identity. The oath was known by the Urdu term *halfnama*, a much more secular word than the alternative term *bai'at*, used to denote a pledge of loyalty to a spiritual leader.

Over time, however, the oath gained a new dimension when outsiders, including the press, began to associate it with the personality cult of Altaf Hussain. The oath became the issue of some serious controversy. According to rumors and newspaper articles, MQM supporters directly and personally pledged their loyalty to Altaf Hussain during huge gatherings in which they were made to sit on the ground in straight lines, army style. According to other reports, the ritual could evoke a form of ecstasy or a state of trance. People were said to collect the dirt from under the leader's feet and prostrate themselves in front of him—a serious religious offense as prostrating for anyone other than God is generally condemned as a form of idol worship (*shirk*).

In social milieus critical of the MQM, the oath-taking ritual was sometimes compared to a passage in *The Terrorist* by H. T. Lambrick. This book is the autobiography of a disciple of the Pir Pagara as written down by Lambrick. In the 1940s the man took part in the uprising of the Hur, the brotherhood led by the Pir, against the British colonial army. The man was captured and imprisoned by the military and interviewed in jail by Lambrick, a colonial officer. The book was first published in 1972 and reprinted in 1995 because of regained news value: terrorism, as we shall see, became a timely issue in the mid-1990s. In the passage at hand the disciple describes his inauguration as a warrior as follows:

> Pir Saheb then ordered us all to lie down side by side, each man to spread his turban and shawl completely over himself, so that no part was visible. My mind was confused: for a moment I wondered whether our Lord was about to have us killed. . . . Then his voice, in a different tone, began to declaim something in words I could not understand, though as I listened they seemed somehow familiar. At length it ended, and Pir Saheb ordered us to arise, in his usual voice. He said: "You have now passed through the shadow of death, and the life that you feel in you is a new life, dedicated for me, your Imam. Go in peace now, and remain prepared for my call."
>
> As I went home through the night along the Sanghar road with a number of others, I asked one of them, an elderly man, what was the prayer Pir Saheb had read over us. . . . The man replied: ". . . [I]f you had ever followed the bier of a Mussulman to the graveyard, you would have known that they are the Janaza prayer, that the Mullah reads at the burial of the dead." (Lambrick 1995: 51).

For those unsympathetic to the MQM, the new recruits of the party took their oath as a rebirth into a life given to them by Altaf Hussain. They believed that the oath signified the moment new recruits left behind the ties of family and neighborhood and became instruments in the hands of their Pir Sahib.

I suspect the oath was rarely experienced as such by the men who took the oath. None of them ever talked about the oath in terms of ecstasy or renewal. Nor did the oath signify a radical rift with family and neighborhood. The bulk of the activists continued to live a community life while engaged in party work, and few could recall even a short sentence of the oath. "That you must remain loyal to Altaf and not work against the party" was the typically disinterested summary of the content.

The oath was nevertheless often mentioned as an important symbol of the MQM's uniqueness. However, rather than the oath itself, it was the controversy, the unconfirmed allegations of *shirk* and the moral indignation of the press, that added a sense of adventure to becoming a member of the MQM. There was shared joy in the fact that one had been involved in a practice that had subsequently been blown out of proportion. The controversy made members proud that they were part of a movement that was capable of worrying a large number of people. Initially a dull formality, it had been turned into a splendid provocation, secret and outrageous. And the shared knowledge that the secret was in fact empty made it even better.

Party Hierarchy

The oath also revealed another aspect of the MQM. Despite its dull and formal character, the oath did make new recruits aware of the strict hierarchical relations within the movement. The reputedly strict and efficient organizational discipline was, in fact, another feature of the MQM in its heyday. This, too, was a matter of pride and admiration for its supporters. It made it impossible, it was said, to misuse party membership and serve one's own interests. The party structure was clear and corruption therefore difficult.

Ironically, given the MQM's attacks on the JI, the MQM's hierarchical structure resembles that of its rival.[15] Like that of the JI, the MQM's structure is based on a series of concentric circles operating at several levels: units, sectors, zones, and finally the general head offices in Karachi and London. Whereas in the JI every circle is headed by an *amir*, the MQM uses the English term *in-charge* so that there is a unit-in-charge, a sector-in-charge, and a zone-in-charge. Decisions are made at the top and come down through all subsequent layers. For instance, if you ask an ordinary MQM worker for a formal interview, he will ask permission from his unit-in-charge, who will take up the matter with the sector-in-charge, etc., so that it takes a couple of days before you get your "no."

Also like the JI, in the MQM every circle is supposed to hold meetings on a regular basis, during which every worker reports on his activities. Every circle furthermore has a "center" (*markaz*). At the top of the hierarchy stands the central *markaz*, also known as Nine Zero, established in Altaf Hussain's home in Azizabad and named after the last two digits of Altaf's telephone number. Here the party's chairman, secretaries, MNAs (members of the national assembly), MPAs (members of the provincial assembly), and other functionaries regularly meet. Nine Zero stays in close contact with Altaf Hussain's residence in London. Altaf himself holds no official position, but every party decision is made in his name.

On a local level, the sector-in-charge and the unit-in-charge are the most relevant levels within the hierarchy. The sector-in-charge (as well as the unit-in-charge) lives within the neighborhood he represents. He is consulted in case of disputes between neighbors, and he makes sure that instructions from higher levels are carried out properly. He often exercises considerable power over the area he controls. When in 1992 the army-led Operation Clean-up came down hard on the MQM, these party officials were the operation's main target. The sector-in-charge in particular was singled out for elimination. Those higher up in the hierarchy often managed to flee the country, while those in the lower ranks could sometimes avoid prosecution by going into hiding or keeping a low profile. Those holding a position as sector-in-charge, however, were identified by the state forces as the crucial link between the party leadership and its supporters. They were also said to be in command of armed militant groups. As soon as the army operation began, they became the target of a propaganda campaign against "terrorists." This army operation cum propaganda campaign also marked the beginning of the movement's decline, which was preceded by the growing tension between Muhajirs and the Sindhi population.

Muhajir-Sindhi Discord Revived

Up until the elections of 1988, relations between the MQM and Sindhi-dominated parties had been friendly, which after the elections resulted in a coalition government of the PPP and the MQM on both federal and provincial levels. Gradually, however, the MQM distanced itself more and more from the PPP. At the local level, too, the MQM changed enemies. Up to 1988 MQM militants were involved in fights with Pakhtun smugglers. They harassed, threatened, and robbed Punjabi settlers in Karachi. There had also been clashes with militants of the JI. After 1988, however, MQM activists were increasingly at loggerheads with Sindhi rivals.

This renewed tension between Muhajir and Sindhi activists started in Hyderabad, emphasizing the difference between Hyderabad and Karachi. The initial pro-Sindhi, anti-Punjabi, and anti-Pakhtun rhetoric of the MQM made sense in Karachi where many Punjabis and Pakhtun had settled throughout the years and where Sindhis were a small minority. In Hyderabad, however, the pro-Sindhi stance ran counter to a long-established animosity between Sindhis and Muhajirs, which dated back to the 1960s. Other Muhajir organizations emerged in Hyderabad, challenging the MQM and condemning it for its collaboration with the archenemy. When the violence between Muhajirs and Sindhis increased and more and more Muhajir victims from Hyderabad turned to the party leadership in Karachi for help, the latter found itself under growing pressure to disengage itself from the Sindhi-dominated PPP. When it finally did, street fighting grew worse and eventually led to acute polarization and incidents of ethnic cleansing.

The MQM in Hyderabad

The distrust between Muhajirs and Sindhis dates back to the language crisis of the early 1970s. Initially groups of Sindhi- and Urdu-speaking students joined the same movement against the military regime in the 1960s, but soon Sindhi groups began to demand that Sindhi be declared the provincial language of Sindh, not Urdu. In January 1971 shortly after the national elections, fighting between Sindhi and Urdu speakers broke out when the Sindhi-dominated Board of Intermediate and Secondary Education made Sindhi compulsory for Urdu-speaking students. Muhajir students took to the streets in Hyderabad as well as the smaller towns of Nawabshah and Mirpurkhas. Sindhi students burnt pictures of Muhammad Iqbal and in retaliation Muhajir students destroyed books in the Institute of Sindhiology. More than a year later, in July 1972, the provincial government of Sindh presented a language bill proposing to make Sindhi the official provincial language. This generated new protest and riots instigated by Urdu-speaking migrant groups (Rahman 1996).

The Sindhi-Muhajir rivalry of those years continued to influence local politics in Hyderabad. Many Muhajirs distrusted the PPP as an essentially Sindhi party and the Bhuttos as Sindhi leaders. Nor did the military regime of Zia-ul-Haq bring Sindhi and Muhajir political organizations any closer together in Hyderabad or rural Sindh, as it did in Karachi where the military became the common enemy of both the MQM and the PPP. The armed uprising of 1983 against the military, which took place in the interior of Sindh under the name of the Movement for Restoration of Democracy (MRD), was primarily instigated by the PPP and remained unsupported by Muhajir organizations. In places like Hyderabad, Sukkur, and Nawabshah, Muhajir organizations tended to respect General Zia-ul Haq as the person who had put an end to what they considered the anti-Muhajir policy of the PPP. Muhajirs in the interior of Sindh remembered the 1970s as an unsafe time amid growing lawlessness, a Sindhi bias in the redistribution of jobs and landed property, and diminishing opportunities for education. While the MQM in Karachi openly celebrated the death of Zia-ul Haq in 1988, several Muhajir organizations in Hyderabad and other Sindhi towns publicly mourned the death of the general.[16] Sindhis took this as an expression of sympathy for the murderer of their martyred leader, Zulfiqar Ali Bhutto.

Given this history of distrust, the friendship with the PPP was an even more spectacular break with former Muhajir politics in Hyderabad than it was in Karachi. Two competing Muhajir organizations challenged the move. One was called the Muhajir Rabita Council (MRC), the other Muhajir Ittehad Tehreek (MIT). The MRC was an organization of the older generation of Muhajirs in Hyderabad, founded by Maulana Wasi Mazhar Nadwi, a former leader of the JI in Sindh who had been expelled from the party in 1976 (Nasr 1994: 234). During Zia's period he was appointed the mayor of Hyderabad and for a brief period became the federal minister of religious affairs. Another member was Ishtiaq Ahmad, who in the 1970s was associated with the Muhajir Punjabi Pathan Movement (MPPM). He would later become an MQM senator, but in the mid-1980s he criticized the MQM's cooperation with the Sindhi separatist Jeay Sindh Movement and the PPP. He and other MRC members attacked Altaf Hussain for being on good terms with G. M. Syed, the leader of the Jeay Sindh Movement, whom they considered a national traitor. They ridiculed the MQM leader by presenting a video of him in the reception room of G. M. Syed, sitting in a submissive pose with his knees together and stammering barely intelligible words in favor of Sindhudesh.[17]

The MIT was a more radical and militant group of young Muhajirs that formed in 1986. Its leader, the medical student Saleem Hyder, claimed to be the cofounder of the APMSO in 1978 and a former friend of Altaf Hussain but also said that he had left the student organization because he was against the adoption of ethnic politics by the APMSO. He condemned this as a denial of the sacrifices made by the older generation of Muhajirs.[18] Nonetheless, both groups occasionally worked together, but more often they were in conflict with each other. The MIT attacked the MQM on two points: its alliance with Sindhi parties; and its supposed domination by Shiʿa Muslims, an accusation that sought to make use of a long history of distrust between Sunnis and Shiʿas among South Asian Muslims. In 1987 and 1988 the two parties clashed violently several times, especially during elections. The MIT vanished from the scene after 1988 but not before it had helped detach the MQM from its Sindhi allies.

The emergence of new militant Sindhi groups also put pressure on the MQM in Hyderabad to retrace its steps. The most vocal of these groups was the Sindh Taraqqi Pasand Party (Sindh Progressive Party) and its student organization. The party was established in a medical college in Hyderabad in the aftermath of the 1983 uprising against the Zia-ul Haq administration. Several students had joined this movement, disappointed with the lukewarm support it received from established Sindhi nationalist leaders. As one former member of the Sindh Taraqqi Pasand Party (STPP) told me: "We fought for Sindh and invited Sindhi leaders to support us. They came to make eloquent speeches and really talked a lot but they were not sincere. We talked to them but they did not listen." Their objective was to actually bring about the independent Sindhudesh of which the former generation had only dreamt and talked. From their perspective, the migrant population as well as the army blocked the fulfillment of the Sindhi national identity. "We did not consider Pakistan a natural country. We did not consider Urdu a natural language. It was a language artificially made up of several languages. How can an artificial language be a national language? What sort of country is it that has an artificial language as its national language? We tried to get rid of this artificial language in the 1970s but then the army intervened and saved the Urdu-speakers. Now the army was on its knees and we were going to finish what had been started in the 1970s." Another one-time supporter of the STPP told me: "The MQM said that they were in favor of Sindh. The Muhajir mayor said that Muhajirs were a peace-loving people. But secretly they all supported the Muhajir bandits who were killing innocent Sindhis in the streets. The army in fact supported them. The army gave them weapons." In short, the STPP was fighting two opponents. There was the internal opponent of the established Sindhi nationalist parties, which were criticized for siding with the MQM. And there was the Muhajir population, allegedly backed by the Pakistani army.

The growing militancy of Sindhi parties was a sign of a more general radicalization in Hyderabad. The Muhajir youth, too, anticipated that the end of military rule would bring about rare opportunities for radical and revolutionary change. The infamous map *Jinnahpur* appeared on public walls, outlining an independent state for Muhajirs consisting of Karachi and Hyderabad with a corridor between the cities. A scattered hope today, it was an adventurous idea for radical students and street fighters in the late 1980s. But it was also anticipated that one could only arrive at total liberation after a prolonged period of fighting the enemy. Today, the years 1986–1990 are remembered in Hyderabad as the years of "battle" or "war" (*jang*). Streets and colleges were regularly the scenes of violence between various militant groups.

The *jang* gained momentum after a controversy in March 1988. The incident concerned the restyling of Hyder Chowk, one of the central roundabouts of Hyderabad. Named after the Sindhi poet Hyder Bakhsh Jatoi, the square had been decorated in 1983 with the blue tiles for which the Sindhi countryside is famous and other pieces of Sindhi folklore. Having won the local elections, the MQM local councilor decided to have the monument demolished and replaced by portraits of several heroes of the Pakistan Movement such as Sir Syed Ahmad Khan, the founder of Aligarh University, and Liaqat Ali Khan, first prime minister of Pakistan. There was a violent clash when Sindhi youngsters tried to remove these pictures. Altaf Hussain intervened from Karachi, declaring that "Hyder Bakhsh Jatoi worked for the emancipation of Sindh from exploiters, so he is sacred to Muhajirs too," while ordering that the pictures be whitewashed.[19] It so happened. But the incident added fuel to the growing tension between Muhajirs and Sindhis.

The divide widened in the aftermath of Black Friday on 30 September 1988. That day the so-called Hyderabad Carnage took place. During the evening rush hour, Sindhi militants drove into the city in jeeps and opened fire indiscriminately at several crossroads in Muhajir-dominated areas. Within a couple of minutes they killed dozens of people and drove off. In retaliation Sindhis were killed in Karachi the following day. More than two hundred people died during those two days.

The incident led to vigorous discussions within the Hyderabad branch of the MQM as more and more members demanded retaliation. In addition, moderate faction within the MQM also had to deal with growing pressure from the MIT, which publicly demanded a division of Sindh to create a permanent haven of refuge for Muhajirs. The reaction from the party leadership in Karachi was thought to be lukewarm as it did not go beyond the standard words of sympathy. The message of Altaf Hussain himself was considered almost cowardly. "We [Muhajirs] have made Sindh our permanent home," he said. "We have buried our dead here for the welfare of the province. . . Muhajirs and Sindhis are one. Please stop fighting each other."[20]

While supporters of the MQM and the PPP jointly celebrated their electoral victories in Karachi in November that year, serious fighting between MQM and Sindhi militants took place the same day in Hyderabad. In other towns and villages in Sindh, Muhajir families began to feel unsafe amid growing Sindhi militancy. In increasing numbers they left their homes and went to Hyderabad and Karachi.[21] In April 1989 the MQM leadership deemed it necessary to come to Hyderabad for a so-called ideological meeting (*fikri nishist*) meant to discipline the local party members. Altaf Hussain himself stayed in Hyderabad for two weeks. He blamed the ongoing tension with Sindhis on "vested interests," which "have infiltrated to create chaos and anarchy." "For the success of any movement an individual must subordinate himself to the will of the collective whole. . . . Personal friendships are like a poison. . . . Individual thinking is injurious for the cause. . . . The *tehreek* [movement] is the fountain head and the centripetal force."[22] While the party secretary, Afaq Ahmad, declared that "the movement in Hyderabad will be organized on scientific lines to make it more effective,"[23] several local party leaders were forced to resign. To a journalist who had asked Altaf Hussain whether his "supporters in Hyderabad want[ed] a more militant line" the party leader replied: "Yes, we have differences of opinion in the MQM but there is no split in the party."[24]

Shortly after that, the MQM changed its Sindhi-friendly policy. It threatened to leave the coalition with the PPP. Altaf talked to opposition leader Nawaz Sharif about the conditions on which to join the opposition. In order to save the coalition, Benazir Bhutto, leader of the PPP, paid a humiliating visit to the MQM's head office in Azizabad, where her huge black limousine got stuck in the narrow alleys. A new agreement was signed, but fighting between activists of the student wings of the PPP and the MQM now also occurred in Karachi. There was also severe pressure from both Sindhi nationalist groups and within the PPP itself on Benazir Bhutto to disassociate from the MQM (Z. Hussain 1989: 18). In October 1989 the coalition eventually broke and the MQM joined the opposition.

Altaf's Hunger Strike

During the summer of 1989 the MQM had launched a new campaign to win back dissatisfied supporters. One slogan read: "Islam is our religion, Pakistan is our country, MQM is our party" ("Islam hamara din hai, Pakistan hamara mulk hai, MQM hamara tanzim hai"). Another said: "We will save the country and the nation with our blood" ("Ham apne laho se mulk aur qaum ko bacaegen"). These slogans were the first signs of a change in rhetoric. Moving away from the language of ethnicity, the MQM returned to the older notion of Muhajirs as the protagonists and defenders of Muslim fraternity and the dignity of Pakistan. This discursive turn signified a change in the MQM's position from an up-and-coming movement into a beleaguered community. It stressed the notions of justice (*haq*), tyranny (*zulm*), and the MQM as the movement of the oppressed (*mazlum*). This was most clearly articulated during the hunger strike that Altaf Hussain undertook in 1990.

The hunger strike (*bhukhartal*) is a well-known, if somewhat worn-out method of protest in Pakistan. One can almost always find some group of hunger strikers near the gate of press clubs or courts of justice. Not many manage to make an impression on the public, but when in April 1990, toward the end of the fasting month of Ramzaan, Altaf Hussain declared that he would start a fast unto death, the reaction to the announcement was anything but indifferent. Twenty young party members reportedly fainted on hearing Altaf's decision. More than one hundred of his followers decided to join the fast.

The hunger strike was meant to protest "state terrorism." While MQM members continued to be in violent conflict with supporters of other parties, the police had begun to raid the houses of Muhajir militants in search of arms. Many MQM members were arrested. This was part of a power struggle between the PPP and the MQM. After the MQM had left the coalition, the PPP sought ways to reduce the MQM's street power. Meanwhile the infamous slogan "justice or death" ("haq ya maut") appeared on many a wall in Karachi and Hyderabad. While the party's irregulars prepared themselves for the defense of their armories, Altaf increasingly gave speeches about social injustice and religious righteousness. "I want concrete assurances by the President, the Prime Minister and others, for the safety of Muhajirs," he demanded.[25]

Devastated party supporters congregated in front of Altaf's house. Dozens of hunger strikers spent their days in open tents that blocked the street, expressing their readiness to give their life to save Altaf's. Families from the interior of Sindh, who had come to Karachi to escape the violence in their villages, came to persuade Altaf to give up his fast. "We cannot afford to lose you now," an old lady cried.[26] Young men shouted slogans against the PPP and Benazir Bhutto. "Let us go out into the streets for a final showdown with the command groups of the PPP," they suggested.[27]

The part of the street closest to the front of Altaf's house was open to women only. During the first few days of the fast, Altaf spoke from there, kissing babies on request. Later on he stayed inside the house. Women were allowed to visit him in groups to look at him and take their children to him. They reported that his face looked pale and unshaven, which had a devastating effect on the crowd outside.[28] Women read the Qurʿan, while others beat their chest as a sign of penance and protest.

This chest beating was significant because it is performed during the ʿAshura processions in the month Muharram. On the tenth of this month, the martyrdom of Imam Hussain, grandson of the Prophet Muhammad, is commemorated in large processions in which symbols of his death (*taziya*) are taken out onto the street. It is primarily, though not exclusively, a Shiʿa festival in which people flagellate themselves with their fists as well as knives and swords. Briefly, the story of the event that is commemorated runs as follows. One day the inhabitants of the city of Kufa call on Hussain, residing in Medina, to lead them into an armed rebellion against the tyrannical despot Yazid. Hussain leaves his hometown with his family to support Kufa. In the Iraqi desert near the town of Karbala, Hussain and his small party meet the army of Yazid. Hussain is cut off from water and deserted by most of his followers, including the men from Kufa. Vastly outnumbered, those who remain loyal to Hussain meet their death bravely. His half-brother Abbas is killed while trying to fetch water for the children. The infant son of Hussain, Ali Asghar, is shot by an arrow, while Hussain, under the flag of truce, requests water for the child. Finally, having seen all his male companions die, Hussain bids farewell to his mother and sisters and on his white horse rides toward his martyrdom. Tyranny continues after his death when his beheaded body is left naked and unburied in the desert. His head is carried into Damascus atop a pole. The women are paraded uncovered through the city.

The story is about several themes, such as betrayal and loyalty, but the themes of martyrdom and tyranny are the most important. It offers several of the most powerful symbols of protest against illegitimate rulers or oppressors. Chest beating is one of them as it evokes the notion of tyranny and oppression. The practice of wearing black clothes, as is the practice during the ʿAshura processions, is also very often used in protest demonstrations. Similarly, allusions are often made to the story in public speeches. This was also the case in what was probably the most dramatic moment during the hunger strike.

Despite his reportedly deteriorating condition, Altaf continued to give speeches over the loudspeaker system that carried his voice far beyond the street. In one of them he read out a list of "martyrs" (*shuhada*) who had given their life for the MQM. He went on to say that "if what I say is beginning to sound like the story of Karbala, it is because our story is like the story of Karbala. . . . Yazid killed Hussain but could not kill his name." Referring to Benazir Bhutto's government as "this Yazid government," he stated that "you can kill Altaf Hussain but you cannot kill the message of *haq parast* [truth-loving]." Painting the sorrow of the mothers, wives, and children of those who had died, he incited Bhutto to put an end to the killing, saying that "you are also the mother of Bilawal [her newborn son]. If you continue your *zulm* [tyranny], who will blame me if I allow my workers to take action?" Raising his voice, he asked: "Will you fight for me?" In the street the answer was a unanimous "Yes."[29]

Altaf ended his hunger strike after six days. Although the government had not met his demands, the fast proved to be successful insofar as it strengthened the link between the party leadership and its supporters. Never before had Altaf been so popular as during this week. It was now "considered disrespectful to refer to Altaf Hussain as anything other than *pir sahib*, *qaid* [leader] or *Altaf Bhai* [Brother Altaf]" (Sarwar 1990).

The fast marked a change in rhetoric during which the language of ethnicity was replaced by a more mainstream Islamic language of justice and tyranny. The aesthetics and emotional power of suffering from oppression, for instance, were exploited with great skill. The unshaven face of the leader showed the hero in agony rather than in victorious euphoria. The central place of women was remarkable too. Suffering, martyrdom, and social justice began to dominate the party's rhetoric in its growing conflict with the ruling PPP.

As we will see in a later chapter, this rhetoric reached its apex during the summer of 1990 when Pakka Qila, the centrally located neighborhood in Hyderabad that is central to this study, became the site of fierce ethnic conflict. The police besieged the neighborhood located within the former citadel of the Sindhi royal family and later shot at unarmed protesting women. In the following weeks, ethnic violence became the order of the day. These events eventually brought down the Benazir Bhutto administration. After the new elections, the MQM became a coalition partner in the government led by the Pakistan Muslim League of Nawaz Sharif.

PERSECUTION AND DECLINE

Apart from the notions of martyrdom, tyranny, and social justice, the party's rhetoric now also increasingly endorsed the discourse of Muhajirs as a beleaguered nation, and MQM speeches and statements increasingly portrayed Muhajirs as the creators of Pakistan. The act of migration was interpreted as a collective sacrifice, in which "twenty *lakh*" (two million) people died and many others left their home and lost property. Despite this sacrifice for Pakistan, however, Muhajirs continued to be the victims of discrimination as the Muslims had been in India. It promoted a feeling of displacement amid a hostile society. However, some interpreted this as evidence that Muhajirs were the natural leaders of a new revolution for social justice. This notion had in fact already been part of the MQM's discourse. On the eve of the 1988 elections, party chairman Azim Ahmad Tariq for instance stated: "We fought for Muslim rights in the subcontinent and our elders established Pakistan. We are now fighting for the rights of all suppressed nationalities. The MQM is a movement for Pakistan's stability and integrity; we have staked everything for it and we will protect it even at the cost of our lives."[30] Muhajirs, having proved their engagement with Islamic justice through their migration, appear as the protectors of the oppressed in Pakistan. Statements like this stress the essentially "middle class" nature of this struggle, extending the notion of the middle class to a growing urban underprivileged population challenging a predominantly rural elite of so-called feudals of various types: *zamindars, jagirdars,* and *waderos.* Over time the MQM began to attack the PPP more and more as a party dominated by feudal landlord families, while the modest background of the MQM's leaders was emphasized as evidence of the essentially middle-class character of the movement. In 1991 it was suggested for the first time to change the name of the party to *Muttehida Qaumi Movement* (United People's Movement), marking the party's aspirations to grow beyond the limitations of an ethnically based movement of Muhajirs only.

Discussions within the party about a change of policy soon led to a split. In the summer of 1991 the breakaway MQM-Haqiqi was formed by three high-ranking leaders of the party who had been expelled from the party on charges of corruption, violation of party discipline, and conspiracy against Altaf Hussain. The three defended their move by protesting the intention to replace *Muhajir* with *Muttehida* in the party's name, saying that the "leadership had become ambitious and greedy... they thought they could reach Islamabad. . . . They were prepared to put the unresolved problems of the Muhajir community . . . to oblivion."[31] According to their rivals in the MQM-Altaf, alternatively called Haq Parast Group, the three worked for the Inter Services Intelligence (ISI), the powerful intelligence agency of the military, which had concerns about the MQM's revolutionary aspirations.

Altaf Hussain's paramount position was reconfirmed in a dramatic and violent way. An MQM member of the national assembly who remained loyal to Altaf called the betrayal of the "chief" "more shameful than raping your own mother, sister or daughter." He also said that "He who betrays Altaf will meet his Waterloo in the shape of destruction of his family. . . . The minimum punishment for betrayal is death. . . . We will enter their houses with bombs on our bodies and destroy them by sacrificing our lives for our noble leader."[32] Slogans on walls also warned that "he who is a traitor to the leader will certainly die" ("jo qaid ka ghaddar hai voh maut ka haqdar hai"). The house of Afaq Ahmad, one of the three Haqiqi leaders, was set ablaze. In Karachi supporters of both factions now fought each other in an increasingly more systematic manner. Enemies were identified, abducted, tortured, and often killed. Of the Haqiqi militants, "fifty or so fled to the United States. . . . The less resourceful went to India or other provinces in Pakistan" (Hanif 1994). In June 1992 these exiled Haqiqi members came back as the byproduct of the first so-called Operation Clean-up.

Operation Clean-up

In hindsight it can be said that growing rumors that the army was about to crack down on the MQM and "restore law and order" preceded this state operation. In 1992 life in Sindh had become disrupted by various militant groups active in cities as well as the rural areas. In the countryside, gangs of criminals (*dacoits*) abducted members of rich families for ransom. They also stopped and robbed trucks and lorries on their way from Karachi to the Punjab and beyond. In the cities the MQM was increasingly accused of abusing its power. MQM strongmen openly carried firearms and terrorized their neighborhoods. The army operation was further foreshadowed by Altaf Hussain's departure to London earlier that year. He officially left for medical reasons, but it is more probable that he was given the option to leave the country before being arrested. When Operation Clean-up started, over one hundred criminal cases were filed against him. All the same, the Pakistani state never seriously pressed the British government for his extradition, as his presence in a Pakistani jail would probably cause a highly inflammable situation in urban Sindh.

The operation was launched in June 1992. At times the operation took the form of a manhunt, which according to official army sources left a thousand *terrorists* and *dacoits* killed (Mujtaba 1993). From this period onward the term *terrorist* became a buzzword. I will say more about it in chapter 6. As several writers have noted, the term *terrorism* is often used to legitimize the excessive use of force, which would not be justifiable within the framework of the rule of law and the principle of human rights (Ivianski 1988; Schlesinger 1991; Taussig 1987; Zulaika and Douglass 1996). This was clearly the case in Pakistan, where state oppression went hand in hand with a propaganda campaign to brand the MQM as a terrorist organization. The army claimed to have discovered many MQM–run torture cells and invited journalists and photographers to report on the discovery. In newspaper reports MQM leaders including Altaf Hussain were accused of sexually abusing young Muhajir girls. Many unverified rumors said that the MQM was sponsored by India or the intelligence agencies of other distrusted states such as Israel or the United States. The propaganda campaign against the MQM reached its apex in the summer of 1995, when Prime Minister Benazir Bhutto gave an infamous speech comparing MQM supporters to rats. Of course, the name of the operation itself—Operation Clean-up, getting rid of dirt—was illustrative, too.

Immediately after the operation the MQM broke with the Pakistan Muslim League, which was held responsible for the operation. Then, while members of the MQM-Altaf group went into hiding, supporters of the MQM-Haqiqi returned to Karachi and set out on a "victory march" through the city. The militants of the MQM-Altaf now found themselves pitched against two enemies, the state forces and the breakaway MQM-Haqiqi. An especially dramatic incident in the rivalry between the two factions took place in May 1993, when Azim Ahmad Tariq was murdered in his sleep. As the former chairman of the APMSO and prominent leader of the MQM, second only to Altaf Hussain, Ahmad Tariq had always been a moderate compared to many of his friends. When Altaf fled from Pakistan, Tariq was expected to take his place. However, Tariq's role in the controversy between the breakaway MQM-Haqiqi and those who remained loyal to Altaf—for a while he refused to take sides—made him unpopular among some. He was shot dead at night in his home. Both factions held marches to mourn his death and accuse their rivals of the murder.[33]

The army operation and the anti–MQM propaganda continued when national elections were held in fall 1993, which had become necessary after the dismissal earlier that year of Prime Minister Nawaz Sharif by the president. The MQM-Altaf decided to boycott the elections. In some districts this led to turnouts of less than 10 percent, which showed how little support the MQM-Haqiqi enjoyed.[34] But the fight between the two groups did not come to an end. Supporters of the Altaf faction of the MQM tried to take back the territories in Karachi they had lost to the MQM-Haqiqi during Operation Clean-up. For months gunfights took place in the streets of Karachi, wounding or killing many passersby. Both factions regularly ambushed each other in a proxy war of semi-autonomous gangs trying to control small patches of the city.

In the spring of 1994, the MQM launched a Jail Bharo Tehreek or "Fill the Jails Movement," a series of strikes and civil disobedience actions to demand the end of the army operation. However, in 1995 the government of the PPP, which had won the national elections of 1993, infused new life into the watered-down army operation. Again, hundreds of MQM activists were arrested or murdered while others fled the country. After the 1997 elections, the MQM reached an agreement with the Pakistan Muslim League and became a partner in the provincial and federal government but kept complaining about the support that the MQM-Haqiqi was said to receive from the military. It again left the coalition with the Pakistan Muslim League in October 1998. Soon afterward military rule was established in the province of Sindh and many MQM workers, freed from jail only shortly before, were arrested once again.

Nonetheless, the influence of the MQM-Haqiqi has been restricted to some areas in Karachi. The group was largely absent in Hyderabad. To be sure, removal and punishment of party members as well as infighting also occurred in Hyderabad, but such incidents were never given a name, a leader, or an organization. However, even though the MQM did not suffer from an internal split in Hyderabad, it was severely damaged from the state persecution of its activists. The local leadership has been in hiding for prolonged periods of time, while other activists have gradually left the movement. The party has never been formally banned, but its head offices have often been closed.

Conclusion

It is difficult to tell how much support the MQM still enjoys in Karachi and Hyderabad. The military takeover of 1999 seems to have thrown the MQM into a state of indecisiveness and impotence. Although there have been signs that the MQM is trying to revive the Muhajir-Sindhi coalition against the military by making statements in favor of Sindh and the Sindhis, the party has sometimes also tacitly supported General Musharraf, himself a Muhajir. In the national elections of 2002, the MQM managed to win in most Muhajir-dominated districts in Karachi and Hyderabad but not as decisively as in the past. Turnouts were far below 50 percent, an expression of people's weariness with democratic politics, which, however, is a general problem in Pakistan and certainly not limited to urban Sindh. On the other hand, no other party has thus far managed to make inroads into the constituencies that the MQM has controlled since 1988.

It is, however, probable that the MQM is no longer as powerful as it used to be. In its early years the MQM appeared as a revolutionary movement siding with the Sindhi opposition against the military regime of the 1980s. At the height of its power, having become the third largest party in Pakistan, it distanced itself from the PPP, returning to the antagonism between Muhajirs and Sindhis, which had been established earlier during the language crisis of the early 1970s. This resulted in a politically isolated position, leading to a showdown between the MQM and the military during Operation Clean-up. Beleaguered, split, its leadership exiled, the MQM fell apart into locally organized groups resorting to anti-state militancy and crime. The party continued to be led from its head office in a northern suburb of London, from where Altaf Hussain tried to stay in touch with his followers in Pakistan by means of videotapes, audiocassettes, the Internet, and speeches addressed to public meetings by telephone. But the days of the MQM evoking high expectations of change seem to have come to an end.

In the remaining chapters I will examine several of the themes discussed in this chapter in a more detailed and anthropological way. Chapter 4 focuses on the elements of provocation, transgression, and the collective effervescence of violence. Chapter 5 discusses the notions of martyrdom and tyranny by analyzing the most severe incident of Muhajir-Sindhi violence since the rise of the MQM. Chapter 6 examines the growing sense of displacement and disillusion among Muhajirs and its ramifications for popular perceptions of the state. I will discuss these themes mainly from the perspective of Pakka Qila, the Muhajir neighborhood built within the old Sindhi citadel, located in the heart of the old city of Hyderabad. I will introduce this neighborhood in the next chapter.

CHAPTER THREE

Pakka Qila

OUTSIDE its walls the neighborhood of Pakka Qila was known as an isolated, closed, and impenetrable community, hostile to outsiders, an image fostered by its geography. The neighborhood lay hidden behind the thick walls of the citadel that had once belonged to the Sindhi royal family prior to the British conquest of Sindh. The fortifications rose up high and inaccessible. Since there was only one entrance to the citadel and no thoroughfare, few outsiders ever visited the place. The small alleys formed a perfect labyrinth in which strangers could easily get lost.

However, outsiders did not primarily point at the forbidden walls to comment on the particularistic reputation of Pakka Qila. It was rather said that Pakka Qila formed one *biradari* (kin group). Many outsiders believed that all of Pakka Qila's inhabitants were related to each other and arranged their marriages according to a strict endogamy. Kin solidarity was also believed to govern economic life. Almost every man in Pakka Qila was taken to be a shoemaker, working in shops and factories owned by their kin group, keeping outsiders out. The system continued, it was said, because young boys left school at an early age, joining the family workshop as an apprentice and learning the skills of the family occupation. To the outside world the inhabitants of Pakka Qila were known as *mochi*, a caste (*zat*) name for cobblers.

My first impressions seemed to confirm these notions of Pakka Qila. I felt like an intruder in a private place when I first visited the neighborhood. Women on balconies heralded my arrival by yelling to each other that a *gora sahib* (white mister) was entering their streets. A woman of respectable age came around the corner, saw my assistant and me, looked surprised, hesitantly put on a veil, and stopped to see where we were going. A man her age stood up from his chair in front of his shop and approached us, friendly but firmly asking what we wanted. We explained and the man offered to guide us through the neighborhood. While we went deeper into the citadel along alleys less than one meter wide, I saw men and women acting as though there was a disturbance in the streets. Women went inside to fetch headscarves. Men, embarrassed to be seen in a loincloth, also withdrew. The public street seemed to them an extension of their small houses. I soon discovered that wedding parties were held on the streets without the colorful curtains known as *shamianas*, which are used in other neighborhoods to separate the party from the public street.

Pakka Qila was indeed a neighborhood dominated by shoemakers. It was said that the fort housed 153 shoemaking workshops. I never counted them, but there were plenty of them. Most were narrow rooms without windows. Although there were a few factories, the biggest of which employed up to forty workers, shoemaking was largely a family business. Many young boys were indeed employed in the family workshop from the age of ten to twelve, which some men saw as a form of training yielding better job opportunities than formal education. Most boys seemed to prefer the work to school. The older men took pride in a boy who was quick to take up the skill.

As a whole, Pakka Qila was one of the major shoemaking centers in Hyderabad and various shoemaking families did indeed work together. They had formed a shoemakers association, which set the prices with clients in the market, negotiated tax with the General Sales Tax Department, and bought leather in bulk from nearby villages to reduce expenditures on raw material. Collectively the Pakka Qila shoemakers also had an influence on shoe fashion in Hyderabad. Early in November, with the coming of the winter, they went to the city with their carts filled with new designs covered with sheets so that other shoemakers could not catch a glimpse of the new fashion before the shoes were actually for sale in the market. This was also a time when the workshops in Pakka Qila were full of workers, for only the biggest companies had warehouses to store shoes in, while others had to produce according to demand.

Hence there seemed to be some truth to Pakka Qila's reputation as a bastion of a shoemaking *biradari* in which loyalty and occupation were based on kinship. But it also became clear to me that Pakka Qila was home to many other families. There were bangle makers, blacksmiths, carpenters, butchers, street vendors, vegetable sellers, tailors, and makers of *biri* (a local kind of cigarette). Like shoemaking, these occupations were considered traditional family occupations. Others held jobs that were not part of a family tradition. Pakka Qila was home to some civil servants, mostly blue-collar, such as peons, bus conductors, and policemen. Some families opened shops, and some men made a living as rickshaw drivers. Apart from occupation, moreover, there were several other loyalties that divided Pakka Qila into smaller social units: place of origin in India; place of residence within Pakka Qila; and, to a lesser extent, religious sect (Sunni versus Shiʿa) and Sufi order (Chishtiyya, Qadriyya, etc.). Taking all these crisscrossing solidarities into consideration, it became impossible to conceive of Pakka Qila as one *biradari*, and Pakka Qila men generally denied living according to the *biradari* system.

It became clear to me that kinship loyalty was not always given a positive connotation. On the one hand, the term *biradari* celebrated the solidarity within the extended family. It was an accepted cultural norm and taken as an Islamic or Asian value setting Muslims or Easterners apart from Westerners, who were believed to be more individualistic. Most men in Pakka Qila also preferred an arranged marriage within the *biradari* for their children. And yet they were also quick to declare that in principle any Muslim would qualify as a future spouse for their children. Too much *biradari* solidarity was clearly not appreciated as it could be seen as a violation of Muslim solidarity. Additionally, it was taken as old-fashioned and part of a past left behind in India. Endogamy, in short, did not befit a modern Muslim in Pakistan.

It began to dawn on me that the opinion of Pakka Qila as a place ruled by kinship solidarity carried a hidden message. It was a subtle way of saying that Pakka Qila was a place where people stuck to pre-independence exclusivist loyalties of caste and kinship. This explained why the inhabitants of Pakka Qila loathed the term *biradari* almost as much as other insults conveying the same message in a more direct manner. These included the caste name *mochi* for cobblers, which hinted at a low caste or even Hindu background; the pejorative term "black" (*kaliya*), which commented on the presumed racial aspects of caste differences; and, perhaps most explicitly, the phrase "son of Nehru" (*Nehru ka beta*), which of course referred to an ongoing loyalty to India. All of these conveyed the message that something was wrong with the sense of national solidarity and proper Islamic mentality of Pakka Qila's residents.

This illustrates how the politics of insult and prejudice played itself out locally in daily life. As this chapter will show, the MQM in its early years managed to mobilize the Muhajir youth in places like Pakka Qila by combatting the stigma of low status and disloyalty that young Muhajirs had to live with. This is an important aspect of the success story of the MQM, which very soon after it had ceased to be a student organization became a neighborhood-based movement, recruiting young men and women in their neighborhoods (*mohallahs*) rather than in educational institutions. The fact that the MQM put forward a self-conscious and proud notion of Muhajir identity in opposition to the low stigma ascribed to them was important in this process.

This chapter starts with an examination of the social stratification of the neighborhood. It will become clear that Pakka Qila is not the homogeneous and exclusivist neighborhood known to outsiders. An inside view reveals the existence of several sub-neighborhoods or *mohallahs* within the citadel, each of which differs from the others in terms of occupation, wealth and power, place of origin in India, and history of settlement. Having outlined the social stratification within Pakka Qila, it is possible to examine the effects of neighborhood politics on the emergence of the

MQM and vice versa. I will argue that the main transformation in power relations brought about by the MQM was the empowerment of the young generation born after migration. Yet, the MQM did not empower all young men equally. The young MQM leaders in Pakka Qila were mostly from the leading families that had dominated neighborhood politics for some time. These leading and indeed shoemaking families form the largest and most powerful subgroup within Pakka Qila. They were also the most successful in turning stigma into pride by taking up the new ethnic Muhajir identity of the MQM.

ARRIVAL AND SETTLEMENT

Most of the migrants who would eventually settle in Pakka Qila arrived in Hyderabad by train. As soon as they left the station, they immediately stood face to face with the impressive southern fortifications of the citadel. Literally meaning "brick fort"—an older mud fort (Kacca Qila) is in the vicinity—Pakka Qila was situated on a low hill, dominating the city. Today new buildings surround the citadel from most sides, the result of Hyderabad's considerable growth since 1947, which has made it into a city of nearly two million inhabitants. However, the view of Pakka Qila from the railway station is still unspoiled and impressive even today.

The entrance of the citadel is on the opposite side, the northern side. Getting there, one passes through several bazaars with cheap hotels and restaurants, most of which are owned by Pakhtun migrants from upcountry. One reaches the grave of Pir Abdul Wahab Shah Jilani, the place where in May 1990, at the height of conflict between the MQM and state forces, the police shot dead a large number of women staging a protest march. The shrine is one of the many holy places in and around Hyderabad. As it attracts many visitors from Pakka Qila, it is locally called the shrine of the *pir* of Muhajirs (*Muhajir ka pir*). The *pir* is a Sunni, belonging to the Qadriyya sect, but next to his grave and connected to it by a narrow alley is a Shiʿa sanctuary. It features a stone on which Hazrat Ali, son-in-law of the Prophet Muhammad, has left the imprints of his knees, hands, and forehead while praying. Both holy places attract pilgrims, beggars, musicians, and pigeons alike.

North of these sanctuaries lies the city center of Hyderabad. The western part of it is colonial in origin and features the Victorian architecture of the old campus, the post office, the city court, etc. Further to the west lies the cantonment, occupied by the army and closed to the general public. Beyond that, nearing the banks of the River Indus, is the new suburb of Qasimabad, almost totally inhabited by Sindhis, many of whom moved

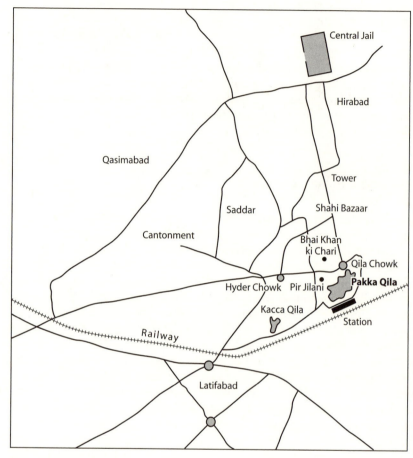

MAP 2. Hyderabad

there in the aftermath of the ethnic violence in May 1990. The segregated area continues to speak of the ethnic polarization of those days. So does Latifabad, the Muhajir equivalent of Qasimabad, a mostly Muhajir suburb separated from both the city center and Qasimabad by the railway track leading to Karachi (see map 2).

The eastern part of the city is built around the Shahi Bazaar, a two-mile-long, winding alley, which used to exude the wealth of this once royal city. The northern entrance is marked by a clock tower. In the south it ends at Qila Chowk, a roundabout opposite Qila Gate, which can be reached from several sides via gentle inclines coming up to the top of the hill. Beautiful pre-independence mansions surround Qila Chowk itself.

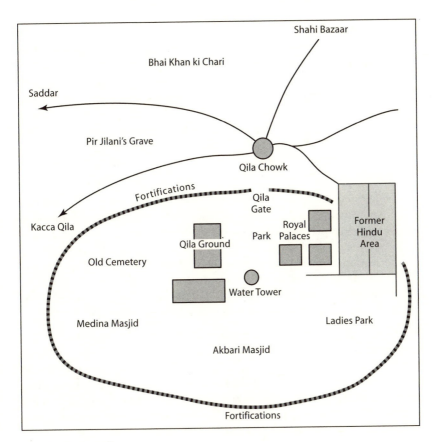

MAP 3. Pakka Qila

Their run-down state gives the place a sense of history, which is contrasted by the hectic atmosphere of all sorts of traffic trying to find its way between the carts and stalls of street vendors.

Entering Pakka Qila through the gate, one sees the former palace on the left-hand side (see map 3). The buildings now house a police station and the archaeological department, whose task it is to preserve the citadel's monumental status. There is a little park on the right that houses several graves, including those of the people who were killed in Pakka Qila during the police operation in May 1990. A little farther, beyond the Mosque of the Date Palm Tree and a little shoemaking factory, lies the British-built water tower, a newer water tank that is no longer in use, and the big open space of Qila Ground. Behind this playground lies a deserted cemetery. The remaining parts of Pakka Qila are residential areas.

The Area of the Hindu-Built Mansions

Pakka Qila was built in 1768 by the Kalhora kings, a local dynasty of Baluchi origin that ruled Sindh semi-independently from the decaying Moghul Empire beginning in the mid-eighteenth century. The Kalhoras made Hyderabad the capital of Sindh. They were replaced by the Talpur dynasty, also of Baluchi origin. In 1843 the citadel fell into the hands of the British colonial army when it defeated the Talpur army at the battlefield of Miani, some ten miles northeast of the citadel.

Before the conquest the citadel was a hive of activity. In the words of Sir Richard Burton:

> The Fort formed at once the place of defence, the treasury, and the residence of the native rulers. The interior was a *haute-ville*, with a promenade round the ramparts; a densely crowded town of wynds, *cul de sacs*, and narrow, crooked lanes; squarelets and guards; Darbárs and mosques, lines and barracks, Palaces and dwelling-houses, harem and stables. Many of the tenements, whilome the abodes of royalty, were spacious, and were made comfortable enough by the [British] conquerors, especially after glass windows, here required for the cold season, were added to the wooden shutters. (1993: 248–49)

But the defeat of the Talpur dynasty marked the end of Pakka Qila as the political center of the province. The British shifted the capital to Karachi, a port town with a mild climate. They continued to use the fort as a military camp and demolished all but the most impressive buildings inside the fort to accommodate troops and ammunition depots. In 1906 parts of the fortification, including the watch tower, were blown to pieces when the ammunition stored within the tower exploded.[1]

Having turned the fort into a military zone, the British controlled the area and granted permission to build houses in the area around Qila Chowk only in the 1930s. Hyderabad was one of the major trade centers in Sindh as was Karachi, and Sukkur and Shikarpur in Upper-Sindh, and like other urban centers in Sindh the majority of the population were Hindu. Since Hindus under the regime of the Islamic kings did not have the right to own land, most of them were in business and trade. They held an excellent reputation for entrepreneurship, stemming from the heyday of the Moghul period when Hindu traders from the Indus Valley used to travel as far as Moscow (Dale 1994). During the years of British control, many Hindus benefited from the upper hand they had over Muslims in matters of trade and literacy (Khuhro 1978: 307–9). Leading Hindu families therefore occupied the area that the colonial army abandoned in the 1930s. Nearly all the mansions built near Qila Chowk still show the names of their former Hindu owners. They also mention the year in which construction was completed, most after 1940. Almost all their inhabitants left soon after 1947. Many of them went to India, while others migrated elsewhere.

While Hindus left, Muslims from India arrived. The influx of migrants changed the population of Sindh drastically. Migrants from India made up at least 25 percent of the population of the province as a whole, including Karachi, which, being the capital city of Pakistan at that time, was still federal area and administratively not yet a part of Sindh. In the major towns and cities, the number of migrants was much higher. Hyderabad probably had the largest percentage of migrants in Pakistan. In 1951 the total city population was 240,000, of which almost 160,000 were migrants (Ghayur and Korson 1980: 213).[2]

Partition initially meant a major redistribution of property. Some Sindhi families occupied Hindu property, adding to their wealth that helped make them highly influential in Hyderabad. Many migrants also considerably increased their wealth. Others lost property. Two factors influenced the redistribution of abandoned property in Hyderabad, one of which was early arrival. The area surrounding Qila Chowk, then being the most posh and modern part of the city, was the first to be occupied. Ian Talbot writes of Hyderabad that "even tonga drivers were found residing in the houses of former Hindu businessmen. They took advantage of the spacious accommodation to stable their animals inside" (1996: 164). Perhaps this is true, although I personally have never heard stories of such extravagance. But if it happened, the continuing process of rehabilitation quickly drove the poor out of the mansions again. It was important to have good connections and relationships with members of the Muslim League, who directed the official rehabilitation schemes. This was the second factor at play. Soon the Pakka Qila mansion area housed members of the Muslim League and high-ranking civil servants. The commissioner of Hyderabad, Nusrat Husain, lived here, as did the family of Qazi Muhammad Akbar, the Sindhi mayor. The family of Mubarak Ali Shah, a migrant who competed with the Qazi family over the central positions within the local Muslim League during the 1950s and 1960s, lived here too.

Situated in the heart of a densely populated area that became increasingly congested, the neighborhood gradually lost its appeal. Over time, the rich families all moved out, leaving behind only their names, which had been given to public places—the Nusrat Bazaar or the Qazi Muhammad Akbar Boys School. They rented out their houses to shopkeepers from outside the citadel. Some of the more prosperous artisans of Pakka Qila have been able to rent these houses to store their merchandise. The somewhat impoverished among the families who first settled here remained.

The area around Qila Chowk is, in sum, a heterogeneous area. It does not have the enclosed and dead-end street character as do the other parts of the fort. Even a few Sindhis and Pakhtun live here, although most non-

Muhajirs who lived here left after the killings of May 1990. In general, this area is not considered to belong to Pakka Qila proper by the inhabitants of the other parts of the citadel.

Ladies Park and Akbari Masjid

Before the end of 1947 all houses were occupied. Meanwhile, the empty space of Pakka Qila had been used as a refugee camp for Hindus who had come from the countryside to Hyderabad to wait for a train to India. When they left the place lay empty again. Arriving refugees considered it "a jungle." They stayed in a reception camp near the station. Here, some migrant families arriving from Agra decided to move to the empty space in the citadel. They felt entitled to it. As one man put it, "[T]he government did not give this land to us. We simply took it. We had the right to live here. [Prime Minister] Liaqat Ali Khan Sahib had invited us to come to Pakistan." These families from Agra built their huts on a piece of land known as Ladies Park. It had been a green spot for the ladies of the royal family, laid out at the feet of a tower from which they could enjoy the breeze during the hot summer. Through hearsay more families from Agra settled here.

These pioneering families all came from one particular area in Agra called Khoja ka Haveli, arriving in Pakistan through a process of chain migration. Khoja ka Haveli was a small neighborhood in Agra consisting of about five hundred houses, most of which were occupied by shoemakers who worked in a factory owned by a Khoja Muslim.[3] A few soon went to Pakistan, but most waited. Then the factory owner sold the factory to a Sikh and left for Pakistan. Hindus and Sikhs who arrived from across the border occupied the houses of the departing Muslims, which accelerated the process of migration among the Muslim population. "The Hindus told us to leave. They said: 'We left our houses in Pakistan, now you give us your houses.' So the rest of us also left." About a hundred households eventually settled in Ladies Park. Today Ladies Park is still the most homogeneous part of Pakka Qila. The majority of the area's households originally comes from Khoja ka Haveli. In addition to shared residence, marital bonds and the shared occupation of shoemaking further strengthen social ties in this area.

Adjacent to this area lies an area now known as Akbari Masjid after the mosque (*masjid*) around which the neighborhood is built. It can be seen as a more heterogeneous extension of Ladies Park. Here, too, shoemaking families from Agra dominate. Located here are, in fact, the largest shoemaking workshops, owned by the most influential Agra families in Pakka Qila. But one also finds other communities forming separate endogamous and occupational groups. They followed the example of the Agra families and settled in Pakka Qila.

Together, Ladies Park and Akbari Masjid form the heart of Pakka Qila, geographically as well as politically. The families living here dominate neighborhood politics and have represented Pakka Qila in the city council. The local MQM leaders have also been recruited from these areas. Moreover, the families living here were strong enough to resist the growing pressure from outside to renovate the citadel, remove the settlements, and relocate the inhabitants to the outskirts of the city. Another area named after the Medina Mosque, located at the far end of the fort, did not manage to escape this fate. Calls for renovation grew louder in the 1960s and were linked to the growing tension between the Muhajir and Sindhi population in Hyderabad. Before looking at the *mohallah* of Medina Masjid, then, it is useful to say a few words about the relations between migrants and Sindhis in Hyderabad.

INSTANCES OF EARLY CONFLICT

The influx of large numbers of migrants in Hyderabad had its share of problems. In spite of calls for national solidarity, a series of disputes did arise. The question of distribution of Hindu evacuee property continued to be a main point of contention. Both locals and migrants felt entitled to a share. Migrants wanted to be compensated for the property they had left behind in India. In Sindh, however, the Muslim League had campaigned for partition, saying that Hindu moneylenders had taken over much Muslim property during colonial times. As a result, several Sindhi families claimed to be the rightful owners of land, shops, and houses left behind by Hindus. Moreover, several Sindhi Muslims ran little businesses in shops they had leased from the Hindu owners. Some of these shops were allotted to migrants who began to exploit the place themselves.

Evacuee property was distributed by the state, which in the early years of partition essentially was the Muslim League—the victorious party of the freedom movement. Competition for wealth and power took place within the Muslim League. In Hyderabad the party was split into two groups: the Sindhi faction, which had run the Sindhi section of the party, and a faction of party members from India who felt they had significantly contributed to the creation of the new state of Pakistan. The center of the migrant party was in the Moti Mahal, the residence of Mubarak Ali Shah, a blind *hafiz*, someone who knows the Qur'an by heart. Born in 1914 in Jaipur, Mubarak Ali Shah turned his house into a cultural center for Urdu speakers, organizing literary nights and meditational music sessions (*qawwali*). These events attracted a large number of Urdu intellectuals, artists, and politicians.

Despite becoming the vice-president of the Muslim League, the *hafiz* did not manage to take over the Muslim League from the Sindhi families who continued to dominate the party. Three families were especially influential: the Mir Talpur brothers, who were the scions of the former Sindhi rulers; the family of Syed Mian Muhammad Shah, who had been the representative of Sindh in the Bombay Presidency Assembly and the secretary of the Muslim League; and the Qazi family, a family of Muslim traders who had settled in Hyderabad in the 1920s. Despite regulations established by the federal government to give priority to the rehabilitation of migrants, existing networks within the Sindhi political elite remained intact in Hyderabad. In the early 1950s Mubarak Ali Shah tried to contest the Sindhi faction of the Muslim League on the basis of a Muhajir identity when he founded the Jam'iat-ul Muhajirin, a party of well-to-do migrant families. However, his attempt never gained momentum and very few in Hyderabad recall the existence of the party, but it was to this party that the chief minister of Sindh, Muhammad Ayub Khuhro, hinted in a speech held in 1954: "My Government will give priority to the rehabilitation of new Sindhis [migrants]. The problem is a stupendous one and it has many complexities. The position has been made more difficult by interested parties who for various reasons are trying to create a rift between the old Sindhis and the new settlers. . . . Formation of sectarian, social and political organizations, especially for the new settlers, has resulted in antagonizing the old Sindhis" (Sorley 1968: 756). In general, then, the local Muslim League remained an arena of competition between Sindhi and migrant families, in which the former tended to have the upper hand. This was in contrast to Karachi, then the federal capital, where migrants did manage to dominate the Muslim League in the early years after independence.

Muharram, 1950

On a popular level, tension between the local and migrant populations took the form of a sectarian riot during the 'Ashura processions in the month of Muharram, in October 1950, in front of a police station just off Qila Chowk. It was an episode that was hardly forgotten in Pakka Qila. Some older men had been part of the riot, while the younger generation had heard stories about it. The riot was documented by a court of inquiry that had been set up to investigate the incident. According to its findings, the following happened.

On 23 October 1950, at 2 P.M., three migrants brought to the city police station near Qila Chowk a Sindhi known as Muhammad Belawal. The man had a bleeding head wound. They also brought with them a four-year-old boy named Shameen. The three had seen the man running with the boy under his arm followed by a large group of migrants. The crowd had eventually gotten hold of him and the man was beaten on his head with a stick. The three had managed to convince the crowd that the man must be brought to the police. Inside the station, the Sindhi claimed that he was the father of the boy. The report does not give the boy's account.

During the first days of Muharram, the month Imam Hussain's martyrdom is commemorated during large ʿAshura processions, there had been rumors in the city that Shiʿas were trying to kidnap Sunni boys. This revived the old fear for Shiʿas as child murderers who need the blood of young Sunni children as a necessary ingredient to the dishes of rice distributed during the ʿAshura processions. As one of the men in Pakka Qila recalled: "The practice was widespread in [Shiʿa-dominated] Iran but it had seldom occurred in India because Shiʿas were a minority there. In Sindh, however, Shiʿas were rich and powerful and unscrupulous. They had been kings over here. [The Kalhora dynasty that ruled Sindh in the eighteenth century was Shiʿa.] They had made this land the land of Ali [whom Shiʿas consider the righteous successor of the Prophet]." According to this man, the crowd was trying to save a migrant Sunni boy from the clutches of a Sindhi Shiʿa.

While the men were inside the police station, the rumor spread that the police had released the Sindhi and killed the boy. The agitated crowd grew rapidly, attracting the attention of a large group of people taking part in the ʿAshura procession. They passed by carrying their symbols of Imam Hussain's martyrdom (*taziya*), stopping to see what was going on. The head constable of the police station called the deputy superintendent from the cantonment station. When the man arrived, he "thought that the Muhajirs who had collected outside the Police Station were acting in the way they usually act in cases where the complaint was against a Sindhi by a Muhajir. In such cases he had previous experience of Muhajirs collecting in large numbers" (Government of Sindh 1950: 8). The deputy superintendent showed the Sindhi man and the boy to the crowd to calm them down. The crowd, however, did not disperse and the policemen subsequently arrested some of the leaders and pushed aside others using their sticks (*lathi*). Some *taziya* were damaged during the operation, which created a stir among the crowd. Slogans like "Hussain's shrine has been martyred" ("Hussain ka roza shaheed ho gaya") were raised, making the mood even more explosive.

The district magistrate, generally known as the "collector," appeared on the scene, listened to the crowd, and promised to look into the matter, which was greeted with cries of "Collector *zindabad*! Pakistan *zindabad*!" ("Long live the collector, long live Pakistan"). Mubarak Ali Shah, as vice-president of the Muslim League, was telephoned by the district magistrate and arrived a little later. Because the crowd had by now grown into the thousands, the *hafiz* addressed the crowd through a public address system brought in from the adjacent music hall known as Radio House. He appealed to the public to be responsible citizens of Pakistan and leave quietly. The magistrate also told the crowd that their conduct was not in accordance with the Quranic injunctions. At that time, self-flagellants made their way into the crowd with a lot of show and noise, beating their drums and waving their dummy swords while rhythmically shouting "Ali! Ali!" The crowd responded enthusiastically to the cries.

In order to quiet the crowd, the arrested leaders were released. But soon more self-flagellants arrived, shouting that Muhajir boys were being kidnapped all over the city. Some of the processionists were said to have been carrying real swords. One boy carrying a knife was heard shouting, "Collector *murdabad*!" ("Death to the collector"), but the constable Syed Hussain Shah, "who is a tall, sturdy Pathan held the boy's hand in his grip and twisted it so making the boy and his knife fall to the ground" (Government of Sindh 1950: 13–4). The policemen again tried to push the crowd aside, but the people responded by throwing brickbats, soda-water bottles, old shoes, and pieces of wood. Thirty policemen were injured.

Meanwhile Mrs. Stacey, the wife of the subinspector who lived in the quarter behind the police station, came into the station and reported that the crowd had broken into her residence in attempting to set fire to her husband's motorcycle. Men from the crowd rushed into the compound of the police station bringing two *taziya* with them, which they set on fire and brought up to the plinth of the police station building. The civilians who were inside, including Mrs. Stacey and Mubarak Ali Shah, "became panicky and fearing imminent danger to their lives requested the District Magistrate to fire at the mob" (ibid.: 16). He ordered that shots be fired into the air, but that provoked even more excitement among the crowd. Then he ordered a fire squad to fire below the belt. The men, most of whom were migrants themselves, hesitated but eventually fired. Four were killed.

The Sindh police rangers arrived in Hyderabad at 6:30 P.M. The crowd was dispersed now but in fury. More dead were found near a mosque in Shahi Bazaar. At 4 A.M. the next morning, Colonel Malik of the rangers reported that "all was well with the city" (ibid.: 19). There were nine casualities, whom he ordered to be buried before sunrise because "he had had experience during the riots at Calcutta in 1926 and 1930 when the police had to fire again to disperse the funeral processionists." A boy succumbed to his injuries later that day. All ten victims were migrants.

The Sunni-Shiʿa Controversy

Of course the report cannot be taken as the only possible interpretation of the riot. The court of inquiry was evidently biased in collecting and selecting data for the report as it had an interest in demonstrating the efficiency and rationality of the state officials in handling the matter. It probably overemphasized the irrationality of others, including the rioters and non-officials such as Mrs. Stacey and Mubarak Ali Shah. Nevertheless, the report does indicate that tension between Muhajirs and Sindhis was not rare in those early years. In this case it took the form of sectarian conflict, a phenomenon with which migrants, especially those from North India, must have been familiar. In North India, the schism between Sunnis and Shiʿas had widened with the surge of Muslim revivalist movements from the eighteenth century onward. Sunni movements opposed religious practices they deemed not to be a part of the practice of the Prophet and his early companions (Schubel 1993: 79). The public processions during Muharram were often the object of controversy and regularly led to violence (Freitag 1989). The conflict hinged on the notion of the Shiʿa as a fifth columnist, excluded from a moral symbolic community.

This early riot can therefore be placed along a continuum that begins with the emergence of modern sectarianism in North India and ends with the widespread present-day phenomenon of both Sindhis and Muhajirs accusing each other of being predominantly Shiʿa. While many Muhajirs refer to Sindh as the "Land of Ali," Sindhis point to the importance of Lucknow in Uttar Pradesh—the province of origin of many Muhajirs—as a major center of Shiʿa learning. Sindhis furthermore often hold that the MQM is a Shiʿa conspiracy. Not only do Sindhis say this, but many Muhajirs critical of the MQM also make the movement out to be a Shiʿa party. The "Islamic" parties in particular have regularly used fierce anti-Shiʿa language to attack the MQM. In 1988, for instance, the leader of the Jamʿiat-i ʿUlama-i Pakistan (JUP), Maulana Noorani, urged its followers to vote for a Sunni candidate, his perception being that the MQM candidates were all Shiʿa (Jafri 1996: 26). Baseless as this is, the accusation shows the potency of the anti-Shiʿa argument.

Related to this is the term *maulai*. The word is a contraction of Maula Ali—Maula being an honorable title—which refers to those devoted to the Prophet's son-in-law Ali. Technically speaking, *maulai* is just another word for Shiʿa, but in Hyderabad it has the connotation of a happy-go-lucky person who leaves everything to God, does not cut his hair, dresses shabbily, smokes narcotics, etc. Some hold the *maulai* responsible for bootlegging and prostitution. In Pakka Qila I was regularly told that the *maulai* had infiltrated the Sindhi towns and villages, perverting them with their immoral behavior. Even the Shiʿa families living in Pakka Qila, who are themselves often accused by Sunnis of living life according to morally loose standards, refer to Sindhi Shiʿas as *maulai* to distinguish themselves from them.

The Grave of Hoshoo Shiddi

Disputes, then, occurred early and revolved around problems of settlement, the distribution of abandoned Hindu property, and the competition over the dominant positions within the Muslim League. But in the absence of a politicized idiom of ethnic strife, the Sunni-Shi'a conflict served as a model to make sense of social tension and competition. A new conflict arose in Pakka Qila toward the end of the 1950s and involved the illegal status of the settlements within the citadel. The city government started the construction of the suburb of Latifabad partly with the intention to relocate the inhabitants of Pakka Qila to this new area. Initially, however, relocation was voluntary and very few families left Pakka Qila.

This question of resettlement was directly linked to the emergence of a Sindhi nationalist consciousness. Groups of Sindhi students and intellectuals began to consider the citadel as a symbol of Sindhi national sovereignty, once occupied by the British colonial army, now still in the hands of non-Sindhis. Concerned with the historical value of the citadel, they wanted the place to be beautified and made into a national monument. This call grew stronger with the spread of a curious rumor, which soon was accepted as a historical fact. It concerned the grave of Hoshoo Shiddi, the commander of the Talpur army that had been defeated by the British in 1843. According to British historical sources, the British commander, Sir Charles Napier, had been impressed by the bravery and strategic skills of his rival and had buried him with military honor at the battlefield of Miani, some ten miles away from the citadel. In the 1960s this army leader and "martyr"—*shiddi* is the Sindhi word for martyr—became a hero for Sindhi nationalists. Moreover, the rumor spread that Hoshoo Shiddi's grave was located within the citadel. I have not been able to retrace the origin of this knowledge, but it soon became an undisputed fact to the extent that government brochures, coffee table books, and foreign travel guides mentioned the grave as one of the places of interest within the citadel. The inhabitants of Pakka Qila soon acknowledged the dangerous potential of this rumor and started looking for the grave of the general. One day, while laying the foundation for a new house, a man uncovered a tombstone, which the community believed to be part of the general's grave. The tombstone was removed and the house was built, but it proved to be ill fated for its inhabitants. Two children were born in it, one crippled, the other dead. The family abandoned the house, which was subsequently turned into a bakery because the dead are believed to stay away from fire.

All this could not prevent the demolition of hundreds of huts and houses in 1962 as part of the operation to clear the citadel of illegal settlements. The operation started at the far end of Pakka Qila, which had been the last part to be occupied. The families in the older settlements quickly mobilized to save the remaining parts from a similar fate. After the intervention of an influential Muslim League member, a resident of one of the mansions near Qila Chowk, they were successful. In effect, only the families who had settled late in Pakka Qila were forced to move.

Only months after the operation, heavy rainfall caused a flood in Hyderabad. The cleared area of Pakka Qila was again used as a refugee camp for those who had lost their homes. A little later, the relocated families started to return to Pakka Qila from the suburb of Latifabad. They found Latifabad, located at some distance from the city center, desolate and without character. Some of the families from Ladies Park and Akbari Masjid had also occupied the open spots, building new houses for their families. As a result, the area around Medina Masjid became a heterogeneous place housing different groups. Families from Ajmer in Rajasthan, India, form a group primarily known as Chishtiyya, or followers of Khwaja Moinuddin Chishti, the great Sufi saint buried in Ajmer. But there are also many families from other places in India, locally known by their caste name, such as *qasai*, who are butchers, and *arain*, most of whom are vegetable sellers. There are also several other smaller groups.

The dispute about the illegal status of the Pakka Qila settlements continued to be raised every once in a while. Those in favor of renovation managed to have the place recognized as a national historical monument. A branch of the archaeological department was established in the quarters of one of the former kings. As we shall see in the next chapter, one of the first acts of the MQM in Pakka Qila was the demolition and looting of the offices of this department by the local youth. The residents finally managed to have their settlements legalized in the mid-1990s. Only the settlements within sixteen yards of the fortifications were not legalized in order to protect the monumental walls from erosion. But those without legal documents also continue to live in Pakka Qila. At the same time, the citadel's status as a national monument was reconfirmed in the 1990s when a postal stamp was issued in honor of the place.

A Shoemaker's Son

In sum, despite outsiders' views that suggest otherwise, Pakka Qila did not form a homogeneous community. It rather consisted of four subneighborhoods or *mohallahs*: the area of the Hindu mansions near Qila Chowk; the far-end area of Medina Masjid; and the centrally located areas of Ladies Park and Akbari Masjid. Each of these different areas qualifies as a *mohallah* as described by Sandria Freitag. In Freitag's analysis, a *mohallah* is largely a nineteenth-century construct of caste and craft groups drawing together in residence units rather than living in clusters as clients and servants around a patron house (*haweli*), as was previously the practice. The artisan population in North Indian cities in particular lived in such *mohallahs*, which coincided with a range of affinities such as caste, kinship, and—in the case of migration—place of origin. Although never an isolated unit, the *mohallah* played a significant role in self-government and religious activities such as the maintenance of shrines and mosques and the organization of processions (Freitag 1989: 118–19).

While it can thus be said that Pakka Qila consisted of four *mohallahs*, an overall Pakka Qila identity also existed within the fortifications of the citadel. But this was a political entity rather than a unit of social organization. The term *qila qaum* or "people of the citadel" was used to denote this supra-*mohallah* form of solidarity. It was a proud name associated with soldiers and kings. It came into existence when Pakka Qila in the 1980s established itself as one of the most MQM–devoted areas in Hyderabad. During the years of war (*jang*) at the end of the 1980s, when Muhajir and Sindhi groups were almost constantly at loggerheads, the notion of *qila qaum* emerged along with the image of the citadel as sovereign MQM or Muhajir territory. The notion of a larger Pakka Qila community was also endorsed during the violence of May 1990, when the place found itself besieged by the police. In Pakka Qila many stories were told recounting how young MQM activists, persecuted by the police, were allowed to take refuge in any home within Pakka Qila. Some of these stories stress that these young males were received and taken care of by young and unmarried women, an unthinkable violation of the norm of female seclusion (*pardah*) under normal circumstances. This temporary suspension of *pardah* fostered the notion of Pakka Qila as a kinship community within which men and women are not secluded. But this notion was largely the result of ethnic violence and the rise of the MQM, and not everyone accepted it at all times. The notion of *qila qaum* was often dismissed as an ideological construct meant to conceal particularistic loyalties. Concretely, the powerful Agra families in Ladies Park and Akbari Masjid, who also dominated the local MQM, were said to endorse the notion of a Pakka Qila community, claiming to represent the citadel as a whole while in fact working mainly in the interest of their own kinship groups and *mohallahs*. The main opposition came from families originating from Ajmer. They sometimes went as far as arguing that the MQM, despite its all-Muhajir rhetoric, was primarily a party of Agra fellows led by Altaf Hussain who himself hailed from Agra. They argued that families from Ajmer were better equipped to lead the Muhajir struggle because Ajmer, being a religious center and a place of pilgrimage, had generated a self-effacing, serving mentality while Agra, as a political center and a former capital of the Moghul Empire, was a place of wheeling and dealing. There were other tactics, too, to undermine the leading role of the Agra families in Pakka Qila, such as accusing them of homosexual preferences, the inability to control their womenfolk, and an assumed infiltration of Shi'a influence.

In other words, the notion of Pakka Qila solidarity, promoted by some while denied by others, was part of internal competition within the citadel. With some exceptions, the shoemaking families from Agra, living in Ladies Park and Akbari Masjid, continued to be the most powerful and dominating also within the local MQM. Their position, however, was not uncontested. The strongest opposition came from Medina Masjid, arousing rivalries on the basis of place of origin prior to migration. This was a remarkable strategy, given the emphasis on migration as a purifying and unifying experience. The remainder of this chapter will give the background for the dominant position of the Agra families within Pakka Qila.

Electoral Politics

Having settled early in Pakka Qila amid many kinsmen from Agra, the shoemaking families enjoyed some economic expansion from the 1960s onward. There was a consensus in Pakka Qila that the 1970s had been the most prosperous years for shoemaking. Typically counting the years in terms of national governments, one man said: "In the years of Ayub Khan [1958–68] prices of shoes gradually began to rise, but the best years were those of Bhutto [1971–77]. Costs were still low and prices went up. In the time of Zia [1977–88], the costs began to rise while prices did not. Profits no longer increased." In addition to economic factors, the introduction of democratic elections also contributed to the Agra shoemaking families, increase in power.

Pakistan had not had democratic elections prior to 1970. In the 1960s the regime of Ayub Khan had introduced the basic democracy system, a system in which the representative bodies were elected indirectly through 80,000, later 120,000, so-called basic democrats, who had been elected in local councils and committees. The system was widely criticized as undemocratic and mainly aimed at cultivating a new rural constituency for the military regime (Jalal 1995: 56). In and around Pakka Qila, it had brought members of the Muslim League belonging to Hyderabad's influential families into the representative bodies. The first democratic elections, held in 1970, however, brought the Pakistan People's Party to power. Mir Rasul Bakhsh Talpur, a member of a Sindhi aristocratic family, became the governor of Sindh. An activist in the freedom movement, he had generously supported refugees and migrants with blankets and food during the early years of independence, also offering them jobs. Later he became president of several labor unions. He encouraged the leading families in Ladies Park to join the Pakistan People's Party, and in return he arranged the construction of a sewage system and the installation of electricity in Pakka Qila.

After 1977, when a military coup led by General Zia-ul Haq brought an end to PPP rule, local elections over the position of unit councilor were held every four years, starting in 1979. The post of unit councilor proved to be an important opportunity for brokerage between the community and the city administration. The unit councilor had direct access to the mayor and was generally considered to be his local intermediary. As the executive powers have a decisive edge over legislative powers in Pakistan, local power brokers, known as *chamcha*, are often very influential. Till the rise of the MQM, the followers of Mir Talpur continued to dominate the local elections for unit councilor. Without exception they lived in Ladies Park and Akbari Masjid. Despite internal cleavages, the leading families were numerous enough to defeat candidates from other communities and *mohallahs*.

These local representatives themselves were the first to benefit from their position. They expanded their businesses and built new multistoried houses during these years. To some extent, however, their wealth permeated the whole community. As employees in new factories several shoemakers benefited directly. Others said it was a form of social security to be related to a wealthy local politician or share a neighborhood with him.

The Quota System

When I say wealthy I mean this in relation to the average income in Pakka Qila. According to the Hyderabad Development Authority (HDA), Pakka Qila is one of the poorest areas of the city. Although everyone in Pakka Qila believes that the standard of living is generally higher for Muslims in Pakistan than for Muslims in India, in 1996 a skilled and experienced shoemaker did not earn more than 4,000 rupees a month, often less, whereas 5,000 to 6,000 rupees was an average income for a skilled laborer in Pakistan. The relatively wealthy, however, earned considerably more. They invested their money in two fields: mechanization and formal education for their children. The sons of the prosperous Agra families in particular began to leave the workshops of their families and pursue higher education.

Formal education enabled these young men to get access to civil service jobs, which were desirable not only for their salary or job security. The salary of a peon, schoolteacher, or policeman is not much higher than the income of a shoemaker, nor do the former jobs necessarily offer more security. Civil servants were mainly envied because they were not stigmatized the way shoemakers were—they did not have the stigma of being a *mochi* or a *kaliya*. In addition, having a civil service job gave one an autonomous position within the family. In time, young men anticipated, the civil service would take them elsewhere, preferably Karachi, Islamabad, or even abroad.

Aspirations to break loose from low social status and social control were most prevalent among the second generation of the more well-to-do shoe-making families. But these aspirations were difficult to realize. Sons of shoemakers from Pakka Qila did not have much access to the networks in which civil service jobs are distributed on the basis of class, ethnicity, kin-ship, and area of origin. They expressed their frustration over these unful-filled ambitions by complaining about the quota system. This system was implemented in 1973 and regulated access to government jobs and educa-tional institutions on the basis of one's ethnic background. In Sindh a distinction was made between urban and rural family background, which in effect was a distinction between Muhajirs and Sindhis. Employers often used the quota system as official grounds for rejecting candidates for whom they did not hold a social obligation to do favors. In the late 1970s, the quota system thus became a major point of irritation for young Pakka Qila residents who had had formal education and were looking for employment.

These two factors—low social status and frustration over the quota sys-tem—played an important role in the first campaigns of the MQM in the mid-1980s. Initially the MQM in Pakka Qila consisted of young men with some formal education no longer satisfied with a future as shoemakers. One of them, a shoemaker's son whom I will call Badruddin, was the first to introduce the MQM in Pakka Qila.

Badruddin

Badruddin went to school but dropped out after ten classes. According to a former friend of his, however, he was very much "a thinker." "His blood always boiled," his uncle said. Instead of hanging out with his peers, he spent his evenings writing the speeches he imagined himself giving one day. But his energy was as yet undirected. He made a tour among several political parties—the PPP, the Jeay Sindh Party, the JI, joining and leaving them one after the other.

Meanwhile he worked in his father's shop. But Badruddin never became a committed shoemaker. He was often away. He went as far as Karachi for his political discussions. There he came in touch with the small group of students who had formed the APMSO in 1978. In the early 1980s he returned to Pakka Qila to start his missionary work. A friend recalled: "In Ladies Park we used to sit outside. Near to our alley was an old school building. It stood empty. One day Badruddin came to us as he often did. He said we had to come to him that night in one of the classrooms. We were all friends and relatives. We went to see him. We were curious."

Badruddin made a speech he read from a pamphlet. It was an early pamphlet of the MQM called "Meri awaz suno" ("Listen to my voice"). His friend said: "It declared that Muhajirs are a nation (*qaum*), that we have a language (*zaban*), a *culture*—the only thing we lack is a country (*desh*). It said that Muhajirs are lost in Pakistan and that we were never given due respect. 'They call us locusts (*makha*), they call us *kaliya*, but we are proud to be Muhajir.' He also sang a song. He asked us to sing along. I cannot remember the words, but the chorus ran like: 'Say with pride that you are Muhajir.' " The classroom meetings continued for several years. Badruddin talked about the injustice done to Muhajirs by the army, Punjabi civil servants, and Sindhi landlords. He talked about the quota system and the lack of education and jobs. At the end of the meeting he would say: "Join my group. Fight the government." His friend finally joined him but he refused to pay the donation Badruddin requested.

In fact, it took Badruddin several years to form a group of about a hundred friends and relatives who supported him. He also did missionary work outside his immediate neighborhood. He was appointed general secretary of the MQM in the interior of Sindh, which included not only Hyderabad but also towns like Nawabshah, Mirpurkhas, and Sukkur. He traveled to all these places. But according to his friend he always returned disappointed.

However, when on 31 October 1986 the MQM chose the large open terrain of Qila Ground to hold its second public demonstration, Badruddin had mobilized a group large enough to make the necessary arrangements. Several weeks earlier the MQM and its leader, Altaf Hussain, had made a name for themselves during the MQM's first public meeting in Karachi. In Pakka Qila, however, Altaf was still a largely unknown figure. "Who is this man?" people asked the organizers. "A Muhajir from Agra," they replied, "who has come back from the United States to work for us." It made people curious. Much to the surprise of the Pakka Qila residents, thousands of young followers arrived in their neighborhood from miles away. They were even more surprised to see Badruddin on the platform next to the speakers from Karachi. He was even given the opportunity to make a short speech himself. Many politicians from all sorts of parties had spoken from that platform on earlier occasions, but never before had someone from Pakka Qila addressed the audience (see fig. 3).

Riots broke out in Hyderabad later that day when MQM supporters burned and looted Pakhtun property elsewhere in the city. The large crowd, the music, and the speeches had evoked an almost festive joy among the youth gathered in Pakka Qila, and in the evening when the manifestation had finished, they paraded through the streets of Hyderabad with their party flags, shouting their slogans, giving full vent to their excitement in acts of violence and destruction against the Pakhtun popula-

FIGURE 3. Qila Ground being prepared for an MQM public manifestation.

tion of the city. A curfew was soon established, but the MQM had made a name for itself and shown its power. "Now all Badruddin had to do was sit in front of his house, while people would come and ask him if they could join him. He only had to write down their names," said his friends.

Some two and a half years later, Badruddin's career as a local MQM leader came to an end when he was accused of treachery and expelled from the party. There were rumors that he had kept party money earned by selling the skins of the animals sacrificed on the occasion of *baqrᶜ id*, the feast of Ibrahim's sacrifice. It was a violation of party rule as well as a religious offense. According to others, however, a younger man known as Kanwar Chota, one of Badruddin's friends and rivals, had set him up. Kanwar had always worked in the workshop of Badruddin's family. Descriptions of both men suggest that Badruddin was an initiator, a pioneer, loyal to the MQM but a little naive and not very practical, whereas Kanwar was younger, more popular, and more streetwise. In 1989, when Badruddin was forced to give up his position, most of his peers had married and found a job, while Kanwar's friends were still single and ready to spend much of their time on party work. As the next chapter will show, this may have been one of the reasons for the change in local leadership.

CONCLUSION

In short, Badruddin was a prominent member of the young generation who, as part of the rise of the MQM, took over local power from the older generation. He belonged to a group of ambitious young men who had had the opportunity to go to school and college, who were no longer willing to accept low social status but failed to find employment outside their community because they lacked access to the networks of job broker-age. The dominant position of shoemaking families from Agra now resid-ing in the central areas of Pakka Qila, however, was hardly threatened.

By sketching the social differentiation within Pakka Qila, I have shown that Pakka Qila is not an endogamous community hidden behind the forti-fications of the citadel; this reputation of a community holding onto par-ticularistic loyalties is as much an ideological construct as its opposite: the equally homogeneous *qila qaum* united under the banner of the MQM. Despite these images of unity, social organization is much more varied and is determined by occupational group, kinship group, peer group, place of residence, place of origin, and religious sect and order. This also accounts for internal competition in local politics, which from the late 1980s on-ward largely took place within the arena of the MQM.

The fall of Badruddin and the takeover of Kanwar Chota as the local MQM leader give an indication of these internal contestations. A lot more must be said about this change of power. It also marked a change in style of leadership. Whereas Badruddin to some extent fits the term "salariat" coined by Hamza Alavi to denote an up-and-coming generation eager to get access to the civil service, he soon lost out to a different type of leader, his younger friend Kanwar Chota, who was not an educated man but rather a man with street power, a masculine man, and to his followers, a "funny" man. The three aspects, then, are the main themes of the next chapter. It will be about the streets, about masculinity, and about *fun*.

CHAPTER FOUR

Fun and Violence

Young men would not say they had joined the MQM for fun the first time you talked to them. Such an introductory meeting would include talk of idealistic visions of an egalitarian world and endless stories of injustice. But in a group sooner or later someone would sarcastically ask whether the speaker was a politician, a historian, etc. Was he preparing for a Friday afternoon sermon (*khutba*) in the mosque? Political rhetoric was not the sort of conversation young Pakka Qila men usually engaged in. Beyond the standardized canon of complaints meant for outsiders was a repertoire of narratives about a youth of breaking taboos, secret outings, and everlasting friendships—songs and gestures full of memory about narrow escapes that would never cease to be good stories. For years the MQM had provided an excellent pastime. Outsiders found it hard to understand what had been so thrilling, but I was fortunate enough to get the chance to see how exciting a movement the MQM could be.

This happened in November 1996 when a party was organized to celebrate the downfall of the Benazir Bhutto administration, which had been dismissed earlier that week. At 5 p.m., Habib, a friend from Pakka Qila, came to inform me that there was much activity going on near the MQM's head office in Bhai Khan ki Chari, a square near Qila Chowk. Habib was in high spirits and said I must come immediately: Altaf Hussain was going to give a speech from London. Habib looked different than usual. A headband in the MQM colors made him look younger than the mid-twenties he was. "We have been waiting for this liberation for four years," he said exuberantly when we walked through the labyrinth leading to Bhai Khan ki Chari. Four years earlier the first Operation Clean-up against MQM activists had been launched.

We entered the little square from the rear. Many of Habib's friends had already gathered there. Some had been hiding from police persecution and Habib had not seen them for months. He embraced them all. They, too, had dressed up in MQM colors or wrapped themselves up in MQM flags. Only those of his friends who had put on considerable weight over the past four years apparently reckoned it was beneath them to wear the outfit they had worn when they were younger. To make up for that, they had put themselves in charge of some task like arranging chairs for journalists and other guests, which were placed comfortably close to the betel nut shop in the corner of the square. Those still slender walked around disguised as *matamdars*, wearing black ribbons in their hair and dressed in black shirts, leaving the top three buttons open. "Black used to be popular," Habib explained: "Girls are very fond of black." Even now I saw a lot of black.

Some younger boys sang "Pardesi jana nahin" ("Stranger, don't go"), the latest hit from *Raja Hindustani*, an Indian film. They jumped on each other's shoulders, building a human pyramid of three levels; the one on top swung his hips and moved his arms. Then he jumped down, confident that the crowd would catch him. Another group of boys moved in from the opposite direction and immediately took up the challenge of building an even more impressive pyramid. Instead of singing movie songs, the slender man on top shouted: "Altaf hamara!" ("Our Altaf"), to which the crowd automatically answered: "*Zinda hai*" ("Long live"). He cried again: "Qaʿid hamara" ("Our leader"), but he lost his balance and fell before the crowd could respond. A wave of laughter welled.

When we tried to find our way through the crowd, I got the impression that everybody looked different this evening. Everybody had done something to his hair or clothes to become somebody slightly different from the person he was in daily life. Some wore Palestinian shawls around their necks, while others dressed in a black uniform that somewhat resembled a kimono. Still others wore army green camouflage jackets or a Sindhi peasant's batik shawl. This *ajrak*, Habib commented, had been out of fashion for a number of years.

From the city side, boys and young men arrived in groups. They announced their arrival by making a lot of noise and spectacle. Some shouted MQM slogans while others sang MQM songs in which new lyrics were added to existing melodies from well-known Bollywood hits. Yet another group entered quite dramatically, accompanied by the sound of a big drum. Behind the drummer his friends shouted rhythmically: "Mast Qalandar Altaf Hussain, Mast Qalandar Altaf Hussain." Habib explained that every group represented a particular neighborhood of Hyderabad. The group showing up as a band of fakirs in the tradition of Lal Shahbaz Qalandar came from a particular section in the suburb of Latifabad. This section was famous for its bravery and loyalty to the movement and had often challenged Pakka Qila's reputation as the city's most fearless MQM bastion. Given that, the reaction of the Pakka Qila hosts to the colorful entry of their rivals was lukewarm. "Our best fighters are in jail," Habib explained, somewhat hurt. Apparently brave fighters also excelled in making a good show. That day Pakka Qila suffered a defeat. But in time, Habib said, they would say that being in jail was a more convincing sign of one's loyalty than shouting "Mast Qalandar Altaf Hussain."

FIGURE 4. Billboard showing Altaf Hussain as an Arabian sheikh.

We reached the party's head office, which was still locked. Although the MQM was not officially banned, its offices had been closed since the beginning of Operation Clean-up. Party officials swarmed like busy bees trying to do all sorts of activities, the purpose of which they would not reveal. Some, however, had a clear task. They climbed ladders in order to tap the electricity lines. They had done so many times for weddings and other street celebrations.

Next to the hustle and bustle stood a small platform of serenity. It looked like a king's bier or a saint's tomb, covered with carpets, green sheets (*chadar*), and heaps of rose petals. On it stood several painted portraits of Altaf Hussain. On the biggest he was painted in a grandiose style that made him look like a head of state. Another one pictured him *en profile* in a smiling, benevolent pose. A third had caught him in action as he shouted into a microphone, his face twisted with anger and indignation and wet with sweat. A fourth, depicting Altaf as an Arabian sheikh (see fig. 4), was considered a joke by Habib and his friends. They agreed that the portrait made him look a bit ridiculous, almost like a woman with that silly piece of white cloth draped over his head. To them, the cloth resembled a *dupatta*, a scarf women wear to cover their hair. On other occasions, they recalled, there had been a picture of him as a Moghul king proudly wearing a turban—a much more masculine piece of headwear than an Arabian bedsheet. But this was also how Altaf Bhai (Brother Altaf) was full of humor, not even sparing himself when he felt like making fun. It seemed appropriate for a leader to appear in several different images during a party his supporters also attended in many different disguises.

Loudspeakers were placed on the platform between the pictures. They would in time amplify Altaf's speech from London, but now they played famous MQM songs that had not been played in public for years. Small children danced. Between Altaf's platform and the male crowd, women sat on carpets, singing the well-known songs while distributing sweets to their children. They seemed quite detached from the men's noise and shows that were going on behind them. Very serious-looking adolescents stood around the carpets, holding each other's hands as a human fence, facing the men. They had tied pieces of cloth around their upper arm as a sign of their official assignment by the MQM head office to maintain discipline and make sure that no one would intrude on the women's domain. "The MQM is a very disciplined party," Habib proudly said. "At meetings of the Jam'iat-i Islami or the Pakistan People's Party, everyone rushes to the front. Women do not dare to go there. The MQM is the only party that provides a safe haven for women."

While women and children were in the front and boys and young men were in the back, older men stood along the side, casually talking to the journalist guests and the betel nut vendor. For hours they would maintain a pose of stopping for a chat while just passing. Young and unmarried women were absent, although we spotted several of them on the balconies and behind the windows of the houses that looked down on the square. We had an argument over who was the prettiest, convincing ourselves that they were looking at us.

The music stopped when the call to prayer came from the nearby Ahl-i Hadis mosque. Some young boys invented a little song on the spot, ridiculing the mosque as a Taliban mosque, referring to the movement that was rapidly conquering Afghanistan, but an MQM official took the microphone and asked for silence and respect for God's prayer, saying that the Ahl-i Hadis were Muslims too. Nothing was going to happen during the time of prayer, Habib reckoned, so he proposed that we leave for a while and come back later. With a couple of his friends we went to a sweet shop at Qila Chowk, where they were soon engaged in telling old stories of how they had miraculously escaped from the police when they disrupted party meetings at Bhai Khan ki Chari. These stories had an easily recognizable pattern. The policemen were stronger and better armed but utterly stupid and slow, and they did not know the area well. Hence the small but smart and mercurial MQM supporter narrowly escaped and then lured the enemy into some dead-end street where he would fall into a pile of garbage or, worse, run into a room full of women who had been informed of his coming and were awaiting him with their shoes ready to beat him out again, meanwhile crying shame that a stranger had violated their seclusion. Subsequently jokes were told about Sindhis. They were difficult to understand because they contained many Sindhi words and modes of pronunciation, but one was about a woman who went to a doctor to complain about a terrible noise in her ear. The doctor asked her to describe the noise, to which the woman responded that it was really peculiar and very different from any sound animals make but that she had heard it once at Shah Abdul Latif's shrine. In this place, much cherished by Sindhis as center of genuine Sindhi culture, people had called this strange annoying noise music.

We went back to Bhai Khan ki Chari. Meanwhile an announcement had been made that Altaf, the "leader" (*qaᶜid*), was talking to the international press in London at the moment and it would take some time before he could address his followers in Hyderabad. While we waited more music was played, in particular the song Habib deemed as the "number-one song" of the MQM, which described Altaf Hussain as the "friend and fighter of the oppressed" ("mazlumon ka sathi aur larnawala"). Everyone sang along. Another song replaced the famous lyrics *Dil dil Pakistan* ("My heart, my heart, Pakistan") for *Dil dil MQM*. Others sang "Ham jitengen" ("We will win")—the national number-one hit during the 1996 World Cup Cricket.

Suddenly a man from the head office took a microphone and began a responsive game with the audience. He shouted "Muhajir," to which the public without being instructed answered: "Zinda hai" ("Long live"). Leader: "Mazlumon ka sathi hai . . ." ("Friend of the oppressed is . . ."). Audience: "Altaf Hussain." Leader: "MQM ka superman . . ." Audience: "Altaf Hussain." Leader: "Altaf hamara . . ." ("Our Altaf . . ."). Audience: "Zinda hai." Leader: "Qaᶜid hamara . . ." ("Our leader . . ."). Audience: "Zinda hai." And so on. As in a Shiᶜa mourning assembly in which people often cry out "Nare Haidari," the game ended when the man with the microphone shouted from the top of his lungs: "Nare Muhajir!" ("Cry out Muhajir!"). The response was an overwhelming "Jiye! Jiye! Jiye Muhajir!" ("Hail! Hail! Hail Muhajir!").

The singing was interrupted by a funny if somewhat embarrassing and pathetic scene. Attracted by the sound of music, a wandering Qalandar beggar, carrying heavy chains of iron on his shoulders, had come up from the nearby sanctuary of Shah Abdul Wahab Jilani, and upon seeing the platform exhibiting Altaf's pictures he instantly ascended into a state of devotion. Out of his pockets he produced a handful of rose petals mixed with small sweets wrapped in paper, and proceeded toward the platform to donate the gift to the portraits. An older man left the betel nut shop and came to stop the fakir, telling the man to go back to Shah Jilani's shrine and make his offerings over there. But the man was determined. He fell on his knees and tried to find a way between the feet of the man in front of him. The crowd laughed when someone from the back jokingly shouted: "Let him perform the ritual ablution (*wuzu*) first." The scene was indeed so hilarious that I began to wonder whether the beggar was in fact being serious. Was he pulling the leg of those who had built the platform, of himself, of everybody else present? Grabbing the iron chains, the older man tried to get the man on his feet again but to no avail. Only when a younger and sturdier man from the head office came to help him did he manage to make the Qalandar understand that Altaf was not a real saint and could not be an object of genuine spiritual devotion.

A little later two boys reenacted the episode. The boy playing the beggar had borrowed from the man the typical headwear fakirs make from three-cornered pieces of multicolored cloth. Making the gestures and sounds of a disciple in a trance he moved toward the platform exhibiting Altaf's pictures. The play became very funny when the second boy tried to stop him and the first folded his hands in front of his chest, bobbing his head the Indian way, blinking his eyes and asking in a submissive voice whether the "master" (*baba*) would be so kind as to let him proceed. A little girl cried: "Muhajir charya hai," which everyone found truly hilarious. *Charya* is slang for mad or silly and mostly used in informal situations, in which case the connotation can be friendly and good-humored. In the context of the parody of the beggar, the word was an appropriate comment on the ambiguity of the improvised play. The fact that the little girl had chosen the slang word *charya* rather than the more common word *pagal* for "mad" made it even funnier. *Charya* would have been an excellent word for Muhajirs to use to express their condescending opinion of the Sindhi as a somewhat naive, silly, slightly stupid, but potentially humorous crackpot. Now the child applied the term to Muhajirs, which unexpectedly articulated an absurd and hilarious intimacy.

For several hours the party went on in this state of ambiguity that made everything that happened potentially funny. Everyone was having too good a time to bother about the delay in Altaf's telephone call. After five hours, shortly after 10 P.M., he finally did call. Not knowing the connection with the loudspeakers had already been made he began by stammering some hardly intelligible words, so while everybody was talking and making jokes we suddenly heard his weak voice mumbling almost helplessly: "Hello? Hello?" Instantly the "number-one song" was struck up again from many sides and as a hymn of welcome the familiar words echoed among the houses: "Mazlumon ka sathi hai Altaf Hussain" ("Altaf Hussain is the friend of the oppressed"). In vain an official from the head office tried to silence the crowd, shouting into the microphone words we could not hear. Only when the chorus had come to an end did he manage to say that the leader had only a few minutes before he had to receive other representatives of the international press. Silence fell upon the square. Then we heard the tone indicating the connection had been broken.

Minutes passed and new jokes were being made that put the party's standard rhetoric in a new context. The joke about the MQM being the only Pakistani party that was not corrupt, for instance, now led to a new joke: it was so thoroughly clean it could not even afford a proper telephone line and subsequently had to tap someone else's line. We heard an electric noise and there it finally was: the voice of the leader. Much more self-assured, he had lowered his voice considerably. "Brothers (*bhai*), sisters (*behin*), children (*bacce*)," he began. He waited a moment—we were anticipating anything—and then said, "As salamo alaikum." To return the greeting, a thunderous "Walaikum salaam" was sent over the heads of the women toward the four portraits on the stage.

The Ludic and the Absurd

There is, of course, nothing special about the fun with which young supporters of the MQM took part in the movement. Several writers have shown that being part of a revolting and violent community can be an adventurous addiction. Bill Buford's book (1990) on English hooligans gives the reader a sense of how funny the collective inventing of cruel and poetic one-liners while watching a soccer match can be. Allen Feldman (1991: 33) quotes a Catholic housewife in Northern Ireland when she recalls the violent days of Belfast 1969: "It was really exciting as a kid watching those barricades built and actually having somewhere to play. . . . We'd play hide and seek and 'You're the Brits and we're the RA.' It was brilliant." A more contemplative ex-activist of the Basque ETA told Joseba Zulaika: "I am not sorry for anything we did, it was great, but we weren't very conscious of what we were doing. We were young . . . we lived another idealism, we experienced it much more than now. But it seems to me now that it was partly absurd, that it all couldn't be very real" (Zulaika 1988: 64–65). These are just a few examples indicating a little researched aspect of collective violence: its potentially ludic, absurd, spectacular, and effervescent character. For this aspect, MQM supporters sometimes used the Urdu term *tamasha*, probably best translated as "spectacle." More commonly, they used the term *fun*.

Fun challenged propriety and questioned the symbolic coherence of dominant discourse in a ludic way. Words and gestures became absurd by taking them out of their appropriate place and applying them to a different context. In this chapter I argue that the ludic and the absurd were highly attractive aspects of the MQM, appealing strongly to the Muhajir youth and in that sense important in recruitment and mobilization. But the ludic and the absurd were more than merely attractive. Their capacity to unbalance whatever seemed fixed was crucial for the creation of a new movement. What MQM supporters called *fun* can be seen as a transgression of ethnic categorization and a ridiculization of high cultural Islamic modernist values and discourses. *Fun* gave young party members and supporters a sense of agency that enabled them to identify with the movement. For them, the movement was much more than discourses on Muhajir identity disseminated by the party leadership. They experienced the MQM as primarily an effervescent sensation of togetherness and power in public manifestations as well as collective activities undertaken in peer groups operating under the banner of the MQM. They felt like active partakers in such activities, rather than passive consumers or onlookers. Lastly, following the work of Don Handelman, I will argue that public meetings such as the night in Bhai Khan ki Chari can be analyzed as events in which the relative absence of models of behavior provides the partakers with ample opportunities to invent new cultural forms, thereby proving their creativity and enlarging their status within their group. Public meetings are therefore not only opportunities to mock the powerful and the pious but also possibilities to rework an internal hierarchy based on reputations of physical prowess, streetwise wit, and daring.

As a last introductory remark I like to say that *fun* may at first sight evoke largely positive associations. For MQM supporters, the phenomena described as such indeed often are their most cherished memories. But as this chapter also demonstrates, fun and violence often overlap. It often takes only a tiny step to go from fun to violence, and it is frequently taken without much consideration.

PUBLIC EVENTS AND PERSONAL PRIDE

To analyze the *fun* in MQM public activities, I make use of the writings of Don Handelman and Gananath Obeyesekere on ritual. That is to say that my understanding of ritual does not follow very closely the footsteps of Victor Turner (1969), according to whom the essence of ritual is in its liminal phase, ritually separated from the everyday life, or those of Maurice Bloch (1974), who argues the opposite, defining ritual as a concise language of power in which the syntax has been formalized to such an extent that it no longer allows for any creativity. As Bourdillon has argued in response to Bloch, rituals are better understood as events that create non-durational concepts of time enabling the partakers to "stand back from the present moment and see it in the context of a continuity from past to future" (Bourdillon 1978: 594). Rituals do not so much create a distinction between linear and nonlinear modes of time. They rather fuse these different modes, enabling one to look at the everyday from a different perspective.

Moreover, as Handelman has argued, this fusion of different time regimes does not only occur in events that are commonly recognized as rituals. Refusing to make a distinction between ritual and other forms of symbolic behavior, Handelman introduces the term "public event," which he defines as "culturally designed forms that select out, concentrate, and interrelate themes of existence—lived and imagined—that are more diffused, dissipated, and obscure in the everyday" (1990: 15–16). I especially find his concept of the "proto-event" useful. A proto-event is a "doing in concert," a highly symbolic event in which the partakers create a new ritual-like situation without any existing template. In some cases a proto-event may become a model for future events. Then "it is the recognition by participants of an emerging design in their practices that enables them to become self-conscious of their creation" (19–21). The public meetings of the MQM are best understood as symbolic public events that open up new perspectives from which to look at oneself and others. They are shaped on the model of early public meetings that can be seen as proto-events.

To understand the character of these events it is useful to consider the distinction Obeyesekere makes between solemn, stately rituals, which he calls "dromena," and "cathartic" rituals, which parody the numinous. Dromena, or "things performed"—a term borrowed from ancient Greek religion—embody cultural, religious, and philosophical values and are characterized by controlled behavior and seriousness, camouflaging conflict and anxiety. Catharses, in contrast, are "vulgar" rituals that move in an opposite, regressive direction. They are characterized by acting out behavior and often levity and obscenity (Obeyesekere 1990: 27–28). They are enjoyed as ludicrous and humorous events, but they are also, as Obeyesekere puts it, relentlessly encroached upon by bourgeois values, causing the demise of such cathartic rituals (44). Although not rituals in the strictest sense of the word, the events of MQM public activities share with the "catharses" described by Obeyesekere an emphasis on the body, the self-conscious parody of high cultural forms and values, and a collective enjoyment of the ludic, of comedy and satire.

Whereas Handelman stresses the element of innovation in the collective symbolic behavior, and Obeyesekere emphasizes the relation between the cerebral and the venerable on the one hand and the vulgar and the ludic on the other, Johan Huizinga mentions the element of competition and contestation within ludic activities and play. Although play, according to Huizinga, has no ulterior purpose—*homo ludens* plays for the sake of playing—and is therefore essentially amoral and arational, it does have a significant effect on social prestige, honor, and self-esteem (Huizinga 1938). This aspect of internal competition through ludic ritual behavior is also present in the public events of the MQM.

31 October 1986

In the 1970s the format of a public meeting had been developed and used widely by the PPP and, to a lesser extent, the JI. Zulfiqar Ali Bhutto had a reputation as an excellent manipulator of such meetings (A. Syed 1992: 68–73). During the martial law of the early 1980s, all political activities were banned, but the ban was relaxed after the nonparty elections of 1985. In the summer of 1986 Benazir Bhutto returned from London and began a campaign of opposition by addressing public meetings all over the country. The MQM started organizing similar meetings modeled on the format of the public meetings of the PPP. Usually starting after lunch, a series of minor speakers addressed the crowd, which gradually arrived in buses decorated in party colors. Vendors selling badges and paper flags, as well as audiocassettes with party songs, lined the public ground. The significance of the speakers would increase after sunset, and the party leader would finally arrive at least two hours late.

As described in an earlier chapter, the first large public meeting of the MQM was held in Karachi in August 1986. The first MQM public meeting in Hyderabad was held two months later on the last day of October on the playground in the citadel, known as Qila Ground. It led to violent riots in the suburb of Sohrab Goth, Karachi, when MQM supporters heading for Hyderabad clashed with the Pakhtun inhabitants of that place. That happened in the morning. What happened in Hyderabad afterward is difficult to assess. It is interesting to note that the party leadership has yet to come up with an official account of this day as it has done with other incidents of violence, such as May 1990. As a result, the participants still tell their own version of what happened, producing an array of inconsistent and contradictory stories. What follows below are statements that were confirmed by at least some and not seriously contested by others.

Altaf Hussain had most probably arrived in Hyderabad a day earlier and had spent the night in a house in the Muhajir-dominated suburb of Latifabad. He probably made a speech there in a place called Ayesha Park, but only a small number of people showed up, and the speech has been forgotten. In the afternoon of the thirty-first, buses arrived from up north, bringing MQM supporters to Hyderabad from villages and towns in the interior of Sindh. They had already been informed about the riots in Karachi. Some say that when they arrived in Hyderabad they demanded a glass of water from a Pakhtun shopkeeper, which he refused to supply. They subsequently looted his shop and burnt it.

At Qila Ground, meanwhile, local MQM supporters had built a platform. Much to the surprise of most inhabitants of Pakka Qila, who still knew very little about the MQM, large groups of young MQM supporters gathered in their neighborhood. There were supporters from Karachi as well as the interior of Sindh. They came, as one man put it, with blood on their hands. They were jubilant, excitedly relating how they had taken on the sturdy Pakhtun and taught them a lesson. They were out for more. Firearms were unloaded from the Karachi buses and sold to the local MQM supporters. One of them, Najeeb, recalled the advertising techniques of the sellers: " 'It is the need of the time to have a weapon,' they said. They asked a small amount of money—'a donation to the party.' Ammunition was five rupees a piece. They would give you an *ajrak* (shawl) to hide the new purchase." With a couple of friends Najeeb bought a gun but he did not know how to use it. Never mind, the man from Karachi said: "Stand guard at the gate and show them your weapon. You must protect our leader." Not quite knowing who was the leader, Najeeb nevertheless placed himself in front of the Qila Gate with the gun hidden in the shawl. He thought he made a good impression standing guard at the place where Sindhi kings and colonial rulers had once passed by, and when he spotted a man with a video camera he could not resist the temptation. He took the weapon out of the shawl, posing like Sylvester Stallone in the film *First Blood*, and shouted: "Take my picture! Take my picture!"

Meanwhile the speeches had started at Qila Ground. All those who would become leaders in the MQM climbed the platform and took the microphone. Badruddin, the MQM organizer from Pakka Qila, was one of them. His reputation grew tremendously. Then someone in the audience who was playing with his newly purchased gun accidentally shot a fifteen-year-old boy who was watching the spectacle from the gallery. While the meeting continued, the boy was taken to a hospital where he died.

Shortly after the evening prayers Altaf arrived. He talked for more than an hour, but few of his words are recalled. He said that Muhajirs had always been hardworking, disciplined citizens, putting aside every penny for a better life in Pakistan. With their blood, sweat, and tears they had earned themselves a decent life. They could now buy televisions and VCRs, he said, but what good are these luxury items if you are not accepted as an equal? "We are not asking anything any longer," he said. "We have come as the followers of Imam Hussain [who fought the tyrannical regime of Yazid]. Do not betray him again [like most of his followers did]. Sell your luxury goods and buy a kalashnikov."

He went on, saying that "we have come in peace. But we were attacked. We will give them tit for tat." He did not explicitly mention the Pakhtun, but when he ended his speech around 8 P.M. many of his supporters paraded to the tower area—a place with many shops owned by Pakhtun.

They waved flags, shouted slogans, and frightened bystanders with their guns. Near the towers they burnt rickshaws and looted shops. Curfew was almost immediately installed. In the following days several MQM leaders and supporters were arrested, including Altaf Hussain himself.

Communities of "Fun"

The meeting on 31 October 1986 stands out as one of the most violent public meetings; other meetings were less brutal. The celebrations that were held spontaneously after the MQM had won the 1988 elections, for instance, were largely without incident. But such nonviolent public events had at least two things in common with the meeting on 31 October 1986. First they transgressed everyday morality. When women went out into the streets to sing and dance alongside total strangers and celebrate the party's electoral victory, they broke the moral inhibitions of their daily existence as much as the young MQM activists who burnt shops and rickshaws. Second, the rank and file of the party gradually lost control over the crowd. The public events attracted so many people because authority was scattered or absent. The MQM leadership could not really control the youths taking part in jubilant, liberating, and sometimes violent events. If it seems plausible that the party to some extent directed the violence on the public meeting in October 1986, it could only do so by inciting its followers to revolt against authority.

How did this revolt and liberation work? The participants explored and experimented with self-images that had previously been unthinkable. Najeeb's story of how he stood guard at Qila Gate is instructive in this respect. In describing to me the person he temporarily became while he exuberantly waved his newly purchased gun, he mentioned several larger-than-life figures, such as Sindhi kings, colonial officers, and an American movie star. He also went to the tower and was party to the looting. Another example of playfully exploring new identities was the widespread use of nicknames among MQM supporters. Names such as *Commando*, *Terrorist*, *Boxer*, *Kaliya* (Black), or *Qasai* (Butcher) were originally meant to comically bestow a new, initially grotesque, exaggerated identity on the bearer. They were also fear-inspiring names, and often, as in the case of names like *Kaliya* and *Qasai*, titles with a stigma usually attached to them became desirable. The bearer of the nickname, however, soon began to cherish his new identity and would not allow anyone to make fun of it. The grotesque was adopted as a reality. In fact, the technique of exaggeration often created an atmosphere in which the absurd became partially serious and the serious became partially absurd. Recall the tomb-like platform at Bhai Khan ki Chari on which four portraits of Altaf Hussain were placed. The suggestion that the exiled leader ruled like an expired and omnipresent saint was ridiculous and offensive when looked at seriously. As a joke, it almost became real. Recall also the slogan "Mast Qalandar Altaf Hussain." To link Altaf to the rural passion of a Qalandar *pir*-turned-patron-saint of the PPP was at first utterly absurd. But it eventually enabled people to imagine the MQM as a movement evoking the passions of loyalty and surrender that resemble those of a religious brotherhood of fakirs.

Fun transgressed and made social boundaries fluid. This allowed for some strategic going back and forth between fun and seriousness. After Najeeb had taken part in the looting, for instance, he began to fear the police would identify him by means of the video that showed him posing like Sylvester Stallone. Several months later he was indeed arrested, but he defended himself by saying that he had only been joking. Didn't the police officer see the smile on his face? Would he pose like this if he really were a terrorist? He had only borrowed the gun for his joke.

I caused a similar form of retreat on the day of Altaf's birthday when a boy proudly showed me the henna on his hand. Henna, associated with brides and weddings, is a powerful symbol. When I asked whether he had done this because of Altaf's birthday, I was too explicit, and the boy said no, of course not, and he turned away indignantly.

The intimacy of *fun* is mostly denied to outsiders. The political rhetoric or stereotypical opinions that are commonly ridiculed within the movement retain their unquestionable truth in the presence of outsiders. The day after the night at Bhai Khan ki Chari, Habib's statement that black shirts are fashionable because black attracts the opposite sex was vigorously denied. How could I think that? Black was the genuine color of protest as it referred to the ʿAshura processions during the holy month of Muharram. But even more illustrative is the conversation a shoe designer, who happened to be a respected Syed bachelor, had with a client about why Altaf Hussain had not yet married. Within the group of people present, we had been discussing the weddings of politicians for some time, mainly commenting on the marriage between Imran Khan—the ex-cricket-star-turned politician—and a high-society British girl, when the client entered the workshop. The designer retreated to a corner to talk to him. Aqeel, my assistant, sitting next to them, overheard their conversation:

DESIGNER: I tell you, in a minute the foreigner is going to ask why Altaf is not married.
CLIENT: Oh? Why do you think so?
DESIGNER: Because it is a very important question. Ha ha.
CLIENT: Why?
DESIGNER: Don't you know? Altaf Bhai is a *nawab*.

Nawab, in this context, meant "homosexual." It was one of the many words used for homosexuals, such as *chakka*, *sufi*, or *pathan*. Commenting on the presumed sexual preferences of a charismatic political leader was common practice in Pakka Qila. During the fiftieth anniversary of Pakistan celebration, state and commerce promoted Jinnah and Iqbal as the inseparable founding fathers of the nation, which in Pakka Qila led people to compare them to a happily married couple. Aqeel was nevertheless astonished to find that the practice also extended to the Pir Sahib of the MQM. But the anecdote did not stop here. As the shoe designer had already foretold, I indeed asked about Altaf's future marriage after the client had left. Trying to be funny myself, I proposed Princess Diana, who was then still alive and a good friend of Imran Khan's wife. Being the eldest person in the room, the shoe designer considered it his responsibility to correct me and he said sternly: "No no, Altaf Bhai will marry a *low-income* girl. A Pakistani and a Muhajir."

Local groups of MQM supporters often take the form of a joking community or communities of *fun*. If you are allowed to laugh along, you have been initiated into their subculture. Paradoxically, *fun* creates a feeling of community while simultaneously commenting on the incompleteness of the discourse of community. Lampooning the conventional language of community, one shows the inconsistency of its rhetoric and the ambiguousness of its symbolism. This is perhaps best illustrated with a reference to the so-called *bhai* culture (brother culture) that has pervaded public life in Hyderabad and Karachi. Since the MQM years, almost anyone addresses another as *bhai*, regardless of age, status, or wealth. Even Pir Sahib is most often called Altaf Bhai. To say, however, that there is a whole collection of *bhai*, such as small, medium-sized, large, and extralarge *bhai*, is a joke only accepted among those who consider themselves part of the egalitarian MQM community.

The MQM peer group–based communities of *fun* can thus be said to share a particular kind of "cultural intimacy" as coined by Michael Herzfeld. In an effort to explain the discrepancy between ideology and ambiguity, Herzfeld (1997) defines cultural intimacy as the shared knowledge that ideology is without truth. Those initiated into this knowledge are free to joke about ideology as such because what binds them together and accounts for the intimacy is not ideology but the knowledge of incompleteness. Another way of putting this is to say that the actions of MQM supporters to some extent resemble those of Gustave Flaubert compiling a satirical *dictionnaire des idées reçues* (dictionary of conventional ideas), thereby poking fun at nineteenth-century French bourgeois culture and revealing its lack of authenticity without altogether rejecting the intimacy of the community (Flaubert 1978).

Poses of Masculinity

While *fun* helps form a feeling of community, it is also part of another aspect of community: internal competition. These two aspects go together. Many MQM supporters genuinely valued the movement for the friendship, constancy, power, and symbiosis it generated. But at the same time the movement was also an arena in which party supporters competed for prestige and power. Again, being *funny* was a powerful way of winning esteem among one's peers. The nature of the game is to apply to the present context by association images, poses, gestures, symbols, and words from another context that is incongruous with the present situation.

This raises the question: Who provides the models to associate with? There is no doubt that this is partly done by the party leadership. The party, for instance, employs copywriters to invent witty slogans. These writers also write the lyrics for songs that get recorded and sold on audiocassettes. On the other hand, the invention of slogans and songs is not a totally centralized affair. The MQM unit in Pakka Qila, for instance, has its own copywriters, employed on a freelance basis. A few days before a public meeting, they have to come up with new and original slogans to be painted on walls, etc. This is apparently a lucrative business. The two neighborhood poets were involved in fierce competition and could not stand each other at all. The younger, a government servant, stuck close to the official rhetoric authorized by the MQM head office in Karachi and often used English: "Nation Needs Altaf," "Save and Serve Nation," "Unity = Power." His rival, the local master tailor who was much older, regularly cited verses from classical Urdu poets and took the liberty to experiment. He wrote the following poem:

> Will you burn your own image, then come with me.
> Will you wipe yourself out, then come with me.
> Turn around immediately if your eyes are on your own house.
> Will you burn down your own house, then come with me.[1]

But even the decentralization of power does not enable the MQM to completely control or direct the imagination of its members. Songs and slogans are often created spontaneously during public meetings or, in Handelman's words, in "the doing of performance" (1990: 19). In that sense, new images, songs, and gestures are the products of crowd behavior. But not everything is equally funny or fit for the occasion. Some patterns can be determined within the more or less spontaneous performances. Most popular are a variety of masculine poses.

Masculinity is not a one-dimensional category. A masculine man might excel in worldly power or physical strength, like movie stars, a rural landlord with a large moustache, or a heavily armed commando. But he can also be an intoxicated fakir, a pain-renouncing *matamdar*, or a Muslim migrant driven by will power (*hosla*). Consequently, those who have not spent innumerable hours in a gym to pump up their muscles opt for a Qalandar outfit, black shirts, or a PLO shawl—images associated with religious faith and constancy. Still others may play a cricket star or a comic dancer. But these are generally for marginal figures not the real *fighters*. Images of physical prowess or religious passion are more appropriate. What is at stake here is honor and prestige.

The public meetings of the MQM provide excellent opportunities to play out images of masculinity and enlarge one's reputation. Not being present is evidence of cowardice. Not to wholeheartedly take part in them might damage your reputation. Moreover, group pressure and peer-group competition make people go over the edge and in that way escalate violence. As Joseba Zulaika demonstrates in his ethnography on Basque militancy, the game of association is not merely a matter of conducting particular political activities on the model of existing cultural practices in the domain of play, leisure, and sports. More than that, the game of association is itself a competition. The person who explores the normative limitations and dares to go a step further takes the lead (Zulaika 1988: 209–30). Caricatures become more extreme. At the same time, paradoxically, the pressure to become one's own joke increases. Standing guard with a kalashnikov at Qila Gate is one thing; the competition for male honor incites young men to take the next step and actually use the weapon. Having taken part in the looting at the tower, Najeeb soon learned how to handle a gun. At night he and his friends would sometimes go up to the roof of his house and fire a series of shots in the air to frighten those who were sleeping.

In sum, the attraction of the movement lies to a large extent in the opportunities it provides for competitive *fun*. It is important to realize that there is plenty of room for individual wit, recklessness, and bravery during MQM public meetings. In fact, such individual performances make the meetings what they are. The crowd, in other words, is not merely or primarily directed by a collective passion or a shared frustration. From the outside, the crowd may seem homogeneous, amorphous, and driven by a collective motive or instinct, as early theorists of crowd behavior such as Le Bon (1897), Freud (1923), and Canetti (1960) have argued. There is an element of collective effervescence or euphoria in large political meetings such as those staged by the MQM, but it would be unwise to explain the escalation of crowd behavior into collective violence from such shared sentiments alone. The internal dynamics of competing for social status on the basis of physical, masculine behavior should also be taken into account. Individual identity is to some extent formed in this internal competition for social status among peers, which at the same time shapes the public events of the movement. This explains why the MQM has become so important to the generation that grew up in the late 1980s. For many, the MQM was the arena of their self-discovery or self-making, an arena they themselves helped create.

It is therefore understandable that the emergence of a renewed notion of Muhajir community and brotherhood occurred simultaneously with a change of power relations. In the remainder of this chapter I look at how this process of shifting positions within the local MQM hierarchy took shape after 31 October 1986 when the MQM had established its presence in Pakka Qila. To do so, I will return to Badruddin and his friend Kanwar Chota, two key players in Pakka Qila introduced in the previous chapter. This is also an example of how collective *fun* spilled over into group violence.

THE NIGHT OF THE BONFIRE

The first public meeting of the MQM in Hyderabad made a big impression in Pakka Qila. The as yet unknown but impressive leader, the large group of determined supporters from Karachi, and the festive violence of that day established the MQM's reputation in the city. For years Badruddin had been struggling to persuade his peers to join the movement, but now he could sit back and wait for new candidates to come to him.

After that day more firearms were sold and diehard activists began to carry their weapons more openly. Young men were shaking off the proverbial reputation of a Muhajir as an urban, smooth-talking but physically weak clerk or shopkeeper. They were now ready and willing to challenge the rural strong: first the sturdy tribal Pakhtun and later the Sindhi landlords (*waderas*) and bandits (*dacoits*). For many middle-class Muhajirs, the greatest wonder of the MQM was indeed how the "Muhajir goat" had successfully pitted itself against the "Sindhi buffalo" and the "frontier ram."

Almost everywhere in Karachi and Hyderabad sport clubs sprung up where the younger generation could train their muscles in bodybuilding, boxing, or karate. At sunset groups of young boys dressed in black uniforms performed their karate exercises in public parks and playgrounds. The gyms were not directly linked to or controlled by the MQM, but both phenomena occurred simultaneously. Foreign sports of boxing and karate replaced the more traditional sports like wrestling and cricket.

This replacement of traditional martial arts by foreign ones was itself a remarkable phenomenon, comparable to similar developments in the Hindu nationalist movements in India. As Joseph Alter has described, traditional South Asian wrestling is more than a sport. It is a way of life, connected to an ideology of disciplining body and mind, which relates to a complexity of ideas on society and the cosmos. Its inherent critique of decadence has had some influence on Indian nationalism in the colonial period (Alter 1992). In the militant Hindu nationalist organization, Rashtriya Swayamsevak Sangh (RSS), wrestling also plays a role, albeit in a reinvented fashion that combines certain images of traditional wrestling with the paramilitary drill of the colonial army and the public school (Alter 1994). As in the case of the MQM, the martial art tradition has significantly changed. But whereas it was transformed by the RSS, it was replaced by other sports like karate and boxing in Hyderabad, even though the notion of martial arts and bodily exercise as an implicit critique of middle-class decadence and social inequality as such has survived.

The adoption of foreign sports in Hyderabad coincided with a changing aesthetic of the male and female body. The traditional wrestler used to be a portly man, and his fat was considered a sign of strength and will power. However, the youth in Pakka Qila had a more ambivalent opinion on the topic. Many boys considered a liking for excessive fatness traditional, old-fashioned, and, interestingly, typical for other ethnic groups. Mussarat Shaheen, for instance—the voluminous female star of Pakhtun cinema—was believed to suit the unsophisticated taste of the tribal Pakhtun. They themselves preferred the relatively slender women and girls from the Bombay cinema, who were considered classy. A beautiful male body, meanwhile, was a body that sported muscles rather than fat. The Pakka Qila youth took the size of the biceps rather than that of the belly as a sign of physical strength. They also found aesthetic pleasure in the technology of modern firearms. This also enabled one to pass for a strong man without being a heavyweight.

In Pakka Qila all this led to the disappearance of the old wrestling club due to a shortage of members. The boxing club, however, welcomed many new members and a new bodybuilding gym was opened just off Qila Gate. Meanwhile, a dispute arose about what to do with the former wrestling pit (*akhara*). The conflict resulted in a rearrangement of power in which the youth of the MQM took over power from the older generation.

The Akhara *Dispute*

The wrestling pit or *akhara* had been abandoned for some time when it became the scene of a "festive" riot. It was early 1987, a few months after the MQM meeting at Qila Ground. The pit lay between the Akbari Masjid, the most central mosque in Pakka Qila, and the Archaeological Department housed in the palaces of the former Sindhi kings. The latter included a small museum, a library, office rooms, and residential areas for its staff. Since the pit was no longer used, the mosque committee decided to use it as an extension of the mosque. The committee mainly consisted of family members and employees of the owner of the largest shoemaking factory in Pakka Qila, which stood several blocks away from the mosque. However, the Archaeological Department also claimed the plot.

The department was far from popular in Pakka Qila. Since its task was to preserve the citadel as a historical monument, it was seen as a dangerous exponent of the state forces that had earlier threatened to clear the entire area of illegal settlements. Besides, most of the staff and officers of the department were Punjabis. They rarely socialized with the local population. One of the staff members was known as a pompous man who acted like an aristocrat and kept a deer on a lead in his backyard. Since the museum never had visitors, they were seen as hostile spongers and local representatives of a despised national government.

Despite the department's claims, the mosque committee began to build the extension of the mosque, and only when it was halfway completed did the department's staff call in the support of the local police. Meanwhile, a group of young MQM supporters had become interested in the matter. The most central figures in this group were Kanwar Chota and a man called Muqeem Ustad. Muqeem was some ten years older than Kanwar, who was in his early twenties, and unmarried. He was called *ustad* (master) because he used to train the local soccer team. Recently he had shifted to boxing and had become the coach of many new pupils in the boxing school.

In addition to the mosque committee and the party of Kanwar and Muqeem, there was a third group interested in the issue of the pit. This group centered around Badruddin, but it took no active part in the *akhara* dispute. Badruddin was still in high spirits because of the sudden breakthrough of the MQM and the rapid increase in local supporters. He seemed to have thought that his time for activism was over. He wanted to be an ideologue, not a street fighter. His role model was Azim Ahmad Tariq, the party's chairman, who also left the canvassing to younger supporters who had only recently joined the movement. After 31 October for instance, young recruits started a door-to-door campaign, visiting neighbors at home to demand their loyalty. But Badruddin would not do that. He did not want to coerce people, and he did not want to coerce people *personally*. His ambitions probably lay outside Pakka Qila as he aspired to an important position within the party. So he kept his distance from street activities, putting his trust in the new recruits grouping around Kanwar Chota and Muqeem Ustad. This proved to be a fatal mistake.

According to former members of the mosque committee, the police only came to the Akbari Masjid in response to the complaints of the Archaeological Department. They showed no real interest and were reluctant to take sides in a dispute in which they had no business. When they were talking with the members of the mosque committee, however, the rumor spread that the police had entered the mosque without taking off their shoes. An official of the Archaeological Department told me later that the police had never entered the mosque and only walked on the plot where the illegal extension was under construction. The argument apparently was about whether a mosque under construction, the legality of which was contested, was already a place of purity. The effect was a gathering near the contested plot of the group of Kanwar and Muqeem and many other adolescents who had become curious.

Initially nothing happened. The police departed, and the members of the mosque committee and the staff of the Archaeological Department went home. But later that night, Kanwar and Muqeem's group decided to go and tell the department's staff to mind their own business and leave the plot to the mosque committee. They called on the residential building but no one answered. Not quite knowing what to do now, someone directed the group's attention to the deer in the backyard. People shouted that the deer was the staff member's sweetheart, hinting that the man was so fond of the animal because he used it for sexual purposes. Somebody else suggested taking the sweetheart (*mashuq*) away. That would force the *nawab*, as they called the staff member, to come outside.

That was exactly what happened. Much to the boys' amusement, the owner of the deer began to defend the animal passionately. Some managed to free the deer, and it panicked and ran off. Others suggested that they "reclaim the deer's dowry," or loot the rooms. The staff and officers quickly escaped. Having brought the electric items, such as television sets, fans, and fridges, to safety, the boys built a bonfire. As it dispersed its warmth in the cold winter night, others broke into the museum and library in search of more fuel for the fire. Royal headwear, robes, and rusty daggers from the king's harem were brought outside. One man recalled how he saw his friends coming out of the museum with "funny hats" on their heads—the cylindrically shaped top hat the Sindhi kings used to wear. When he saw them he also ran into the museum. He and his friends walked out again parading like kings and soldiers. They danced around the fire with royal robes around their shoulders, cutting the flames with the antique swords and daggers.

The fire seemed to have made an impression. In stories about this night it was always vividly recalled. The spooky silhouettes it produced seemed to have contributed to the somewhat unreal, festive atmosphere. The night was widely remembered as a night of great fun, one of the most memorable events of their youth. Despite the spirit of joyful destruction, however, the antique copies of the Holy Qur'an, which had been kept in the library, were saved. One of them appeared for sale in the nearby Shahi Bazaar several years later.

Qila Qaum

The Archaeological Department disappeared from Pakka Qila for a long time after that night. The staff and employees were moved to Karachi, from where they lodged their complaints about the destruction of the highly valued relics of Pakistan's past, outraged that neither the police nor the army had intervened.[2] The office was formally reopened in 1988, but until May 1992, when Operation Clean-up was launched against the MQM, it did nothing.

For the local population, the expulsion of the Archaeological Department symbolized the establishment of MQM sovereignty in Pakka Qila. Until May 1990, Pakka Qila was relatively free of state interference. Only then was a station of the Rangers—a paramilitary force—installed in the former kings' buildings. For more than three years, Pakka Qila would be a symbolic free town of the MQM. The notion of a takeover of power was strengthened by the multitude of royal symbols during the night of the bonfire: the *nawab* and his deer, the royal palace, the antique robes and daggers and headwear. Soon Pakka Qila as a whole became a symbol of conquered royal power.

As indicated earlier, the notion of a citadel community or *qila qaum* has its roots in those early days of MQM power. No longer a refugee camp or a mere residential area, Pakka Qila regained its image as a bastion of power. The MQM youth walked around proudly displaying their guns as the Sindhi or British colonial soldiers had done. Even during the time of my fieldwork, the phrase *qila qaum* connoted full sovereignty. For example, like others elsewhere, most men in Pakka Qila did not fast during the fasting month of Ramzaan—in any case not on a daily basis. But in the park of Pakka Qila one quite openly drank tea and smoked cigarettes, whereas in other parts of the city this was done in more secluded places. When I asked whether we should not keep up appearances in the park, too, I was answered bluntly: "No. Why? We are *qila qaum*." It sounded like: "In our park we do what we want. Here no one can tell us our business."

From the night of the bonfire till May 1990 Pakka Qila became off-limits to outsiders. In the words of Allen Feldman, it became "a sanctuary." In his ethnography of Catholic-Protestant violence in Northern Ireland, Feldman has described the spatial structure of violence in terms of two opposing sanctuaries, each controlled by one of the conflicting groups, divided by a neutral interface. Sanctuaries are considered sovereign, private areas that are defended by means of barricades and so on. The ultimate ambition of the opponent is to intrude on this private place through guerilla tactics or mass processions. Violence inside the sanctuary is not the same as violence at the interface. At the interface violence is expected, but an attack on the sanctuary is considered a violation of sovereignty (Feldman 1991: 17–45).

The perception of Pakka Qila as a sanctuary in ethnic conflict was played out dramatically in May 1990 when the police raided the citadel. It was considered a violation as serious as the violation of the seclusion (*pardah*) of a private home. Never before, I was told, had the enemy entered their homes, touched their women, or forced men into a state of submission inside their own homes. The result was an acute feeling of being without shelter, which dramatically heightened a sense of community solidarity. I will return to this topic in the next chapter. But to fully understand the drama of May 1990, it is important to keep in mind the notion of sovereignty that is inherent in the term *qila qaum*, the origin of which lies in the night of the bonfire.

Pleasures of War

The establishment of *qila qaum* did not mean that all differences within the neighborhood were now forgotten. On the contrary, the *qila qaum* was initially a project of a rather small group of MQM supporters, most of whom had recently joined the movement. The majority of the population was as yet not involved in local politics whatsoever. The MQM was still primarily a party of the youth. For other people the change of loyalty only came in May 1990.

Kanwar Chota and Muqeem Ustad became influential figures after the night of the bonfire. They rapidly built up a large following. One reason for this was, I think, the community-building capacity of the night itself. Although many boys had joined the crowd just for the fun of it, the illegal activities during the night stirred their imagination of an outlaw and adventurous collectivity. But there was a second aspect. Whereas the older generation during the *akhara* dispute had submissively negotiated with the police, and whereas Badruddin continued to "talk big" about an all-Muhajir platform while staying out of the dispute, Kanwar and Muqeem had actually done something. To their followers they had shown their courage and had come out victorious to boot. Things rapidly got out of hand, however, and what had started as a series of practical jokes and other instances of rude humor and vandalism soon took a more serious and destructive turn.

This partly had to do with the escalation of practical jokes caused by the wish to show one's courage, strength, and sense of humor within groups of friends. But that was not the only factor. The wider context of ethnic contest in Hyderabad and beyond, the "war" (*jang*) among various militant organizations, was important too. The connection between these two factors—peer-group dynamics and the wider political context—can perhaps best be illustrated by finishing a story I have already started. That is the story of Najeeb, the boy filmed at Qila Chowk at the first MQM public meeting on 31 October 1986. His story shows that fun did not necessarily cease to be fun when it became violent. In fact, the *jang* could at times be pleasurable and hilarious.

A Fine Punjabi Lassi

I liked Najeeb a lot. Always slightly ironic, he appeared to me more of an observer than a participant. Although he had joined several groups of friends involved in MQM work throughout the years, he never became a diehard MQM activist. Once his friends tried to persuade him to take the oath of the MQM and to become a true party worker. It was an honor and a duty alike, but Najeeb turned down the offer. To be sure, he did not do so for ideological reasons. He was not much of an idealist. He just did not see the point of taking an oath, which he thought was worthless. After a few years he stopped hanging out with the MQM boys. He was disappointed after the expulsion of Badruddin, who happened to be one of his best friends. He left voluntarily, and over time he became more critical of the MQM. He still supported the party and thought it had done much for the emancipation of Muhajirs, but he had grown weary of the violence and coercion. The MQM, he said, had been a good idea, but it had attracted the wrong people. When I asked him whether this included himself, he grinned and said it probably did.

His uncle owned a rickshaw. Najeeb sometimes worked as a rickshaw driver at nights to make extra money. Although his family was poor and not related to the core families of Pakka Qila, he was quite popular on the street where he lived. He was usually good-humored and physically strong, he did not speak the fancy language Badruddin sometimes did, and he had a little extra money because of the rickshaw driving. He had also been present the night of the bonfire, even though he was slightly older than most of the boys who had been there.

One day Badruddin asked him to loan the rickshaw to Kanwar Chota, who needed transport. Najeeb became interested and asked what sort of transport. "Weapons," said Badruddin. This excited Najeeb. "Okay," he said, "but I will drive the rickshaw myself." So he did and after that was asked several times more. Usually he would be asked a couple of days beforehand. One night the two men who had been carrying the goods told him to take a different route than usual. Najeeb thought that the guns had to be delivered somewhere else, but instead he was asked to stop in a posh residential area. The two called on one of the villas, demanded cash at gunpoint, which they got, and left. Knowing that the house owner had seen his face, Najeeb was on edge for a couple of days. But nothing happened and the next time he was asked to get his rickshaw ready he went again.

"We lived like kings," he said. He talked about those years in a mixed tone of repentance, nostalgia, and amazement about what they had done. "It is like talking about my little brother," he once said. "He is the one who does the stupid things." He told me about the evening they went to eat sweets in a Punjabi-owned dairy. "We had no money but we were thinking about what to do with ourselves, so we said, let's go and have a fine Punjabi lassi." The phrase "fine Punjabi lassi" came from the signboard of a recently opened, fancy dairy shop, advertising the sweet or salty yogurt drink known as lassi. The shop was in Saddar, the uptown shopping center, not a place Najeeb and his friends would normally go to. They went inside and asked for lassi and sweets, and then more sweets and bottles of coke, and they ate and ate, convulsing with laughter in anticipation of what was going to happen when the shop-owner discovered none of them had a single rupee on him. Finally they rose and the owner asked them to pay.

> So Salman said to me, "Najeeb, go and get the money from the rickshaw." The man said, "What nonsense? Who keeps his money in a rickshaw?" We said, "Why not? If you do not believe us, you can come with us. We will show you." The man followed us outside and we showed him the ammunition and we said: "How much do we owe you?" "No! No! Go away!" he shouted. "What? Don't we have to pay?" "No. No. Nothing. Go away."

Frightened to death the man ran back into his shop. It was still a great story to Najeeb, and he said he would love to go back and enjoy a free and "fine Punjabi lassi" again. In fact, the storytelling itself, together with the great dramatic skills with which Najeeb related the episode, brought back the gay atmosphere of those days to the extent that I initially laughed, too, realizing the brutality of the story only later.

Najeeb, like many others his age, commonly used the word *jang* with much bravado when he talked about these years. Since the *jang* offered an opportunity to break away from social restraints and live life dangerously, it was an adventurous time for many. They impressed others who were not as involved in the MQM as they were with their thrilling tales of how they had broken laws, rebelled against norms and values, and gotten away with it. As Najeeb said, it was "raj hamara" ("our rule").

Kanwar Defeats Badruddin

Then came the so-called Hyderabad Carnage or Black Friday on 30 September 1988. That day Sindhi militants killed many Muhajir commuters at rush hour while spraying bullets out of fast-moving jeeps. The incident was part of growing ethnic tension in the months prior to the first free elections after eleven years of military rule and a dramatic response of Sindhi militants to the everyday provocation of MQM activists. It led to vigorous discussions within the MQM on how to respond to the assault. Some wanted revenge. Others argued that the killings could have been masterminded by the army's secret intelligence agency to provoke more violence, which would eventually lead to the postponement of the elections, which were due later that year. Most of the MQM members from Pakka Qila took the militant stance and demanded immediate retaliation. But they had to deal with opposition from within as Badruddin sided with the moderates. Badruddin and Kanwar Chota had a fierce argument. Kanwar called Badruddin a coward, and he responded by saying that Kanwar was too young and too stupid to understand politics. Kanwar said he understood politics very well, but Badruddin was making the same mistakes the older generation had made. They had always been waiting, putting their trust in the future. "If we wait a little longer, then all of us will be dead," Kanwar said. In Karachi, meanwhile, Sindhis were attacked to avenge the Muhajir victims in Hyderabad.

Matters were still in limbo the morning the brother of K. B. Jaffar was shot dead. K. B. Jaffar had been a well-known figure in the Muslim League in the 1950s and 1960s. He had made it into the national assembly in the time of Ayub Khan. He was a respected old man and continued to live in a big mansion near Qila Chowk. His brother was a respected old man, too. He had himself been involved in politics during the 1970s as a member of the Pakistan People's Party and had been leading a quiet life since then. One early morning, about a week after the killings, he opened the door to his balcony and was shot in the head by a sniper. In Pakka Qila, everyone thought Sindhis were responsible for the assault, considering it a murder to avenge the death of the Sindhis in Karachi the previous week. The attack was especially frightful because for the first time the enemy had hit a target within the walls surrounding the neighborhood.

Groups of armed men patrolled the streets of Pakka Qila at night and guarded the gateways. Women brought food and tea to the patroling men, carried ammunition, and went door to door to recruit more volunteers. The patroling continued for weeks. Kanwar Chota was one of the men who organized the operation. More than a daring fighter, he now became the leader of a collective defense operation. He blamed Badruddin for having been weak in the face of acute danger.

Badruddin was forced to resign several months later. Accused of having plundered the party's monies collected during the feast of sacrifice, he left the city. There were rumors that Kanwar had set him up. Others recalled that Kanwar had stood up for his friend when someone had spoken publicly against Badruddin. It was said that Kanwar had even carried Badruddin's luggage to the bus bound for Karachi.

CONCLUSION

In sum, the MQM had been an underground movement of small groups of friends before the public meeting at Qila Ground, but it attracted much larger numbers of male adolescents and young men immediately after that. One of the benefits of joining the movement was the opportunity it provided to take part in ludic peer-group activities. A still relatively small but armed group, the MQM turned Pakka Qila into a bastion of diehard MQM fighters, a *qila qaum*. When the violence entered their "sanctuary," those with a reputation for bravery presented themselves as capable defenders and managed to outmaneuver other groups that favored negotiation and elections.

The fight between Badruddin and Kanwar reflects a more general trend within the MQM. The ethnic ideology of the initial leaders—mostly students or men who had had some formal education—was replaced by a street culture of masculinity promoted by younger, more recent recruits. Education ceased to be an indication of status. Kanwar, for instance, never felt the need to hide his illiteracy. Like Altaf Hussain himself, who in those days used to sneer at intellectuals, calling them insincere, decadent, and useless, Kanwar almost always suspected the educated. Once a mother called on him in his capacity as the leader of the local MQM, powerful enough to settle local disputes. She complained about a schoolteacher who did not let her son pass a dictation even though, she claimed, he had hardly made any mistakes. The teacher was called upon, and when he produced the paper to show the corrections, Kanwar laughed, keeping the paper upside down: "*I* cannot see any mistakes, it looks fine to *me*," and ordered the teacher to let the boy pass.

As for Najeeb, he gradually withdrew from the MQM. When asked why, he once answered: "I found a job." On another occasion he replied: "I got married." He regretted his decision only once, he said, in May 1990 when he sat trapped with his young pregnant wife in a dark house, frustrated and unable to take part in the resistance. I will turn to this episode in the next chapter.

CHAPTER FIVE

Making Martyrs

VIOLENCE, then, was to some extent the byproduct of the paramount role within the MQM of peer groups, bound together by a subculture in which competitive masculinity, physicality, and *fun* were key values. But that was not what violence looked like in May 1990. In May 1990, Pakka Qila was besieged by the police, a protest march led by women ended in a massacre, and the weeks that followed can perhaps best be described as a period of ethnic cleansing in anticipation of a new partition. This was no longer a period of irreverent rebellion by groups of young males. It was instead a time of acute danger and resistance in which women took center stage. It was also a time of terrifying rumors about gruesome acts of tyranny and equally awe-inspiring instances of martyrdom. Above all, it was a summer when the notion of Muhajirs as a beleaguered diasporic nation became more relevant than ever.

In the time of my fieldwork, some six to seven years later, the incidents of May 1990 continued to constitute a rare moment of truth for the Pakka Qila residents. The collective memory about these unfortunate days left little room for personal stories derivative of the collective narrative. It was very rare for people to question or doubt the main facets of this historiography. Surely it was not a *fun* matter. Whereas the MQM peer groups resembled joking communities, May 1990 produced a moral community, excluding the "Other" through moral condemnation and the symbolism of sacrifice and displacement. For the Pakka Qila residents, May 1990 had revealed once and for all the real but often hidden face of the Pakistani state, dominated by hostile Sindhis, who do not grant Muhajirs a place within Sindh or Pakistan. It was also an argument about a deep cultural antagonism between Sindhis and Muhajirs, divided by different mentalities that transcend everyday life. May 1990 had established, as it were, how fundamentally different Sindhis and Muhajirs were. More than that, this interpretation of May 1990 as revealing the insuperable nature of ethnic differences spilled over into areas far beyond the citadel itself. In Sindh and beyond, Pakka Qila is today still associated with the May 1990 events, which stand out as the most outrageous and brutal example of state persecution against Muhajirs. The Pakka Qila Operation, as the events are commonly known, has thus had a huge impact on ethnic relations in Sindh as a whole.

This chapter engages several of these themes while others are dealt with in the next chapter. I begin this chapter with a discussion of how May 1990 is collectively remembered in Pakka Qila. I will then move on to a reconstruction of the culmination of the events, the protest march of women shot at by the police, in order to analyze a process of progressive ethnic polarization. This was, I will argue, an unpredictable and complex process of violent action and discursive interventions in which the notions of martyrdom and motherhood were of special importance. Lastly I will examine how the violence changed direction. Starting as a violent conflict with state forces, the trouble soon evolved into ethnic clashes. To explain this we must shift the attention from the symbolism of martyrdom and motherhood to memories of partition and the notion of restoring primordial purity. This section also takes up the issue of diaspora in Muhajir identity, a theme that will be explored more fully in the next chapter. The next chapter will also discuss the impact of the state on ethnic relations, as well as the changing popular perceptions of the state.

Violence and Purity

Central to this chapter is the notion of purity—ethnic, religious, or national—and how it relates to large-scale violence. This is a central theme in recent studies on ethnic and religious violence. But my approach to the subject differs somewhat from a number of influential studies on ethnocide and genocide. Several studies start from the assumption that the drive for ethnic or religious purity is a given, implicit in any nationalist project or, indeed, modernity. Violence can then be explained as a reactive attempt to radically come to terms with the uncertainty, ambiguity, or pollution of everyday reality, which violates the desire for purity. Slavoj Žižek (1989), for instance, uses Lacanian concepts to argue that the perpetrator of brutalities desires to reach a register of experiences that transcends language, a largely subconscious "Real," that is an inherent and insatiable part of man's psychology. In a more historical argument, the notion of national purity is linked to modernity, generating a desire for sharp social boundaries and classifications. This desire becomes more pressing with the growing uncertainties and imbalances that are the result of globalization and postmodernity. Ethnic violence is explained as a radical refusal to come to terms with the confusion created by the insecurity of social hierarchies and identities in the context of mass migration, the spread of transnational mass media, and other developments that damage the position of the nation-state as the privileged site for identity formation (e.g., Appadurai 1999; Bauman 1997; Daniel 1996: 43–72; Hayden 1996).

My problem with these theories lies not in their treatment of the concept of ethnic or religious purity itself. The notion of social purity is indeed often envisioned as much grander and heroic than the confusing diversity and maddening incompleteness of everyday life. It is clearly a powerful vision and part of the imagination of the nation. But I am not so sure whether the large-scale processes of postmodernity and globalization cause the anxiety that stirs the imagination to such an extent as to lead people into violent action. More specifically, I doubt that violence is the outcome of this modern, nationalist desire for purity of identity. The case presented in this chapter seems to suggest instead that violence is constitutive of identity. For some time and in reaction to the idea that violence can be explained from the modern desire for purity, I took the opposite position, thinking that the notion of purity emerged during and because of large-scale violence. Now I think this opposite position is also too simple. It also presupposes the possibility to separate ideology and agency, purity and violence, whereas it seems to me more fruitful to take their interconnectedness as a point of departure for analyzing ethnic violence. This means examining the seemingly chaotic and unpredictable sequence of actions and reactions by different groups of actors as they respond to each other's actions and reactions as well as to rumors, calls for mobilization, physical coercion, and more. In other words, violence and its various ideological interpretations form one interrelated process. Ethnocide and the desire for primordial social purity feed upon each other. The one does neither exist independently from nor prior to the other. They are one of a kind, and we need to examine the historical, context-specific process of how this pair comes about without taking one as the shortcut explanation for the other.

What I propose, then, is an interpretation of the interconnectedness between violence and the desire for primordial purity that does not start with the anxiety caused by ambiguity of identity. From my stay in Pakka Qila I would suggest that ambiguity, rather than a problem, is the normal state of affairs in everyday life, and people do not seem to be worried about it much. Daily life can best be characterized as filled with skepticism, bargaining, humor, irreverence, and unfinished conversations. It is, to borrow a phrase from Lawrence Rosen, a constant "bargaining for reality," an ongoing process of negotiating the meaning of the terms and relationships of which reality is composed (Rosen 1984). That does not mean that the notion of ethnic/religious purity is absent. It is communicated through religious myths and symbols, memories of shared life crises, and nationalist discourses based on such myths and memories. Most of the time these wisdoms can be negotiated, contested, or even ridiculed or dismissed as hypocrisy. In highly tense situations such as incidents of exceptional violence, however, they offer an immediately available conceptual framework with which to make sense of an extraordinary and life-threatening situation. They can help overcome humiliation, shame, and guilt, as well as restore dignity and self-esteem. They are forced upon people in frantic public debates and symbolically loaded collective actions. In this chapter I will describe this process as a "condensation" of normally negotiable beliefs into a singular existential truth.[1] A conviction that leaves no room for other memories or beliefs, the notion of primordial purity may in specific cases be the basis for further violent reactions.

Ethnocide, in other words, is a process of "schismogenesis" (Werbner 1997), in which ethnic antagonism is at once produced and expressed. In analyzing the May 1990 violence, I will start from a perspective on "Muslim politics" offered by Eickelman and Piscatori, while also making use of Arjun Appadurai's remarks on ethnocide, combining these various insights with a somewhat eccentric reading of Victor Turner's interpretation of martyrdom. Eickelman and Piscatori (1996: 8–12) argue that Muslim politics is to a large extent conducted in the language of Islam but that language itself is subject to a great deal of bargaining, cajoling, and jockeying. Muslim political discourse may limit and direct but rarely determines action. The practice of bargaining and negotiating did not stop as the situation in Hyderabad grew more tense. If anything, it intensified as several groups of actors raised the stakes by expressing their demands and complaints in highly loaded language. These symbolic interventions took place in an acutely tense atmosphere filled with violence, fear, and death; distorted information was transmitted via loudspeakers installed on mosques; and ethnic prejudice was expressed in religious terms. Amid this chaos, the process of condensation, of thickening the meaning of ethnic-religious language, began. The increasing "thickness" of symbolic action and language decreased the bargaining possibilities and reduced the chances for retreat and concession. To illustrate what I have in mind, let me briefly discuss Turner's interpretation of the martyrdom of Thomas Becket. The way this twelfth-century archbishop of Canterbury ran into a deadly conflict with King Henry II shares some similarities with the way the Hyderabadi women taking part in the protest march approached the police in May 1990.

I should stress here that what I find useful in Turner's interpretation of Becket's martyrdom is his description of it, not his theoretical framework. The latter revolves around the concept of "root paradigms," which I find less helpful than his narrative of the symbolically loaded negotiations between the king and the archbishop, leading to the latter's death. Turner begins by saying that Saint Thomas was at first only reluctantly holy. He relates the story about how Becket hesitated to give his cloak to a poor man suffering from the winter cold and only parts with it when pressured by King Henry, who was then still his friend. "Henry bullies Becket into being good" (Turner 1974: 70), knowing that Becket had a reputation for living a life of "sumptuousness and magnificence" (71). Then the text moves on to the conflict between the king and the archbishop. The king sought to curtail the powers of the Catholic Church, which resulted in the personal struggle between Henry and Becket. This, however, was a gradual affair, in which "breach soon became crisis and crisis grew so severe that available, formal means of redress proved inadequate, throwing back the situation into deeper crisis and preparing the way for the ultimate drama, six years later, of the murder in the cathedral with its symbolic deposits of martyrdom and pilgrimage" (79).

Becket found himself increasingly under attack as King Henry put more and more pressure on him and most of his fellow bishops abandoned him. He was in bed with fever when rumors reached him that the king wanted to imprison him for life and mutilate him by gouging his eyes out and cutting off his tongue. Describing the grim atmosphere of this "Black Monday," Turner suggests that Becket at this point remembered the "*via crucis* pattern of martyrdom" (84) as the only possible solution for him. The following day was Tuesday, which suddenly became significant to him because he recalled that all important events of his life had taken place on Tuesday. He decided to confront the king with a "spiritual sword" (85). The following morning he went to the St. Stephen Chapel, a place heavy with symbolism of martyrdom. He conveyed that he carried the sacred Host under his cassock for protection while proceeding to the room where he would face the king. He also carried a cross, saying, "I carry it to protect myself and the English Church" (89).

This act put enormous pressure on King Henry, who, despite everything, shared Becket's belief in the holy symbols with which his enemy confronted him. "When he heard that Thomas was coming with cross and Host he may well have gone into a blue funk." Henry realized that "he could only use direct force against him at the expense of giving him what he wanted and what would strengthen the church's position at home and abroad—the martyr's crown" (92). He refused to meet Becket under these circumstances. Frantically consulting his advisors, the king finally decided to challenge his claim to holiness by lodging an appeal to a higher religious authority, the pope, accusing Becket of having perjured himself.

Becket, however, had no way to retreat. He "had burnt his boats behind him" (93) by presenting himself as a martyr. To retreat now would mean making a fool of himself and desecrating the holiness of the symbols he carried with him, doing precisely what Henry had just accused him of. Becket finally did what the residents in Hyderabad could not: he escaped into exile in France. On his return six years later, he was murdered in the Canterbury cathedral.

I think this story shows the escalating effect powerful symbols can have when evoked amid an acute conflict. Becket's beliefs, which would otherwise offer him some room to maneuver and compromise, closed in around him from all sides as he tried to defend his position with their help. He faced a lack of alternatives, a moment of loss experienced as a moment of truth. Using Appadurai's term (1996: 149), his beliefs "imploded," that is, the gap separating reality from its representation vanished so that symbols became reality. The symbols evoked by him became thick with meaning, providing him with no option other than to proceed into reckless high-risk acts. A similar process leaving little room for retreat or reconcile unfolded in Hyderabad in May 1990, leading to the shooting of protesting women near Pakka Qila and ethnic cleansing in the following weeks.

SILENCE AND SPEECH

Considering the number of discussions I have had with Pakka Qila residents about the events of May 1990, I know surprisingly little about what actually happened in Pakka Qila during those days. Most of these discussions took place in the little park next to the graves of the seven victims who were shot by the police during the operation and were buried in the park because curfew prevented their families from taking their bodies to the graveyard outside the citadel. One would expect that the presence of the dead would evoke memories and stories of how they had been killed and buried. One would expect that people would go on from there and talk about their own fears and anxieties. One would, in short, expect these graves to function like a monument where people could remember their own experiences and at the same time give them a place in a shared memory and shared grief. But nothing of the sort was true. Apart from my first week in the neighborhood, when I was taken to the graves and made to read the epitaphs, no one ever felt the urge to elaborate on the victims, how they had died or how they had lived. As a group they signified the injustice of May 1990. Individually they only meant something to the nearest relatives and friends.

There was more than simply a difference between the collective memory and individual memories. There was a friction, illustrated by the man who came to the communal garden on a motorbike every Thursday night. He would not say a word apart from a short greeting and go immediately to the grave of his brother. He would wash away the dirt with the water from a communal tap. He would water the flowers he had planted beside the grave, and then he would leave. When I tried to talk to him about his brother, he would shrug his shoulders and mumble: "Politicians talk." Then he would start the engine of his motorbike and drive off to his house outside Pakka Qila where he had moved after 1990. I found his silence significant. Silence was apparently the only way to stay aloof from the standardized canon of stories in which May 1990 was collectively remembered. More than that, the fact that he had moved elsewhere gave him the choice to remain silent.

The relatives of other victims were willing to give me their version of the May 1990 episode quite readily. One man told a story about a cousin who had been lying in the street for more than twenty-four hours. When the police finally retreated shortly after midday on 27 May, he was dead. He also said that he and his family had decided to bury the body in the park when they found out that the city was still under curfew and realized that they could not reach the cemetery. They buried the body next to the grave of Nawab Muzaffar Khan, a politician and founder of the Muhajir Punjabi Pakhtun Movement, who died in 1981. The man claimed that his family had chosen the park as a burial place because the grave of the Nawab was already there and he was considered a true Muhajir leader. Since his cousin had died as a martyr for the Muhajir nation, he deserved to be buried next to the Nawab.

Another man, who had lost a sister, contested this. He said *his* family had made the decision to bury the dead in the park. He explained that his sister had been hiding at home with her children while her husband was being held captive in his workshop. After twenty-four hours she ran out of water and decided to try and reach the nearby house of her parents to fetch some water for her children. On the way back she was shot and left to die in the street. On 27 May, at 2 P.M., they took her body to the Qila Gate in order to go to the cemetery but found that they could not go there. Meanwhile the other victims had also been brought to the gate, and then it was decided to bury them all in the adjacent park, next to the Nawab. He said that he thought that either his family had made the decision or it had been the decision of all the families together. In any case, it had not been the decision of the man who had lost his cousin.

The final resting place of the victims as martyrs beside a former Muhajir hero appeared important to these men. At least, it was important enough that the issue as to who had been responsible for singling out this spot that would affirm their status as Muhajir martyrs was mildly contentious. The man who had lost his sister insisted that some kind of collective burial had taken place, whereas the man who had lost his cousin said that each family had held a private funeral and that his family had been the first to do so. Perhaps the latter was at least partially right—I had never heard anybody else talk about a collective funeral for the victims—but that is not the most intriguing point. The debate itself about the status of the victims as Muhajir martyrs and the question of who had taken the initiative to make this possible are more relevant. In the collective memory, the dead were a group of martyrs rather than individual victims.

This collective narrative of what happened during the police operation highlights several aspects at the cost of others. One aspect emphasizes the moral perversion of the Sindhi police who were said to have looked like longhaired, unshaven, rural bandits, were drunk on liquor, and emptied their bladders against the walls of the mosques. Another aspect concerned the police violation of rules of seclusion and privacy (*pardah*). The fact that the police had entered the citadel was seen as a form of disrespect for the neighborhood's autonomy. The fact that policemen entered private homes was of course an even more serious violation of *pardah*. There were also allegations of rape, but a fact-finding team of the Human Rights Commission of Pakistan reported that it had not found any evidence to support the allegations (Jafri 1996: 401). A third element revolved around the police's lack of respect. Many stories were about old men being beaten up and young men being forced to denounce Altaf Hussain. Men took up arms to avenge the humiliation and defend the privacy of their homes and neighborhood, killing two policemen. Finally, the collective memory centered around the women's march, when the police shot and killed several women despite the fact that they were carrying the Holy Qur'an above their heads as a moral shield of protection.

Although most of this was hearsay, this does not mean that the stories are not true. On the contrary, most allegations have been confirmed by the Human Rights Commission report as well as several journalists working in Hyderabad during those days. It does, however, indicate that the public memory is derived from newspaper reports, rumors, political rhetoric, and discussions with neighbors rather than personal experience. In private some men did tell me bits and pieces of their personal story. They contained considerably less violence and heroism and far more fear and frustration. Most of them had been made to stay in dark rooms or workshops with the windows closed. Some men hinted at the frustration and shame they had felt as they sat trapped inside their homes, unable to defend their family. They dreaded the memory of having been exposed to the neighbors in a humiliating pose of subjection. One man mentioned the lack of a bathroom and how he had to defecate while his colleagues and neighbors were present. It had been a devastating experience for him and he did not like to recall it. In public it was better to tell a story that enabled a man to regain self-esteem and prevented him from becoming a silenced victim. In those stories women did the suffering while men played a more active role.

This may explain why there was so little room for deviation, doubt, or questions, let alone jokes. Irreverence and debate would upset a collective memory that enabled men to cope in a socially acceptable way with the pain and humiliation they faced during the siege. They had to continue living within the neighborhood and to do so many individual experiences were collectively repressed. Instead they resorted to a narrative about immoral policemen and suffering women. In the wider context, this restored the reputation of Pakka Qila as a bastion of fearless and devoted defenders of the cause of Muhajirs. The victims-turned-martyrs confirmed Pakka Qila's central place within the Muhajir nation.

It would, however, be deceptive to argue that the collective memory turning shame and humiliation into heroism and meaningful suffering was only constructed after the violent events had ended. The interpretation of violence is a form of competition over who is wrong and who is right, who loses face and who retains honor, and this discursive conflict was already in full swing the moment the brutalities were committed. The process of stripping the violent clashes of their complexities, particularities, and individual experiences had already started during the violent incidents themselves. I will demonstrate this point in the next section by turning to what is remembered as the climax of the conflict: the protest march led by women.

A Reconstruction of the Women's March

The protest march was the climax of a prolonged period of tension in Hyderabad. On 14 May a dispute between different groups of students escalated into clashes that spread to the entire city center. Three people were killed and a curfew was enforced. For eleven days the curfew was lifted for only a few hours a day. On the eleventh day, 25 May, the government decided to send the police into Pakka Qila, which it saw as a hotbed of revolt and unrest. The police, consisting of several forces from predominantly rural districts surrounding Hyderabad, entered Pakka Qila to establish a police station within the walls of the citadel and to clear the neighborhood of arms. The police besieged the area, closing off all exits. They entered houses and workshops in search of weaponry. They shot at people breaking curfew and leaving their houses. MQM militants nonetheless managed to escape and mobilize resistance outside the citadel. Some shooting between the police and MQM militants took place within Pakka Qila. As a result of the siege, the water supply from the water tower in the citadel was cut off, disrupting the water supply in large sections of Hyderabad.

On 27 May at 10 o'clock in the morning the women's march began, reportedly in the Muhajir-dominated suburb of Latifabad. By then the city had been under curfew for over three hundred hours with only twenty hours of breaks. Some journalists reported that MQM suporters had contacted them and informed them about the march before it began. According to the police, armed men were hiding behind the women with the intent to bring new arms into the citadel. To the inhabitants of Pakka Qila, the march was a spontaneous action of mothers and wives who protested against the brutal violation of their rights. They demanded that the water supply be restored so that they could again take care of their families. At the same time, the demand for water had a profound religious connotation. At the battlefield of Karbala it was Imam Hussain whose water supply had been cut off, and several of his men had died while trying to get water for the women and children in their camp. Cries for water can still be heard during the annual processions of ʿAshura when the battle and its martyrs are commemorated. While the women's march proceeded, heading for Pakka Qila, its religious symbolism increased. Not only did the women carry the Qurʾan above their heads, they also shouted slogans such as "Ya Ali madad" ("Ali is our help") and "Yazidi hukumat murdabad" ("Death to the Yazidi government").

When the procession reached the ascent to the gate of the citadel, it met a line of policemen, resting on their knees, with another row of colleagues behind them. The women began to recite the confession of faith (*kalima*). What follows is the eyewitness account of Ali Hassan, a senior reporter working for various English and Urdu newspapers and magazines.

> One policeman walks toward the processionists, and, pointing his rifle at them, orders the women to halt. The women defiantly keep on marching forward, and the policeman shouts: "I said stop, or else I'll shoot!" Rehmat Bibi, a 34 year-old mother of four, shouts back: "We have come to die. Open fire!" She adds that she knows the police cannot fire, "because we are carrying the Holy Qurʾan on our heads." "You are mistaken," shouts back the policeman, pointing the barrel of his rifle toward Rehmat Bibi's forehead. The woman does not seem afraid of the consequences, and continues to move forward. The policeman presses the trigger. Rehmat Bibi falls to the ground, and another woman, who screams "Ya Allah" and leaps to pick up the Holy Qurʾan from beneath her, is hit by another bullet. (Hassan 1990: 34–35)

Other policemen started to shoot. While some women dropped to the ground, others rushed into the nearby shrine of Pir Abdul Wahab Shah Jilani. Some thirty people were killed.

The ʿAshura Ritual in Pakistan

The process of making martyrs had already started during the march. The symbolism of Imam Hussain's martyrdom prevailed throughout the march, reaching a climax when the women met the police. The symbols of Karbala, providing one of the most powerful examples of martyrdom in Islam, are often used in political rhetoric and in political manifestations. It is for this reason that various authors have emphasized the importance of the story of Karbala as a model for political action. Although I endorse this view, it is also important not to overestimate the impact of Karbala as a model for collective action. The fact that Karbala can be a model for action does not explain why people follow that model. Mark Juergensmeyer, for instance, writing about the impact of Karbala on the Islamic Revolution in Iran, argues that the mobilization of Shi'a Muslims against the regime of the shah can be explained from "the communal guilt for not having defended . . . Hussain, when he was attacked and martyred by the vicious Yazid" (Juergensmeyer 1988: 83). This, I think, stretches the symbolic power of Karbala too far. The present-day conflict in which the symbolism of Karbala is evoked is too complex to explain people's behavior merely from the "logic of religious violence" (83) as provided by the Karbala myth. Even more problematic are the remarks made by Stanley Tambiah in his account of the May 1990 events in Hyderabad. He suggests that the slogans raised by the women were modeled on similar slogans raised by Iranian Islamic revolutionaries and that they were "adopted and translated in Pakistan" (Tambiah 1996: 174). This is a rather grotesque remark as these slogans refer to Islamic heroes and stories known to all Muslims—the Prophet's son-in-law, the story of Karbala—and anyone who has ever witnessed a lively political debate in Pakistan knows that there is hardly a need to import political slogans from abroad.

To understand the courage or stubbornness of the women when they proceeded in spite of the warnings given to them by the police, I think it is important not to simply take the Karbala myth as a one-dimensional and all-important model borrowed from abroad. The interpretation of the Karbala myth is to some extent dependent on the way it is communicated through ritual, in this case the 'Ashura processions, and the performing of these rituals is subject to historical change. It is therefore important to pay attention to the 'Ashura processions in present-day Pakistan. Moreover, I doubt whether the Karbala myth alone accounts for the escalation of violence. There were other cultural "logics" at play, notably the gendered notions of motherhood and male honor. Before discussing these notions, however, I will first look at the 'Ashura ritual commemorating Imam Hussain's martyrdom in Karbala.

It is first necessary to call to mind the evocative power the Karbala myth has as a means to rebellion and mobilization. We have already seen an example of this in chapter 2 where I discussed Altaf Hussain's hunger strike and his use of Imam Hussain's martyrdom to portray the prime minister as a modern-day Yazid. Particular forms of symbolic action derived from the 'Ashura procession can have a similar impact. The wearing of black clothes or the beating of one's chest, for instance, refers directly to the 'Ashura processions. In general, there is a long tradition of using symbols derived from the 'Ashura processions to reject state authority (Freitag 1989: 251).

In Pakistan, however, the 'Ashura ritual has also confirmed the right defended by the state to publicly perform religious practices. This has a lot to do with the tension between Shi'as and Sunnis, which builds during the month Muharram when the 'Ashura ritual is performed. The Shi'a-Sunni tension is an old phenomenon, but it has become more serious since the 1980s. Initially urban Sindh remained largely unaffected by this renewed upsurge of so-called sectarianism, which began in the north in cities like Peshawar, Jhang, and Lahore, for some time paralyzed Gilgit in the northern areas, and has spread to the southern Punjab (Abou Zahab 2002). In Sindh contentious politics followed an ethnic rather than sectarian logic, and it was only in the mid-1990s, when the influence of the MQM was on the wane, that Shi'a and Sunni militants began to operate in Karachi and Hyderabad, too. Here the 'Ashura processions had aroused an atmosphere of tension and controversy throughout the years (Zaman 1998).

Appreciating that religious sectarianism could undermine the nation as much as ethnic separatism, the state downplayed sectarian differences. Jinnah always said that he belonged to "the same sect as the holy Prophet," careful not to mention the sect in which he was born. Denial of differences has since then been the policy of successive Pakistani governments. The national census, for instance, does not ask for one's sect. All the same, the state has made it its task and duty to protect Shi'a public ceremonies. After the Pakistani tests of nuclear bombs in 1998, for instance, when the long list of public holidays was cut short in order to make up for foreign financial sanctions, the two Muharram holidays escaped this measure. When the Zia-ul Haq administration proclaimed that the Islamic law (*shari'at*) would be the supreme law of Pakistan, Shi'as were allowed their own interpretation of the Islamic law (Nasr 2002). That does not mean that there has not been any discrimination against Shi'as in predominantly Sunni Pakistan, but state policy has always been to grant religious sects a large degree of autonomy in ritual matters.

The state has played an important role in the protection of 'Ashura processions. During the processions there is a clear division of tasks between state forces and groups of young men dressed in black escorting the processions and keeping order. Although highly visible, the latter mainly serve a ritual purpose. In contrast, the police and paramilitary forces, who place themselves discreetly on strategically located rooftops, guarantee the processionists' right to proceed. The state also determines the route of the procession and seeks to regularize the procession up to the point of manipulating the content of the sermons given along the route (Rehman 1989). In short, the state has created a clearly demarcated ritual space within which people have the right to perform their rituals. The sovereignty of the procession is therefore not so much an alternative to the state's sovereignty but complementary to it and defended by it. This was an important factor in the escalation of the women's march. In addition to the model of Karbala, the protesting women also acted upon the model of the ʿAshura processions, demanding the right to proceed and expecting state forces to defend this right.

Motherhood and Male Honor

However, for most people in Hyderabad, or indeed elsewhere in Pakistan, the violence directed at the women's march was outrageous not primarily because of the ritual resemblance to Karbala and ʿAshura but because of the issue of gender. The perceived vulnerability of the women qua women was stronger than their perceived vulnerability as followers of Imam Hussain. Similarly, the fact that the police had shot at women was condemned more vigorously than the fact that the police had shot at people carrying the Qurʿan above their heads and shouting slogans reminiscent of Karbala. Most people, including those unsympathetic to the MQM, thought the police were wrong merely for shooting at *women*.

Although gender roles differ according to class and ethnic group, most women in Pakistan live in seclusion while men dominate public life. It is rare for women to come out in the streets in such a contentious way, and when they do, this by definition makes an impression. The fact that women left the family domain was seen as an indication of how seriously wrong the police were: no respectable woman would risk her dignity if she had not genuinely been aggrieved. Their demand for water was therefore symbolically loaded for yet another reason. It reminded one of Karbala, but more important, it also symbolized the sanctity of the family and the mother who was trying to take care of her thirsty children during the hot summer days.

It does not come as a surprise, then, that the women were later portrayed as desperate mothers no longer able to take care of their children. Not only the MQM but the public at large, ranging from Islamabad-based journalists to the inhabitants of Pakka Qila, condemned the police for taking on defenseless women. However, it also appears that the marching women were more than just caring mothers. The water supply is often cut off to the poorer areas of Pakistani cities, occasionally for weeks, and although this sometimes leads to petitions and other means of protest, prolonged lack of water rarely results in a women's demonstration. It is most likely that the women and other partakers had several motives for taking part in the demonstration. Anger and frustration about the lack of water may have been one of them, but they had probably also been informed about the battle in Pakka Qila. They had no doubt heard about the shooting. It is possible that MQM activists were also taking part in the protest march. Several militants from Pakka Qila had managed to escape from the citadel and had met up with their comrades from other parts of the city. These activists were determined to take back the citadel in order not to lose their arms supplies. They were also concerned about their friends and families. In short there were several possible reasons to organize and take part in the demonstration, but they all found a mutual target in the water tank of Pakka Qila.

When the women started out, they raised slogans reminiscent of Karbala as moral arguments to present their case to the audience and mobilize others. The simple demand for water symbolically accused the state forces of violating moral norms as it at once referred to Imam Hussain's martyrdom and the sanctity of motherhood. These slogans and symbols, as well as the prevailing tension, turned the march into a quasi-religious demonstration that was not quite like the annual ʿAshura procession but not very different from it either. When the women met with the policemen blocking their way, they began reciting the *kalima* and raised the Qurʾan to demand their right as Muslim citizens to take part and proceed in a public demonstration of faith. They did not come to die, they came to march, and standing in front of the police they called to mind the state's duty to protect the public performance of religious ceremonies.

How, meanwhile, did the police react? We do not have accounts of their mood and actions before the women reached the point where they blocked the road. Ali Hassan reported that a policeman ordered the women to stop and opened fire when they refused to do so. Hassan's report continues as follows:

> At this point, the other policemen on the scene also open discriminate fire, pointing their guns directly at the processionists. A terrible stampede ensues as everyone attempts to run for shelter. Screaming women rush into the shrine of Abdul Wahab Shah Jilani, located nearby, and take refuge there. The men, meanwhile, continue to spray bullets in all directions while chasing the protestors. "They are prostitutes," screams one policeman hysterically. "Don't allow them to get away alive." Within no time, the crowd has disappeared from the scene, leaving the injured screaming for help. In the stampede, many of the injured and dead are trampled under the boots of the policemen. "Let's teach them a lesson," screams a policeman who comes close to me. "Look, I'm a journalist," I tell him, before he can open fire. "Who asked these people to come here?" he asks me. "They only came here to urge the authorities to restore the water supply in the fort area," I inform him. "I haven't eaten either since last night," says the policeman. Suddenly a policeman hurls abuse at me, and tells a colleague to hit me. But we are interrupted by the appearance of an old man from a hut nearby. "Who are you? What do you want?" shouts a policeman. The man refuses to answer and remains silent. (1990: 35)

Other journalists reported similar stories about policemen going berserk, screaming abuses about Muhajir women being prostitutes and about Muhajir men being the sons of prostitutes, inciting each other to finish them off. "Get these Muhajir bastards," they were reported to have screamed.

I can think of three possible interpretations of the police's reactions and especially of their "hysterical" screams and abuse that accompanied the shooting. Why, for instance, did one policeman shout "They are prostitutes!" before chasing the women? Such cries were possibly an attempt to deny the women their claim to respectable motherhood with which they challenged the police in the first place. The fact that they were facing women placed the policemen in a predicament much more awkward than if they had been confronted by protesting men. The police had two options, both of them equally uninviting. Since the women did not allow themselves to be stopped and were there in much greater numbers, to hold them could only be achieved by the use of force. That would turn the police into brutal killers of innocent mothers. But to let them pass would turn the men into weaklings defeated by women. Calling them prostitutes may have been a last-ditch effort to avoid an inevitable social emasculation.

The problem with this interpretation is that it does not explain why the police opened fire with a vengeance. They could have used the sticks they usually carry. That, too, would have been a violation of women's untouchability, but they might have been able to stop them with considerably fewer victims. This would suggest that they were not merely trying to avoid social emasculation but that they were suddenly on a mission to avenge. In this interpretation, the scream "They are prostitutes!" is an expression of an immediate and intense hatred and anger caused by the fact that the women had dared to publicly question their status as honorable men and Muslims.

The third possible interpretation differs from the previous two insofar as it ascribes considerably less meaning to the screams and abuses of the policemen. In this interpretation, cries about prostitution and the immorality of the ethnic opponent are taken as conventional articulations that of course express some form of frustration, anxiety, or confusion but say little about the nature of the crisis. People call each other prostitutes and bastards all the time in quarrels between neighbors, business disputes, traffic accidents, etc. Alternatively they use ethnic abuses. Abuses and insults referring to perceived sexual practices and ethnic background are on the tip of most tongues. They are usually not meant to incite people to take drastic actions such as murder. Hence, cries like "They are prostitutes!" or "Get the Muhajir bastard" reveal very little about the predicament of the police.

What remains, then, is the fact that the police did something out of the ordinary. We may speculate that this resulted from complete confusion caused by the absence of options. In a highly tense situation, played out in a quasi-ceremonial protest march, the symbolically loaded language of motherhood and martyrdom left the police no room to retreat in a way that was acceptable to them. While the women pushed forward, self-conscious about their righteousness, there was no way the police could avoid losing face. They went berserk.

PARTITION REPEATED

For several hours panic and frenzy prevailed in Hyderabad. A large crowd gathered at Shah Makki Road, which connects Pakka Qila to the suburb of Latifabad. People were shouting, running, and arguing amid the ongoing noise from loudspeakers installed on various mosques. "Come out of your homes," voices from the loudspeakers cried. "Muhajirs are being killed. Save them. Help them." Other voices made desperate appeals for people to donate blood and bring cots and bedding to the hospitals. Ambulances from the Edhi Foundation, a charity organization, were driving between hospitals, most of which were already too full to be able to treat more patients. Large crowds blocked hospital entrances and tents were put up in the compounds to accommodate more wounded. People arrived pushing carts of dead bodies. Women queued to donate blood. Doctors performed surgery in the corridors. There were rumors about another massacre in a section of Latifabad, across the railway track. It seemed as if the entire city had come out in the streets, frantically asking for information (Hassan 1990: 35).

Around 2 P.M. army trucks loaded with armed soldiers from the cantonment area appeared in the city. They were passionately welcomed by Muhajir crowds shouting, "Help us! Help us! Pakistan Army, help us!" and "Save us! Install martial law!" The military forced the various police squadrons to go back to their respective districts. The police were yelled at while they left the city. Outside the city, however, they were reportedly welcomed, garlanded, and offered soft drinks by a group of Sindhi youth.[2] In the city, the military made announcements from vehicles, asking people to return to their homes.

The night was reasonably quiet, but the next day the violence welled again. But this time the nature of the riots had changed to ethnic violence. Beginning in Karachi, groups of armed Muhajir youth began to attack Sindhi residents. "Fierce clashes broke out between armed militants and contingents of police and the paramilitary Rangers. The clashes were followed by a grim series of killings, in which scores of people were gunned down—most of them Sindhis."[3] Similar attacks, in which any Sindhi or Muhajir could be a target for retaliation, were reported from other places in Sindh. A train traveling from Karachi to the interior of Sindh carrying mainly Sindhi refugees was ambushed by gunmen and sprayed with bullets. In Hyderabad, too, the violence started again, lasting ten consecutive days, with attacks on Sindhi and Muhajir localities by militants belonging to the rival ethnic group. Automatic guns, hand grenades, and rocket launchers were used. Additionally, people were reportedly strangled or hanged. Women were raped. Houses and shops were looted and burnt. On 15 July a bomb exploded near the railway station killing several people. In the new predominantly Sindhi suburb of Qasimabad, a camp was established to give shelter to Sindhi families who had been forced to leave their homes in the city center. Elsewhere in Hyderabad, Muhajir refugees from villages and towns in the Sindhi countryside began to arrive in considerable numbers.

According to some journalists working in Hyderabad, the violence of the summer of 1990 differed from earlier ethnic violence. It was no longer conducted by militants of ethnic organizations alone. The so-called *jang* or little war, which had been ongoing in Hyderabad since 1987, was mainly a clash of armed activists of rival organizations. Now a much larger number of people managed to obtain weapons and ammunition. Traders with links in the underworld of Hyderabad reported that the demand increased so rapidly that the price of ammunition skyrocketed. As a result, people who had never touched a weapon joined in the fray whenever a riot broke out.[4]

It is, however, extremely difficult if not impossible to verify these reports through anthropological research. I found it highly problematic to figure out what people in Pakka Qila had been doing during these days. The more people were willing to talk about the siege and the women's march, the more reluctant they were to say anything about what followed. And if they talked, they told stories in which they portrayed themselves as victims. I met people, now living in Latifabad, who had been forced to leave their homes in a Sindhi village. They told me how their Sindhi neighbors had looted their homes or shops and how they had fled to Hyderabad. But it was very difficult to find the perpetrators and make them tell their story. Eventually, some men in Pakka Qila told me that they had been involved in murder, but they would stress that they had done so as retaliators on behalf of the victims. Those accounts typically started with a long story of a friend or a relative killed by a Sindhi neighbor or employee, ending abruptly with the assertion that they had chased the man and taken his life. More people claimed that they had been involved in armed clashes with the police. These stories were most often told with a gravity that underlined the dedication and sense of duty with which they had managed to face the high risks of such encounters. When asked for motives, they would either mention their devotion to the cause of Muhajirs or recall the death of a friend shot by the police. From these stories I did not get the impression of frenzy, fury, and wild rage—these moods had been present, people said, but only on the part of the enemy. The enemy had acted like wild beasts, while they considered their own violent acts as proportional and necessary. In contrast to the stories about the *jang*, which were told with a great deal of bravado, the accounts of the summer of 1990 were all within the limits of what was considered morally justifiable. Moreover, all my informants emphasized that they had never engaged in senseless looting, arson, or rape. Accusations of rape were especially vigorously denied.

Naturally, such stories say little about the atmosphere of those days. More than anything else, they demonstrate the impossibility of saying anything substantial about the moods and motives of the people involved in large-scale ethnic violence. Such events are of course unfit for the anthropological method of participant observation (Nordstrom and Robben 1995), while the information obtained through oral history is made up primarily of interpretations highly colored by political interests, image management, and feelings of guilt or shame, denial, etc. In addition, inquiries are mostly met with silence. As a result, most recent studies on ethnic or religious group violence typically lack any kind of concrete research data derived directly from the perpetrators.

However, if we turn our attention from the individual acts of violence to the memories people convey about their predicament during the crisis, it is possible to get an impression of the prevailing atmosphere and the modes of interpretation with which people tried to make sense of the chaos. For example, people have memories of conversations that shed some light on how they evaluated the situation. Such memories testify to the sorts of debates that were going on at the time as well as the social pressure put on them or that which they put on others to act according to a particular interpretation of the violence. From these discussions I want to suggest that the episode was increasingly interpreted as an imminent partition, following the logic and experiences of the earlier partitions of 1947 and 1971. This is confirmed by newspaper reports comparing the situation to a civil war reminiscent of earlier partitions. From the discussions I had in Pakka Qila about these days, I got the impression that people anticipated the division of the province of Sindh. Some fled to Karachi. Others prepared for a final showdown with the Sindhis, in which it would be decided whether Hyderabad was going to be the capital city of a new Sindh without Muhajirs, or the second city (second to Karachi) of a Muhajir-dominated province or state, for which various names, from Muhajiristan to Jinnahpur, circulated. Many made explicit comparisons with the exodus of Muhajirs in the aftermath of 1947.

To conclude this chapter I will examine the memories people had of conversations in which they talked about the ongoing violence in terms of another partition. It is not possible to explain individual acts of violence from these interpretations, but these conversations shed some light on the deep antagonism of which the atrocities were an expression.

Fathers and Sons

One set of discussions concerned the decision whether to flee to Karachi or fight in Hyderabad. Some families from Pakka Qila, anticipating defeat, packed their bags and took a bus to Karachi to escape the imminent violence in Hyderabad. This met with a great deal of criticism from neighbors, who considered this an act of cowardice. One man recalled: "Those who left were called 'weak of heart' [*buzdil*]. We said that they were women, not men." The phrase "weak of heart" was connected to the opposite concept of "will power" (*hosla*), commonly used to describe the state of mind necessary for migration. To leave India in 1947 was widely considered an act of will power. But to leave now was an act of cowardice. As one man explained: "We cannot be on the move forever. We came to Pakistan because it was our country. This is not 'enemy territory' [*dar al-harb*], like India. This is 'Islamic territory' [*dar al-islam*]." Another man said: "If you leave the country [*mulk*] where your grandfathers are buried, you feel weak at first. You feel empty. It takes a long time before you feel strong again. It took us twenty or thirty years to feel strong again. If we leave now, we will once again feel weak. This is our home now and we cannot leave it again. If we go to Karachi now, they will come after us. Then where do we go from there? That is the end. They will drive us into the sea." Another man recalled that "we considered those who left as cowards. When Sindh is going to be divided, Hyderabad will be the place where the final battle will take place. We have to stand up for ourselves and fight." He also explained that Hyderabad is surrounded by Sindhi territory, unlike Karachi, and that therefore every man was needed to defend the city and retain it as Muhajir territory.

Similar conversations were taking place between different wings of the MQM. The radical wing of the MQM student organization, the APMSO, was reportedly planning large-scale violent operations to drive Sindhis out of the city, inciting young Muhajirs to join them by saying that "Sindhis are non-Muslims, like Bengalis."[5] They met resistance from more moderate circles within the MQM. This led to discussions as to whether the time was ripe for a division of Sindh and the establishment of a separate Muhajir province. Several MQM strongmen in Hyderabad went into hiding to continue the fight in a military fashion, anticipating civil war and the partition of Sindh.[6]

A different set of debates took place between fathers and sons. As several residents of Pakka Qila recalled, a son tended to be more radical, trying to convince his father that a moderate position would be detrimental for Muhajirs. One young man recalled:

> We had a gun in the house. Many of us had one at that time—for self-defense. My father wanted to take it and bury it before the police would find it. He said that the police would arrest me and torture me if they found the gun. He also told me to stay at home. So I asked, "What is the difference? If they manage to catch me, they will arrest and torture me anyway—gun or no gun." Then he said that I must hide and wait till the trouble was over. So I argued, "If we all hide, then who is going to defend our rights? Where will we end up if all we do is hide and flee all of the time? They will never allow us a place to live if we do not fight for it." We had a big fight. I had never had such a big fight with my father. Eventually I just took the gun and left. I thought my father would never forgive me for that. But when I returned, he was very emotional and said he was proud of me.

Another man, a father, told me a similar story. He, too, had had an argument with his son. For some time the son had wanted to join the MQM but the father had always managed to dissuade him. The son had never taken part in public meetings or other actions held under the banner of the MQM. Then, on 25 May, he was working in a shop when the police operation started. The police entered the workshop and gave everyone inside a severe beating, screaming in Sindhi: "Where is your brave leader now that you need him?" When the police left Pakka Qila, the son was determined to join the fight despite his father's objections. He was not angry with just the police; he was also angry with his father, whom he told: "You have always told me that we should have been more courageous in 1947. You have always told me that we should have fought. If we had fought hard enough, Pakistan would have been much bigger. We would have had the whole of Kashmir, Junagadh, Ajmer,[7] a much larger portion of the Punjab. . . . You always said that it had been a mistake to simply pack our belongings and leave." The father recalled that he had not been able to respond. He gave his son permission to join the others. "How could I stop him this time?" he said.

In a similar account, another young man also confronted his father with his own words. The father often complained about the younger generation's weakness and inconstancy. He regularly argued that the Muslims of India had managed to win themselves a separate homeland against the superior forces of two enemies, the Hindus and the British, whereas he claimed that the younger generation could not even effectively deal with one enemy, the Sindhis, who were cowardly to boot. "The MQM is fighting a woman," he said, alluding to Benazir Bhutto, "and still they cannot win." The scorn of his father had led the son to look for a different sort of reason that would explain the differences between 1947 and the present. In his opinion, World War II had been crucial for the Muslims since it had weakened the British, and without the support of the British the Hindus were weak. Similarly, he reasoned, the Punjabis supported the Sindhis and they could be defeated once they lost that support. The fact that the army—a Punjabi institution from his point of view—had pushed back the Sindhi police seemed to him to be writing on the wall. The Sindhis stood alone now and this was the right opportunity to prove that his father had been wrong about the younger generation. He therefore joined the militants in order to establish a Muhajir homeland that would end the displacement of Muhajirs amid hostile Sindhis.

Partition as a Model

What I take from these examples is that amid the violence there was strong pressure to read the situation in light of the partition of 1947—and to a lesser extent the partition of 1971—to justify further militant actions or to incite people to join the fight. People experienced and talked about the ongoing situation as an event similar to earlier crises and recalled the heroism as well as the failures of the past to assess the present situation and decide how to react to it. The memory of earlier partitions helped people make sense of a hectic situation. Partition was a model for further actions and a powerful argument to persuade others to follow suit.

A central aspect of this partition model is the notion of Muhajirs as a diasporic people. The sense of isolation, of being on the run, of being deprived of a place of one's own, is evident in the above-mentioned examples, as is the call to end the pattern of flight and migration. It is important to note that even today the residents of Pakka Qila are convinced that the police operation was aimed at driving Muhajirs out of the city of Hyderabad. It is believed that the Sindhi-dominated administration of the PPP was not willing to allow Muhajirs a place to live in Sindh and wanted to force Muhajirs to move to Karachi. Eventually, Muhajirs would not be allowed to live in peace there either. It was often said that "they want to drive us into the Arabian Sea. We Muslims used to rule India, but we were driven to the westernmost corner of the subcontinent, and even here we will not be granted a place of our own." Statements by Sindhi politicians that Muhajirs had to become "new Sindhis" added fuel to such fears. Some radical Sindhi politicians, sensing that Muhajirs were not willing to do that, went so far as to say that there was no place for Muhajirs in Sindh. Immediately after the violence in May 1990, for instance, Federal Minister Syed Ghulam Mustafa Shah threatened to demolish the settlements within

Pakka Qila in order to put an end to the violence and to end the Muhajir occupation of the former royal palace of Sindh.[8]

The fear of displacement was also enhanced by the plight of the so-called Biharis, Urdu-speaking Muslim migrants who went from India to East Pakistan after 1947. After Bangladesh gained independence in 1971, most tried to go to Pakistan, but not all were successful and large groups of them have resided in refugee camps in Bangladesh since then. Successive governments of Pakistan have not given them permission to come to Pakistan. This has been taken up by the MQM, which, if only for rhetorical reasons, has made the rehabilitation of these migrants one of its most important demands. For Pakka Qila residents, the Biharis in Bangladeshi refugee camps reflected their own fears of displacement. This made it even more important to defend Hyderabad. More than merely a city of residence, Hyderabad was a place where history could be forced to take a turn. By defending the place instead of fleeing again, Muhajirs could secure for themselves a territory of their own and end their destiny as migrant people. Left in the cold by the others, one insisted, Muhajirs could rely only on themselves. The alternative would be ending up in a UN refugee camp in some distant desert.

For the Pakka Qila residents, then, the present situation differed from 1947 in several ways. First, migration in the aftermath of independence was considered a flight from un-Islamic territory and therefore comparable to the *hijra*. In May 1990, however, it was argued that Islamic territory was under attack. Flight would now be a violation of the injunction to defend Islam. Second, it would be an unmanly act. In 1947 migration had been a matter of will power (*hosla*), but now it was a matter of will power to stay and defend oneself. Third, flight offered no vision of a better future. In 1947 the famous cry "Calo Pakistan" ("Let's go to Pakistan") was a promise of prosperity and freedom. To leave now meant accepting defeat and displacement.

Despite the differences, Pakka Qila residents clearly also saw similarities with earlier partitions. They often talked about their opponents, the Sindhis, as if they were Hindus or Bengalis. The phrase "Sindhis are non-Muslims like Bengalis" illustrates this very well as it combines both previous partitions: the non-Muslim Hindus and the Bengalis. Another example is given by a report of the Human Rights Commission: "The Hindu population had also become extremely vulnerable. It was victimized by Muhajir extremists for its [alleged] support to Sindhi nationalism. A number of Hindus were killed in the incidents of violence in the city" (quoted in Jafri 1996: 403). The fact that Hindus were associated with the Sindhi opponent must almost certainly have been the result of rumors about a perceived solidarity between Sindhi Muslims and Hindus—Hindus do not normally engage in ethnic politics because they are in a far too vulnerable position to do so.

Examples like this suggest that the historical particularities of the different partitions were blurred when people began to perceive the May 1990 carnage as a reiteration of earlier partitions. The partition of 1947 had established the division of territory as an option to deal with social tension. A new partition in 1971 generated demands for more divisions elsewhere in Pakistan, notably among Sindhi nationalists. MQM leaders, too, although never demanding a separate state, regularly warned the government not to repeat the mistakes of 1971 by pushing Muhajirs up against the wall. Among the radical MQM youth, the notion of an independent Muhajir province or state was alive. But most of the time the division of Sindh was a distant option. In the summer of 1990, however, it suddenly became a real possibility as the large-scale and life-threatening violence elevated the fears for displacement and a life in diaspora.

The Reaction of the MQM to May 1990

While Pakka Qila residents used earlier experiences of partition to make sense of the violence, the MQM put forward its own interpretation, mainly focusing on the killing of the protesting women by the police. In an immediate reaction from London, where he was receiving medical treatment, Altaf Hussain spoke of a "genocide of Muhajirs," comparing the incident to the 1919 massacre of Jallianwala Bagh in Amritsar, where British troops led by General O'Dwyer shot dead 379 unarmed people. In fact, Altaf said, the Hyderabad incident was worse because "whereas O'Dwyer was a foreigner and a non-Muslim, the perpetrators of such heinous crimes in Pakka Qila were Muslims as well as fellow countrymen."[9] MQM chairman Azim Ahmad Tariq said that "the blood of Muhajirs which flowed in the streets of Hyderabad will one day become the symbol of the greatness of the Muhajir nation."[10] Furthermore, many speeches were made comparing the killing of the women to the story of Karbala. The latter is significant because I found that in Pakka Qila the Karbala myth was hardly mentioned to cope with the crisis. Whereas partition provided an interpretative framework for the violence in Pakka Qila, the MQM in its rhetoric referred to the Karbala myth. This indicates that both parties were engaged in different kinds of battles. While the Pakka Qila residents anticipated another partition, the MQM tried to increase the pressure on the PPP government to resign. The MQM leadership was not aiming for a separate Muhajir province or state; it primarily tried to discredit the government of Benazir Bhutto.

While making martyrs of the murdered women by linking the Pakka Qila incident to the story of Karbala, the MQM was nonetheless careful not to turn them into individual martyrs. None of those who were killed were given a name and a face. Producing individual martyrs has in fact never been party policy. The way the MQM deploys Islamic traditions of martyrdom, such as Karbala and the *hijra*, focuses on numbers rather than individuals. For instance, no effort has ever been made to compare the death of MQM militants or supporters to the martyrdom of saints executed by the state. Instead, in the tradition of Karbala and the *hijra*, we see large numbers of believers make their sacrifice while following a supreme leader.

The facelessness of MQM martyrs shows that the party found it less important to pay homage to its followers than to identify its enemies. If it was the main aim of the MQM to discredit the government and its leader, the references to the Karbala myth were primarily meant to compare the Bhutto administration to the tyrannical regime of Yazid. In fact, the MQM had already started to talk about the government led by Benazir Bhutto as "this Yazidi government" before the summer of 1990 (see chapter 2). References to Karbala increased dramatically during the violence to undermine the legitimacy of the PPP administration. This, indeed, proved successful. On 6 August, some six weeks after the police operation in Pakka Qila, the President dismissed Prime Minister Benazir Bhutto, mentioning her handling of the crisis in Hyderabad as one of the reasons for dismissal. Altaf Hussain responded by saying that "a Karbala of twenty months has come to an end."[11] The government of Benazir Bhutto had lasted twenty months.

Another reason why the MQM has not produced martyrs with a face is the paramount position of Altaf Hussain as the "leader of the movement." During the summer of 1990, Altaf, as during the time of his hunger strike, again appeared as the only person people would turn to make their sacrifice for the cause of Muhajirs and the MQM. This was illustrated by the crowds who welcomed him on his return from London shortly after the dismissal of the Bhutto government. "Pir Sahib," they shouted, "I am ready to offer my head for you."[12] Many of those who were present were recent refugees from the interior of Sindh, including Hyderabad, who had escaped the violence and come to Karachi, some of them lodged in refugee camps. Complete families came to welcome Altaf, turning to him as their savior. "God alone and you on earth are to help me," a woman explained. "We were looted and forced to migrate long ago. We worked hard for forty years and built a new home. That too was snatched away from us. We came here and you have helped us."[13] In this statement, the fear of displacement fueled by the recent crisis is again evident. But it is also clear that the MQM did not use this increased anxiety to demand Muhajir autonomy within or without Pakistan. It rather downplayed popular references to a new partition, instead referring to the crisis in terms of the Karbala myth in order to damage its main rival, the PPP led by Bhutto.

CONCLUSION

The Pakka Qila crisis, then, did not lead to a new division, separating Sindhis from Muhajirs, although many inhabitants of Hyderabad did leave their homes in mixed neighborhoods, settling instead in residential areas dominated by their ethnic group. A typical story about the summer of 1990 relates how Sindhi and Muhajir friends, both living in the "wrong" neighborhoods, exchanged houses to escape the rage of their neighbors. For some time MQM militants hoped for an autonomous Muhajir province or state, while others feared that a new partition would force them to leave their homes once again. But with the dismissal of the Bhutto government and the subsequent elections that brought the MQM back in office as a coalition partner of the Pakistan Muslim League, such hopes and fears gradually subsided. A delicate peace was restored in Hyderabad. In the former royal palace of Pakka Qila a police station was opened, but until 1992, when Operation Clean-up against the MQM began, its presence was largely symbolic. No policeman dared patrol the labyrinth of narrow alleys in the residential parts of the citadel.

Six years later, during the time of my fieldwork, May 1990 was collectively remembered as a crisis that temporarily stripped reality from its ambiguous, bargaining incompleteness. Many felt the deep antagonism that appeared in the violence of 1990 to be more real and more true than the fussiness of everyday social relationships. At the same time, the collective memory of 1990 hardly allowed for complexity or personal idiosyncratic memories. To that extent, it can be said that May 1990 had been turned into a "transhistorical" episode devoid of the particularities and subjectivities of the event, like the partition of 1947 or the battle of Karbala. All the same, despite the fact that many Pakka Qila residents felt that the crisis of 1990 had revealed the "deep truth" of ethnic relations in Pakistan, the notion of ethnic purity had nonetheless lost most of its relevance as soon as the violence abated. Daily life had been allowed to regain its imperfect self again.

To conclude, my interpretation of the violence of 1990 can be seen as a reversal of the anthropological theory on life crises associated with Van Gennep and Victor Turner. According to this theory, the ritual process moves from structure via the liminal phase into a new structure. Ambiguity resides in the liminal phase of being betwixt and between. I believe that May 1990 constitutes an important life crisis for the Pakka Qila residents for exactly the opposite reason. May 1990 stands out as a rare moment revealing an unambiguous "truth" about ethnic relationships, while daily life is characterized by the insecurity and incompleteness of ethnic categories and identities. As a rare moment of condensed or thickened symbolic meaning, May 1990 has been woven into a tapestry of earlier highly significant episodes, such as the partition of 1947. These moments continue to resonate in everyday life as negotiable convictions, and they may provide people with an interpretative framework in future crises.

For some, the "truth" of these moments is frightening and dangerous. But their diminishing relevance in everyday life also accounts for the sense of nostalgia that pervaded Pakka Qila during the time of my fieldwork. I will turn to this sense of loss and disillusion in the next chapter, which also discusses a third form of violence associated with the MQM. After the provocative violence of young male peer groups in the early years of the MQM and the martyrdom during large-scale crises such as May 1990, full-time militancy became prevalent in the 1990s, along with state persecution and a growing sense of isolation among the Muhajir population. The next chapter, in other words, is about popular perceptions of the state, about "terrorism," and about the recurrence of the diasporic Muhajir identity.

CHAPTER SIX

Terrorism and the State

NOSTALGIA looms large in Muhajir identity. But it is not primarily a longing for a place left behind in India. It is rather nostalgia for the early years of arrival and settlement, the 1950s and 1960s, which are remembered as years of hope, progress, and peace. In retrospect, the ideal of Pakistan as a place of social equality and solidarity seemed to make sense then. There was some discussion in Pakka Qila about when the years of optimism ended. Some said it was the loss of East Pakistan in 1971. Others mentioned the language riots between Sindhis and Muhajirs that same year. A third group identified the national elections of 1970 as the turning point. But everyone agreed that the downfall started in the early 1970s.

This feeling of nostalgia is not restricted to Pakka Qila. It also pervades recent publications on the history of Karachi. The volume *Karachi: Megacity of Our Times* (Khuhro and Mooraj 1997), published on the occasion of the fiftieth anniversary of Pakistan's independence, is a good upper-middle-class example. The book is full of sentimental journeys back to more orderly, gay, and safe years, in comparison to which present-day Karachi appears as a hellish place. But the Festschrift-turned-elegy only repeats a melancholic way of remembering the past, which one can also find in novels and short stories written earlier. In Shaukat Siddiqi's famous novel, *Khuda ki Basti* (1991), Karachi is a hectic place that never sleeps, home of many wandering souls looking for a place of their own. But it is also a city of lights, possibilities, and an anti-establishment spirit—very different from highbrow Lahore or disciplined and sterile Islamabad. Karachi was a city of migrants looking for a compelling life, a life in dignity: "[E]ven the slums looked like paradise for me. For here I was at least free," wrote M. A. Seljouk in a story entitled *The Bandit* (quoted in Rahman 1997). The picture painted of Karachi is one of opportunity, humor, tolerance, and diversity. The real Karachi is a metropolitan disaster of infrastructural mismanagement, environmental destruction, unemployment, and political violence.

One finds a similar migrant nostalgia in Hyderabad, even though it has not been expressed in a literary form. Here, too, many migrants recall the city of their younger days as a place of national solidarity and economic opportunity. In such memories there is no room for traffic jams, corrupt state officials, ethnic tension, or unemployment. And in Hyderabad, too, optimism has been replaced by nostalgia. Today stories on migration no longer emphasize the pioneering spirit but lament the sacrifices. There is more attention to what has been lost than to what can be gained.

In Pakka Qila nostalgia was reflected in a well-developed distrust of the political process. Hardly anyone managed to mention the word for politics, *siyasat*, without a tone of contempt and disgust. Politicians were generally described as vultures who "eat your brain" (*dimag khana*) with their hollow phrases and false promises and were blamed for the ethnic disharmony of the recent years. The general feeling in Pakka Qila seemed no longer to be one of anger but one of frustration. "I am fed up with this situation," I was told time and again. This even affected the degree of support for the MQM. Even among the most dedicated to the cause, the desire to find a job and start a family seemed more acute than the spirit to fight on and dedicate one's life to the MQM.

One of the reasons for this weariness with the party could have been the meager prospect of success. Up to 1992 the MQM had been upbeat, its ranks had been expanding, and its supporters had been more and more confident that the promised MQM revolution could be realized. Then the Pakistani state came down hard on the MQM in Operation Clean-up, which sent many of its leaders abroad. With most of its leaders in exile and most of its militants dead, men who enjoyed neither the respect nor the experience of the early leaders now led the MQM.

Even the most devoted found it difficult to hide their sense of disillusion. In January 1997 Altaf Hussain was scheduled to give a speech to encourage party members on the occasion of the imminent national elections. For days expectations rose higher and higher. Several young men anticipated that they would finally be liberated from their state of inactivity and that they would be given a new sense of direction. After the speech, transmitted by telephone from London and amplified locally on a large playground, disappointment was tangible. "He said nothing new," one young man commented. "He said the same things two years ago." His friend tried to make excuses for the leader: "He works hard for the nation in London. We must have patience." "That is what *he* also says," the first speaker answered, "but he has been telling us so for years."

I must stress this feeling of disappointment because it set the tone of many conversations I had in Pakka Qila. Those who had been between fifteen and twenty-five years old some ten years ago had grown accustomed to an atmosphere of great expectations, victories, and excitement. On some rare occasions that excitement returned, as during the public meeting near Bhai Khan ki Chari I described in chapter 4. But there was also a widespread feeling that the splendor of those days was gone. The promise, whatever it had been, had not been fulfilled. The leadership of the MQM was partly blamed for this failure. Comparisons were made with other independence movements that had been successful. One young man said, "Why did Ireland become independent? Because the Irish had a one-cause program. They only demanded independence. Nothing more, nothing less. The MQM has dozens of demands but we forget about the most important one: the demand for a separate Muhajir homeland." Another said, "Compared to Jinnah, Altaf Bhai [Brother Altaf] is not so great. We are stronger now in Pakistan then we used to be in India. Yet, Jinnah won Pakistan for us while Altaf Bhai did not get us independence."

It would be misleading to say that support for the MQM and its leader was waning in Pakka Qila. The MQM was still the only political party that mattered in the neighborhood. During the elections of 1997 most inhabitants abstained from voting altogether, but those who did go to the polling station voted for the MQM. This was again the case during the elections of 2002. But the support was not unconditional. Many said the party was losing momentum and the devotion suffered correspondingly. Critics within Pakka Qila, including many who still supported the MQM for want of an alternative, pointed out that the MQM was no longer the ideological and revolutionary movement that worked for the good of all Muhajirs. Instead the MQM had become a political party like any other. Making quick money, it was said, had become the main objective of the party workers. They used their reputation as MQM strongmen to demand free food in restaurants and tea stalls. The movement, the critics within Pakka Qila said, had turned inward and forgotten its vision of justice and liberation for all. Since the leadership was away in exile, there was no one around to correct undisciplined party workers.

In a word, many felt that the ideology of Muhajir solidarity, which had characterized the MQM in its early years, had gradually given way to common political corruption. In addition, most Pakka Qila residents were not happy with the party name change that replaced *Muhajir* with *Muttehida*. Some said it was a tactical move provoked by the experience that anything presented under the banner of Muhajir was bound to be sabotaged in Pakistan. Others felt that the party was turning away from them. In any case it contributed to the sense of insecurity, confusion, and disappointment.

This final chapter, then, takes us into the ethnographical present—the present of my fieldwork in 1996 and 1997. In Pakka Qila the present seemed a much gloomier place than the past. I will examine this nostalgia from three different angles. I will first explore the disappointment with the MQM and link this to the theme of "terrorism"—the word that the MQM of the second half of the 1990s is most often associated with. Paradoxically, this stigmatization of the MQM by the state, along with real acts of state oppression, is perhaps most instrumental in preventing the movement from falling apart. Next, I will look at the more fundamental sense of disillusion with politics in general and with the state in particular. It is this particular form of disillusion that accounts for the present-day crisis of governability and accountability in Pakistan as well as a sense of nostalgia for authoritarianism. Although these are often-mentioned themes in political science studies today, their social causes and implications remain largely unexamined. Finally, I will return to the themes of displacement and diaspora, about which I have already made several remarks in the previous chapter. My conclusion is that the diasporic aspect in Muhajir identity is of a rather recent date. It does not find its origin in migration as such but is better understood in relation to the expanding atmosphere of nostalgia and disillusion of the 1990s.

TERRORISM

As Martha Crenshaw argues, it is possible to analyze militant groups from at least two angles. One approach is to study the group in terms of its ideology and the strategies used to bring about its objectives. It is, however, also possible to look at a militant group as a community whose main objective is sustainability and accommodation of its members. "The incentives for joining a terrorist organization, especially one that is already established and of known character, include a variety of individual needs: to belong to a group, to acquire social status and reputation, to find comradeship or excitement, or to gain material benefits" (Crenshaw 1988: 19). These are much more profane incentives than idealism.

There was a marked tendency in Pakka Qila to argue that the MQM had ceased to be a revolutionary movement driven by ideals and had become an inward-looking organization mainly concerned about its own survival and the well-being of its members. One set of terms used to describe this transition was the pair *dayan* and *bayan*: right and left. The MQM was believed to possess both a right side and left side. Right or *dayan* represented the search for justice (*insaf*) and truth (*haq*). It was also translated as the peace-loving, ideological, or sacrificing part of the movement. The *dayan* part of the movement worked for the well-being of all Muhajirs. Left or *bayan* constituted the "political" and compromising part of the party. It focused on personal gain and the search for individual prestige. According to public opinion in Pakka Qila, the left, corrupted, *bayan* side had gradually taken over the authentic, right, *dayan* side of the MQM. Membership in the MQM had become a profession rather than a conviction. It was an easy way to become affluent and to develop a fearsome reputation. New recruits joined the movement on the promise of earning easy money, not for ideological reasons.

More than that, Pakka Qila residents increasingly found these self-concerned MQM militants to be as arrogant as the people they were supposed to fight and replace, such as corrupt policemen, bureaucrats, and politicians. The practice of forcing people to pay "voluntary donations" (*bhatta*) to party members had spread widely. Within the neighborhood, MQM workers acted as the legislative, executive, and judicial powers all in one. They strongly dissuaded people to consult state institutions such as the city court in case of conflict and advised people to come to them instead. Some people found the MQM way of administering justice a lot quicker and more just than the way of the state, but others complained that justice continued to be as arbitrary as ever. Decisions and verdicts made in the MQM head office in Bhai Khan ki Chari were binding and there was the threat of physical punishment for disobedience. At the far end of Pakka Qila was an old brick barrack where violators of party discipline had reportedly been punished. Especially feared were the Black Tigers, black-uniformed MQM strongmen, trained in at least one of the martial arts. It was also common to say that the MQM forced people to obey "at gunpoint." This English phrase had become a buzzword.

I do not think that much of this was new in 1996. There had been complaints earlier about the MQM terrorizing its own neighborhoods. But this naked power had always been dressed up by the movement's *dayan* side. The notion of making sacrifices, of self-effacing loyalty to a good cause, always excused incidents of power abuse. The notion of revolution and sacrifice was promoted through a range of practices and discourses. These included the personality cult surrounding Altaf Hussain as well as several social welfare programs and charity festivals. There used to be the Muft Kitab Bazar, or Free Book Market, where books were distributed to students from poor families, or Ramzaan melas, festivals during the fasting month of Ramzaam, when food, money, and equipment—sewing machines, for instance—were given to widows and the disabled. The party's charity organization, the Khidmat-i-Khalq Committee, collected alms and distributed millions of rupees to the victims of political violence. Such practices had virtually come to an end. Even Altaf Hussain no longer served as the centripetal force of the movement. He was no doubt still held in high esteem, but, residing in faraway London since January 1992, he was on the verge of becoming a barren icon of distant grandiosity, gradually fading away.

Paradoxically, the language of terrorism came to the movement's rescue. Introduced by the state to legitimize its extrajudicial methods of persecution during Operation Clean-up, terrorism was originally intended to spread fear and exclude MQM militants from the moral community of Pakistani citizens holding citizen rights. But as Edmund Leach (1977: 27), among others, has noticed, one man's terrorist is another man's free-

FIGURE 5. Painting on a wall in Hyderabad showing an image of an MQM fighter or "terrorist."

dom fighter or martyr. The image of the terrorist usually resonates with particular societal fears, but they can also contain a certain aesthetic and awe that some people find attractive. In other words, the appropriation and reversal of the terrorist stigma into a new *dayan* image of a self-sacrificing, persecuted freedom fighter was one of the techniques the MQM used to resist the state operation against the movement. To be sure, it was not the only technique the MQM applied. The party also endorsed the language of human rights in a campaign, largely designed by the party office in London, that combined press releases, fact-finding documents, Internet sites, and exhibitions of photographs. In his telephone speeches from his home in London, Altaf Hussain continued to talk in terms of oppression (*zulm*) when commenting on the state operation. But in the MQM strongholds in Karachi and Hyderabad, the number of images of broad-shouldered fighters with heavy guns in their hands painted on public walls rapidly increased (see fig. 5). The MQM youth, moreover, compared these fighters to foreign Muslim militants operating in places like Palestine, Kashmir, Chechnya, or Bosnia. Reversing Orientalist notions of Muslims as prone to fighting and fanaticism, they argued that the MQM militants were driven by the uncompromising devotion to the faith characteristic of true Muslim males. Although the MQM never sided with radical Islamist groups locally known as *jihadis*, the reversal of the terrorist stigma generated among MQM militants a mixture of faith and violence that resembled the interpretation of *jihad* as military action.

Remarkably, these party activists simply accepted and adopted with pride the term *terrorist*—in English. Alternatively, they called themselves *goonda* (thug) *dacoit* (bandit), *dahshatgard* (brute), or another term akin to terrorist. They made no effort to argue that they were freedom fighters rather than terrorists. For them, "terrorist" was an honorary nickname, like "freedom fighter" or "martyr" (*shaheed*). But there was also an almost comic element to the adoption of the term terrorist. Two young boys welcomed me:

> SHAHID: You are in Pakka Qila now. We live here. This is our *desh* [country]. We
> are *qila qaum* [fort people]. We shoot every policeman who dares to come here.
> MOEEN: We are *pakka dahshatgard* [real brutes].
> SHAHID: Commandos.
> MOEEN: *Acche* fighters [good fighters].
> SHAHID: You see Moeen here—he is very brave, like Rustam. Hahaha. He is a
> *qasai* [butcher] too.

If we were to take these two good-humored boys seriously, we would have to conclude that the population was made up of terrorists, commandos, and other fighters brave as the legendary Iranian prince Rustam. But their boyish appearances made all that seem absurd. Used in this sense, the concept of terrorism was primarily meant to ridicule state propaganda against the MQM.

Together with the speeches on oppression (*zulm*) and human rights, then, the partly serious, partly ludic reversal of the terrorist stigma to some extent helped prevent the movement from falling apart. In a time when most party officials down to the post of sector-in-charge were either eliminated or abroad, and when dissatisfaction with the party was on the rise, stressing the sacrifices made by party activists qua "terrorists" was one way of upholding the notion of the MQM as a genuinely idealistic movement. It could not entirely prevent the decline of the party, but it helped maintain the image of the MQM as a still thrilling and extraordinary movement. Hence, the MQM still had some credibility in Pakka Qila. The state, the subject of the next sections, had considerably less.

CORRUPTION AND THE CRISIS OF GOVERNABILITY

When Nasr (1992b) argued that the rise of ethnic violence and the imminent collapse of democracy was the result of a "crisis of governability" caused by a decay of political institutions and an erosion of state authority, he expressed in academic words a widely held public opinion in Pakistani society. I have come across many people who argued that ethnic violence is bound to take place when the state loses its grip on society. They would recall that the ethnic violence of the late 1980s took place during the transition toward democracy after eleven years of authoritarian military rule—a process that to some extent resembled the fall of the military regime in the late 1960s, which had also come about in a period of large-scale social unrest. Whereas the relationship between the erosion of state power and increasing political violence seemed beyond debate, I often witnessed lively discussion about how to interpret this relationship. Some people would blame authoritarianism. They would argue that prolonged oppression would sooner or later lead to revolt. Others took the opposite stand and put the blame on the weakness of the state.

To be sure, I agree that the changing relationships between the state and society form an important point for consideration to understand the rise of ethnic violence and ethnic identities, but I also believe that neither the weak state thesis nor the authoritarian state thesis sufficiently addresses what is at stake. To begin with, there is empirical evidence that does not support either opinion. Surely the thesis of a weak or collapsing state is difficult to maintain when one considers the large number of military, paramilitary, and police forces that have been brought out into the streets of Karachi and Hyderabad since the late 1980s. It seems unlikely that the transition to democracy has lowered the capability or readiness of government leaders to use force against civilians. But the notion of the authoritarian state is also problematic. Effective state control presupposes a high degree of efficiency in coercion. There seems to be enough evidence, however, to suggest that the Pakistani state agencies and government bodies are too fragmented and internally divided to keep large numbers of citizens firmly under control.

What is more, it is not uncommon for a Pakistani to express both profound nostalgia for authoritarianism and a deep distrust of state officials. This puts the notion of collapsing state authority in a different light. It seems that what is collapsing is the authority of particular state *officials* and state *institutions*, whereas the *idea* of the state as a legitimate power remains unaffected. This may seem obvious or trivial at first. When there is a shortage of honest state officials, the longing for an authoritative leader grows. There is, however, more to the disparity between the state as an idea and the state as a configuration of organizations. I think this disparity offers a fertile ground from which to explore the contradictions and complexities of people's perceptions of the state.

Here I largely follow Philip Abrams's suggestions for the study of the state. Abrams (1988) suggests that the state is not only a *system* of power centered in government and more or less dominant in any modern society. The state is also an *idea* of legitimate authority. As such it is reified in speech and symbolized in state rituals and monuments so that it becomes a thing or a body that makes demands, requires loyalty, can be threatened or smashed, for which sacrifices can be made, etc. This has several important ramifications. First, the state is seen as transcending society. It may lead to the belief that state officials are, or can be, neutral arbiters who are not at the same time part of society as members of an ethnic group, a class, an extended family, etc. From the point of view of social groups, the state becomes "somebody else." Second, a high degree of coherence, unity, and autonomy is attributed to the state. Third, this discursive boundary between state and society is a technique of power that creates an authoritative body to which obedience or loyalty is required.[1]

Extending this view, it can be said that resistance or rebellion hinges on the same technique of separating state from society. In a study of a northern Indian village, Akhil Gupta (1995) shows that the villagers make a sharp distinction between the state and themselves in daily discussions on corruption. Through this theme of corruption, they develop the abstract notion of a bureaucratic and impartial state. They assess local state officials on the basis of this abstract principle, finding them wanting. This enables them to explain everyday incidents of power abuse in terms of moral decay that pervades the state but has no effect on society. Rather than a principle of authority, the state becomes the site of moral corruption. This notion, in turn, can be turned into social critique.

Corruption is a big theme in Pakistani politics. It was also on the tip of everyone's tongue in Pakka Qila. I think these discussions tell us a great deal about state-society relations in Pakistan today, and corruption will therefore be my focus in the following discussion on the crisis of state accountability. I will first look at the issue as it features in national politics and then continue to discuss what Pakka Qila residents have to say about corruption and the state.

Corruption and Accountability

Recently the Pakistani state has discovered its own crisis. After the dismissal of the Benazir Bhutto administration in November 1996, a commission was installed—the Accountability (*Ehtasab*) Commission—to combat corruption. The operation was given enormous publicity and presented as a massive effort to cure the Pakistani state of a contagious disease that had spread rapidly over the previous ten years or so. It was said that the objective was to restore bureaucratic transparency, which had supposedly once characterized the Pakistani state. Practices labeled as corruption were treated as alien to the system of governance, even though it was admitted that corruption had affected many parts of the state and had become a serious threat to the system.

The theme of corruption had been used earlier. When Bhutto was dismissed on the charge of corruption in 1996, she was not the first prime minister to face this allegation. Muhammad Khan Junejo in 1988, Benazir Bhutto in 1990, and Nawaz Sharif in 1993 were all dismissed on the same charge. And when Nawaz Sharif was dismissed a second time in 1999, corruption was once again one of the charges against him. These decisions invoked the ideal of the transparent state threatened by a less than transparent state performance. They promoted the notion that transparency was the norm and corruption an abomination. This, however, could only be maintained by ignoring the common practices of Pakistani politics.

Politics in Pakistan is highly personalized. Politicians usually flock around the party in power, which explains the common phenomenon of "floor-crossing," or *lotaism*, where politicians strategically change parties to increase their personal influence and wealth. In turn, leaders of established political parties like the Pakistan Muslim League and the PPP give favors to representatives of rich and influential families in their home districts to induce them to campaign for their party. Moreover, the implementation of regulations concerning development schemes, the issuing of leases, the distribution of jobs, etc., are based on personal networks, patron-client relations, extended family loyalties, and, increasingly, money. More generally, one can say that Pakistani politics is conducted according to the rule of reciprocity, or returning favors, which is a widely accepted norm in everyday social relationships but increasingly under attack in the political system.

When in the 1990s Nawaz Sharif accused Benazir Bhutto of corruption, or vice versa, it was difficult to believe that the political leaders wanted to put an end to a political culture both of them participated in. But this accusation was tied up with calls for reform that can now be heard everywhere in Pakistani society. Such calls get support from abroad. For instance, during the time of my fieldwork, Pakistan was second on a list of the most corrupt countries in the world. It led to many public comments. Some joked that it was to be Pakistan's tragic fate never to be the best in anything, be it cricket or corruption. Others countered that Pakistan had originally been at the top of the list but the government had bribed the makers of the list to put some African state in first place. In opposition to this skepticism, the Accountability Commission in 1997 presented itself as a truly bureaucratic enterprise. The national television network showed the chief ehtasab commissioner behind a huge pile of documents. He was also shown solemnly speaking with the president and high court judges against a background of high-ranking uniformed soldiers. For weeks the president and the interim prime minister issued statements that the bank accounts of every politician and every bureaucrat would be investigated and that no exception would be made.

Before long the commission itself became subject of controversy. After its installation the new government of Nawaz Sharif revoked most of its powers. The commission complained about the lack of cooperation from the government. Some files mysteriously disappeared. The "accountability benches" of the high court simply did not take up cases against high-ranking bureaucrats. Overnight lawyers lost interest in cases they had been working on for months. The government increasingly tried to use the commission to damage its political opponents. The commission that was supposed to restore transparency itself became opaque, leading to new accusations of corruption. When in 1999 the army under the leadership of General Musharraf took power, it immediately renewed the promise to restore transparency and accountability. As a result of all this talk about corruption, the legitimacy of state institutions is rapidly eroding.

The Postcolonial State

In the postcolonial period the political, bureaucratic, and military elites not only copied the institutional organization of the colonial state (Jalal 1995; Wheeler 1970; Ziring 1971), they also borrowed its style. The civil service was shaped in "the best traditions of colonial bureaucratic authoritarianism" (Jalal 1995: 37) and reading Ayub Khan's autobiography (1967) one gets the strong impression that the same is true for the military in which most of the high-ranking officers had been trained in the military academy of Sandhurst. The image state officials tried to promote of themselves bore a close resemblance to the public servant as a parental figure as glorified by the British colonial government. As Muneer Ahmad wrote in a study on the civil service in the 1960s in Lahore, "A section of the public service still seems to be devoted to the concepts of personal rule. For example, the officers of the Civil Service of Pakistan are still encouraged to adopt the role of *mai baap* (parents) to the people" (1964: 103). Many people continued to look at state institutions as foreign bodies, as they had done in colonial times. The unwritten dress code of civil servants continued to be pants and shirt. In Hyderabad people still located the state in the colonial parts of the city: the cantonment where the military resides; the city center with the church-like buildings of the former university campus; and the British colonial architecture of the central police station, the city administration, and the city court.

After 1970 the PPP had to bring the state apparatus under its control. The Civil Service of Pakistan was radically transformed whereas the nationalization of industries also added to the transformation and expansion of the state (A. Syed 1992: 120–40). New state institutions were founded, such as archives and conference buildings, aimed at renewing state prestige. This was especially important for the PPP, which initially lacked the authority of the military. These measures were primarily meant to drape the young PPP, which had inherited only half a state after the partition of 1971, with the trappings of state power. In addition, they also provided means for the redistribution of jobs.

The moment the state began to expand, however, it also began to fragment. This was partly the result of democratic elections. The political elite increasingly had to deal with groups gaining power through the democratic process. This process is going on even today. In Hyderabad, for instance, the elite exists of several established families tied together through social activities, marriages, and a common education. The colonial gymkhana or club still functions as an exclusive meeting place of the higher echelons of society. In ethnic terms the club is mixed. The languages spoken are Oxford-English and cultured Urdu while the young generation brings in its American accent. The families are either of the landed gentry, high-ranking members of the former Muslim League, or from a high-level bureaucratic or military background. One also sees many members of the two established political parties, the Pakistan Muslim League and the PPP. The older generation has been educated at the universities of Aligarh or Bombay. The younger generation studies abroad in the United Kingdom or the United States. Wedding parties can be regarded as extensions of the socializing in the gymkhana. The same goes for *iftar* parties that are held daily during the month of Ramzaan when it is time to break the fast at sunset. In these circles, too, one finds a great deal of nostalgia. People talk melancholically about the former days when national politics largely took place within their circles. Democratic elections gave power to parties that are not socially connected to the established elite, such as the "Islamic" parties and the MQM. The MQM has been a particular threat. Very few of the Muhajir elite families supported the MQM, and those who did were harshly criticized and ridiculed within their own circles up to the point where they were no longer invited to parties. In more covert ways, however, many links were established between the MQM and the established elite. These contacts were largely based on money. By means of private arrangements the latter bought the political favors of the new representatives. As one member of the elite told me, referring to the perceived low-caste status of MQM members: "Butchers and cobblers had never been part of our considerations, but now we have to receive them in our homes and do business with them."

This is a national trend. Behind the democratic scene, the postcolonial elitist families continue to wield considerable influence. But their influence is waning, a process that accelerates as more and more upper-middle-class families retreat from the public sphere to spend their time and money in private businesses. They live in enclaves aptly called "ghettos of the rich" (Hasan 1997) in relatively scenic locations—Karachi's narrow strip along the ocean, the Himalayan foothills of Islamabad—never far away from an international airport. As a result, Karachi has been called a "divided city," where the rich live in splendid isolation from the rest of society.[2]

State Violence and Secret Agencies

Democratization brought about not only increased political contestation but also more blatant use of state violence. As Thomas Blom Hansen (1996a: 351) argues, democratization transforms the state as it expands the "overt manipulation of central symbols" as well as increases the use of "covert strategies of undermining of adversaries." In the 1970s Zulfiqar Ali Bhutto masterfully deployed public humiliation as a political tool (Wolpert 1993: 239–40). As Anwar Syed (1992: 260) writes, during the rule of Bhutto "talk of violence became more profound in political speech than it had been before." His son Murtaza used murder as a political strategy (Anwar 1997: 179). State violence and public humiliation became more common in the 1980s. Public whipping was part of the "islamization program" by the military regime, while human rights commissions reported an increase in police and military brutality. In the more remote rural areas in particular, state forces regularly used rape to punish and humiliate. Human rights continued to be violated during the 1990s. According to human rights activists reporting on conditions in the central jail in Hyderabad, practices such as rape, urinating on a prisoner's body, or making prisoners squat in front of superiors are more common today than in the past.

Another phenomenon related to the heightened political contestation and the crisis of the state are the increasing activities of intelligence agencies as well as the talk thereof. The Inter Service Intelligence (ISI), run by the army, is the most well-known, efficient, and powerful agency. But in Hyderabad other state forces such as several police departments and the Rangers, a paramilitary organization, also had their own intelligence agencies. Given their secret nature it is difficult to learn much about them. But I got an impression of how widely they have infiltrated society. A man who said he was a secret intelligence agent asked for information about my activities in Pakka Qila. A couple of days later I mentioned this to a friend, whom I knew to be well-integrated in political circles. He suggested that the way to get rid of him would be casually informing the right persons about the harmless character of my work. The way to do this was to make a tour around the city and visit the persons my friend knew to be informers of some agency, drink a cup of tea, have a chat, and leave a benign impression. It took us a couple of days, visiting travel agencies, petrol stations, post offices, tea stalls and restaurants, shrines, offices of lawyers and NGOs, the press club, and several shops and workshops in the bazaars.

The *agencies*—another English word that had entered the vernacular—were also omnipresent in speech. Most political rumor in Hyderabad was about the agencies. They were generally believed to be all-powerful manipulators of politics. Almost all important political developments and events were said to be masterminded by them. An often-mentioned example is the founding of the MQM, which many people believed to be an ISI manipulation. The idea behind it was that the army in the mid-1980s needed another popular party in Sindh to break the back of the PPP, which was the main opponent of the military regime. To some extent the idea of omnipresence was fostered by the agencies themselves. They regularly showed traces of themselves, which generated more rumors. It made the situation in Hyderabad to some extent comparable to the socialist state of Romania prior to 1989, where the state spread distrust through the semi-secret presence of the Securitate in order to suppress anti-state activities (Verdery 1996).

Unlike Romania, however, the Pakistani state appears to be highly fragmented. The many intelligence agencies operating independent from and sometimes against each other are a case in point. The fragmentation of the state is partly the result of the fact that every new party in power adds its own state institutions to the already existing apparatus. Very often the new ruler does not seek to abolish institutions installed by his predecessor or to replace its staff. That could arouse too much resistance. Instead a new and competing institution is installed, staffed by people known to be loyal. As a result, state institutions compete rather than cooperate. During Operation Clean-up, for instance, the Pakistan Muslim League government brought the military to Sindh to curb the power of local police forces, most of which were known to be loyal to the PPP. A very different example of the fragmentation of the state has to do with the national history taught in schools. From Urdu-language schoolbooks, schoolchildren learn that Muhammad Ali Jinnah was born in Karachi. Books of the Sindhi Textbook Board, however, tell students that the Great Leader (*qaᶜid-i azam*) was born in Jhiruk, a Sindhi village near Thatta, south of Hyderabad.

On the one hand, the fragmentation of the state is a check on totalitarianism. On the other hand, it adds to the growing perception of the state as unreliable, volatile, and arbitrary. In addition to the image of the state as increasingly operating in a semi-secret and uncontrollable manner, this perception of unreliability critically affects the legitimacy of the traditional political elite. More than anything else, democratic elections express this quickly eroding faith in politics. Turnouts have been steadily on the decline, reaching an all-time low in 1997 with a turnout at just over 30 percent. People in Hyderabad took this as a powerful protest against successive governments.

The only state institution that at least to some extent has escaped this negative perception has been the army. Many people looked at the army as the only neutral and disciplined guardian of national unity. Given that, the absence of popular protest against the military coup of 1999 hardly came as a surprise.

Popular Perceptions of the State

What I have been suggesting thus far is that the widespread talk about corruption in Pakistan does not necessarily indicate an increase in corrupt practices. The expanding corruption discourse is rather a part of an ongoing transition in democratic politics that includes the rise of new popular-based political parties such as the MQM, the retreat of the postcolonial elite into the private sphere, and a changing, fragmenting state that increasingly and more openly deploys violence and secret agencies to rule. The fact that corruption has become a major theme of the political agenda signifies a demand to end the hegemony of the postcolonial elite, which for decades has dominated through a political culture of family networks and patron-client relations. In that sense, allegations of corruption have a much wider impact than merely on the person against whom the allegations are made. During the 1990s the leaders of the two main political parties, the Pakistan Muslim League and the PPP relentlessly accused each other of corruption, creating public distrust of democratic politics in general. Over time, however, popular-based parties employing the politics of identity, such as ethnic or "Islamic" parties, have also discredited themselves. In such a general atmosphere of disillusion, an authoritarian nostalgia emerged giving the military coup of October 1999 some legitimacy.

In Pakka Qila the theme of corruption was intermingled with ethnicity. That is to say that in Pakka Qila, too, the crisis of democratic politics was explained in terms of a corrupt state, but in addition the corruption of both state and politics was explained as an ethnic phenomenon. Pakka Qila men talked about the state as something they had lost to other ethnic groups, which were subsequently blamed for corruption. As Muhajirs, and therefore as Pakistani citizens, they felt entitled to a share of the state, but they also felt the state was being taken away from them by other ethnic groups. And these other ethnic groups—Punjabis, Sindhis—had not only captured the state but also used its institutions to enhance their own interests. Corruption not only caused Pakka Qila citizens to become disillusioned with the state and politics but also made them feel displaced as Muhajirs, foreigners in their own country.

In a sense, Pakka Qila residents identified strongly with the Pakistani state. As the direct outcome of Muslim nationalism, the state was for them a prize South Asian Muslims had won in their struggle for independence. As Muhajirs, having left India, they felt they had critically contributed to the success of this struggle. They had intrinsically linked their personal history of migration to a national history, interpreting their travel as a sacrifice for the new state of Pakistan. More than that, there was also the tendency to think that the state could not have been established without the efforts of Muhajirs. As the most educated, urban, and modernized South Asian Muslims, Muhajirs felt they had the mentality and the experience to run a state. Very often Pakka Qila residents told me stories about how Muhajirs had had to explain to local Sindhis the small—but to them important—details of running a modern state. Instead of sitting on carpets and rugs, for instance, one should use a table and chairs for meetings. The practice of documenting, and having these documents signed, countersigned, and stamped, was equally new to Sindhis, the stories in Pakka Qila asserted. The Pakhtun from the mountainous areas in the north were another people who did not understand the ways and laws of a modern state. They were considered a tribal people rather than primarily a rural people like the Sindhis. Their tribal customs such as blood feuds, could be admired as evidence of virility, but the Pakhtun were also said to hold onto their traditions with great stubbornness. It was difficult to convince them that in a modern and urban context authority lay with the bureaucratic law, which, most Pakka Qila men agreed, should be in line with the Islamic law (*shari'at*) in the Islamic state of Pakistan.

If they, as Muhajirs claiming to have significantly contributed to the state of Pakistan, felt entitled to a proportional share of its fruits, very few in Pakka Qila actually had access to state power and state resources. One man worked as a policeman and a few others were low-ranking civil servants, but for most residents of Pakka Qila the state was an impenetrable bastion. It was generally considered a waste of time and energy to apply for a job in the civil service because a Pakka Qila resident would never be allowed to join unless he was willing to pay a bribe as high as one year's salary. Other experiences with the state were equally negative and alienating. To have one's citizen rights upheld by civil servants, one had to rely on personal contacts or be willing and able to pay a considerable amount of money. The police were often hostile and condescending, setting up checkpoints to relieve passersby of their money. The police station housed in the palaces of the former Sindhi kings was seen as a foreign occupation.

As I already said, these negative experiences were explained in terms of ethnicity. The state was considered captured, and by extension polluted, by other ethnic groups, more precisely, by Punjabis and Sindhis. The police, for instance, was considered to be Sindhi dominated, in spirit if not in actual numbers. Punjabis were believed to be in control of the white-collar sections of the state. Put crudely, the Sindhis were said to rule the streets whereas the Punjabis dominated the assemblies, the courts, the officers' messes, etc.

Both groups were said to have captured the state by means of their unique form of solidarity, both equally in violation of the Pakistani principle of Muslim fraternity. Punjabis ruled by virtue of their kinship groups (*biradaris*). The abbreviation PIA, for instance, officially stood for Pakistan International Airlines, but to the Pakka Qila residents the real and concealed meaning was *Punjabi* International Airlines. The state-owned company—considered one of the most attractive suppliers of jobs in Pakistan, which, moreover, offered the opportunity to escape the country—was believed to be controlled by Punjabis defending their stronghold by way of kinship or *biradari* ties. A typical Punjabi extended family, it was said, distributed strategically important posts among brothers, uncles, and cousins. One was sent into the army, another covered the bureaucracy, a third took care of the landed property, numbers four and five did the dirty political work in the Pakistan Muslim League and the PPP respectively, number six started up a family branch in the United States, another joined the PIA. If one branch suffered, the others would make up for the losses. The Sindhi way of domination was described as following the vertical, "feudal," loyalty of patronage networks headed by a landlord. These landlords, known as *wadera* or *zamindar*, had their servants and clients in a firm grip. Anyone who tried to escape was said to be punished by the landlord's private army of heavily armed *dacoits* or rural bandits.[3]

From the Pakka Qila perspective, national politics was equally ethnicized. Although the two main political parties presented themselves as national parties, behind the scenes the PPP was dominated by Sindhi landlord families of which the Bhuttos were the primus inter pares. The PML was felt to be primarily a party of a limited number of Punjabi *biradaris*, as symbolized by the powerful positions former Prime Minister Nawaz Sharif and his brothers held within the Punjabi provincial administration. It was for ethnic reasons, then, that both parties were believed to be hostile to the MQM. Since Sindhis and Punjabis were more numerous than Muhajirs, chances were slim that the captive state could ever be freed.

Disillusion gave way to a renewed sense of diaspora. Captured by other ethnic groups, the Pakistani state now belonged to other people. It no longer felt like the Pakistan they had come to, the Pakistan of the 1950s and 1960s, which was so widely recalled as a land of hope, optimism, and national solidarity. Conquered from within, Pakistan had become a state ruled by internal foreigners, as it were, in which Muhajirs were like strangers and second-class citizens. It may be useful, then, to once again take a look at the self-imposed diasporic position of Muhajirs in Pakistan.

Reviving Diaspora

As several writers have argued, nationalism is a discourse that critically depends on the notion of territory (Anderson 1992, 1994; Appadurai 1990; Van der Veer 1995). The world of nations is a world divided in bordered contiguous tracts of land, each of which signifies the unity of its inhabitants. In such a world, migrants are often seen as a problem—"uprooted," an "abomination," "alien" (Douglas 1966; Malkki 1995; Sassen 1999). Exile (being cut off from the homeland), "internal exile" (the autochthonous population shares its territory with new settlers), as well as diaspora (the nation in search of a homeland) all contribute to the often ambiguous status of a migrant identity. Faced with such an ambiguous status, migrants may look backward to find consolation and certainty in a home in the past (Gardner 1993). Others may champion the hybridity of their identity as a gateway to the best of both or even multiple worlds.[4]

Given these recent debates, it seems only a matter of time before a book appears that takes up the issue and applies it to Muhajirs to argue that what we have here is another case of a migrant people crushed between nations and now stuck in limbo without a homeland, suffering from a diasporic national identity. That, however, would ignore the fact that displacement did not come with migration as such. Displacement and diaspora, now such central themes in present-day Muhajir identity, have come to haunt Muhajirs only much later. Individually, the first generation of migrants may always have had fond memories of their birthplace. For a long time, however, such nostalgia was hardly part of Muhajir public identity. Migration was rather interpreted as a renewal, a second birth into a new national community, a first step toward liberation and prosperity. This began to change in the 1970s, and in the 1980s the MQM gave voice to this growing sense of displacement. But the move back into diaspora only gained momentum in the 1990s along with a growing pessimism about the possibilities of positive change.

As argued earlier, Muslim artists and intellectuals in North India first formulated the notion of diaspora in the nineteenth century. Several Urdu poets wrote melancholically about the Indian Muslims as essentially foreign to the Indian soil, "guests," who had already stayed too long. A cultural Muslim elite itself therefore largely imposed the foreignness of Muslims. The diasporic identity was part of that. Having lost an empire and a civilization in India, Muslims had no other place to go to (Jalal 1997). The trope of loss and decay was firmly established and continues today, but with the founding of the Muslim League and, later, the rise of the Pakistan Movement the self-imposed foreignness ceased to be a source of melancholy and instead became the basis for national action.

Migration was at the core of Pakistani nationalism. Pakistan was conceived as a homeland of an essentially diasporic people, tracing their roots to foreign territories such as Persia, Central Asia, and Arabia. Besides, the process of nation building was compared to the Islamic exodus or *hijra*, reinterpreted as a move away from particularistic loyalties in favor of a national identity. Initially, then, Pakistani nationalism ideologically lacked a territorial basis. Muhammad Iqbal, for instance, was critical about a territorial notion of the Pakistani nation as it ran counter to his belief in universal moral values (Masud 2002). Pakistan was imagined instead in Islamic traditions of travel. With the emancipation of regional groups, more and more territorial, mystical, and "ethnic" elements were added to the national identity. It was to this change that groups of Muhajirs reacted by founding the MQM.

This reaction of the MQM—especially the youth who were at the heart of the movement—was much more innovative than is often acknowledged. It was far from a conservative and reactionary movement that tried to defend the privileged position of the Muhajir middle class in Pakistani society. The movement came out of marginalized neighborhoods like Pakka Qila. It presented a picture of Muhajirs that radically differed from an earlier image of Muhajirs as shaped by Islamic modernism. The movement created a culture of street humor, physicality, and competitive masculinity, which challenged the high cultural, Islamic modernist, formal education–oriented culture of middle-class Muhajirs. There was not much room for nostalgia and diaspora in this movement either.

Originally a youthful and subversive movement, the MQM became increasingly violent over time. Initially the MQM was primarily a movement of practical jokes and irreverent humor, but the *fun* had the tendency to escalate into festive spectacles of arson and destruction. The state retaliated with a vengeance, which the MQM tried to counter by a language of oppression and justice. While the rhetoric of tyranny and martyrdom increased, the violence evoked memories of partition and new visions of national purity in Pakka Qila. Several years later, violence had become routine and included extrajudicial methods of state persecution as well as the collection of *bhatta* and other forms of power abuse by local MQM activists.

The notion of diaspora returned with the advent of large-scale ethnic violence, state persecution, and a widening gap between state and society giving way to popular distrust of state institutions and nostalgia for authoritarianism. During my fieldwork in 1996 and 1997 there was a general fear that eventually a new partition would occur, pushing Muhajirs to an even more marginal position. No one expected help from inside Pakistan once that happened, and many were also skeptical about the chances of foreign intervention. Muhajirs felt that the outside world, including the

United Nations, was generally hostile to Muslims and did not expect support from abroad if there was a civil war in Sindh. In this way, the foreign negative images of Muslims added to the widespread diasporic identity among Muhajirs.

Many people thought they had few or no options left. One opportunity, open only to a few, was further migration. There was a great eagerness, especially among young people, to leave Pakistan and settle elsewhere. The West in particular appeared highly attractive. But with the West, as well as the Middle East, practically closed, some tried their luck in East Asia—Japan, Taiwan, Singapore—where several reportedly lived as illegal laborers.

There were also signs of renewed zest for Islam among the youth. A new missionary pietist movement had arisen calling itself the Dawat-i Islami. Launched in Karachi in the early 1980s, it began to attract more followers in the mid-1990s, especially from the post–MQM Muhajir generation. Dawat-i Islami disciples were easily recognized by their green turbans and seamless white garments. Modeled on the much older proselytizing movement known as the Tabligh-i Jam'iat, the Dawat-i Islami embraced more expressivist practices such as ecstatic and meditational *zikr* sessions. It generally had a more Barelwi outlook than the more modernist Tabligh-i Jam'iat. It called itself strictly apolitical, which in itself was a political statement in line with the general public contempt for politics, and it looked at the green mosque of Medina rather than the national assembly in Islamabad as its center. The movement had a very large center in Karachi and a smaller one in Hyderabad. Although it was too early to tell then what its impact would be, it seemed to have the potential to grow and was watched with apprehension by MQM activists.

Aspirations, then, again lay abroad—in Medina as well as the consumer societies of the West. To some extent these aspirations reflected a revived diasporic identity, based on a tradition founded in the nineteenth century, buried under optimism in the postcolonial era, then rejuvenated along with growing disillusion with the state and an even greater disappointment with the Muhajir Qaumi Movement.

Epilogue

THIS BOOK is an historical ethnography of the Muhajir Qaumi Movement, its rise, its heyday, and its imminent decline, seen from the perspective of Pakka Qila, one of the movement's strongholds in the city of Hyderabad. I have tried to show how the MQM has changed since its advent in the mid-1980s. Initially the MQM was a hopeful movement, which provided its supporters with ample opportunities for enjoyment, laughter, public spectacle, and the illusion of living life out of the ordinary. When it grew larger, it entered the established arenas of national and provincial politics and became a threat to other, more established political parties, with which it was increasingly in often violent competition. The MQM leadership began to distance itself from a peer-group culture of street humor, masculine and dangerous play, ethnic pride, and irreverence for high cultural Islamic modernist traditions. Instead, it took to a language of tyranny, justice, and righteousness, steeped in Islamic traditions of martyrdom and sacrifice—in particular the story of Karbala and the *hijra*. By focusing on the events of May 1990, when Pakka Qila found itself under attack by state forces, I have tried to demonstrate how and in what context the vision of national primordial purity is produced. State oppression became better organized and more effective, especially after the creation of the breakaway MQM-Haqiqi, as well as the launching of Operation Cleanup, the military operation against the MQM accompanied by a political campaign to make the MQM out to be a "terrorist" organization. This campaign significantly curbed the powers of the MQM and isolated many of its hardcore members, who became full-time professional party workers, often willing to engage in high-risk activities. For its ordinary supporters, however, the MQM became less and less appealing, as it could no longer provide prospects of radical change, empowerment, or enjoyment. On the other hand, state persecution and the stigma of terrorism also enabled the MQM to maintain its image of a movement driven by a self-effacing and awe-inspiring determination to fight the powers of tyranny and evil. The hope of earlier days, however, was gone and an atmosphere of nostalgia prevailed, which is part of the political crisis in Pakistan today, throwing Muhajirs back into a diasporic identity.

In describing these changes, I have rejected the idea that the MQM can be analyzed as the project of an upcoming, would-be middle class, aspiring to take the seats now occupied by the established political and cultural elites. Instead I have argued that the MQM signifies a larger transformation of politics in Pakistan. One of the characteristics of this transformation is that the middle class is losing its politically paramount position. The postcolonial elite no longer determines the styles, discourses, and arenas of politics. In effect, Sindhi or bazaar Urdu can now be the language of political speech as much as cultured Urdu or English. The physically potent politician, backed by a gang of armed strongmen, now competes with his educated, *ashraf*, urban colleague. Partly because of the rise of the MQM, the streets of formerly marginal neighborhoods have become important sites of political action in addition to the established political arenas such as assembly halls, press clubs, and university campuses.

To analyze the MQM as a part of this transition, I have found it helpful to use the concept of the ludic or *fun*, the latter being a popular term among MQM supporters to denote their own activities. Seemingly simple and clear, *fun* is actually a rather complex concept. It is made up of several aspects, some of which are worthwhile to recall here.

I have described *fun* as primarily a peer-group phenomenon. One of the more important findings of this study is perhaps that peer groups of young men are among the most relevant social groupings in which to study present-day nationalist identity and violence. This has hardly been appreciated thus far. Very little research has been conducted on young male peer groups and their relationship to questions of nationalism, religion, and identity. The study of nationalist and religious discourse in Pakistan, and perhaps in Islamic and South Asian studies in general, has primarily focused on the family, the patriarch, the saint, the clergy, the urban intellectual, and the politician. This has had clear implications for the interpretation of particular cultural institutions. One example is the notion of male honor. Male honor has mainly been analyzed functionally in relation to the family, but there seems to be enough evidence to suggest that profound expressions of masculinity and male sovereignty are found outside the family in the peer groups of young men. Feminist studies have challenged the emphasis on the patriarch, but they have hardly probed into domains outside of and alternative to the family. This is all the more problematic given the fact that a very large proportion of the population in societies like Pakistan consists of people in their teens and twenties who spend a great deal of time in gendered peer groups in schools, streets, gyms, social movements, Internet communities, and religious organizations.

Studying nationalism in such groups is likely to shed a different light on the topic. The youth almost by definition stand in an ambiguous position toward dominant discourses. When cohorts of the young and impatient want to provoke a generational conflict, they have to distance themselves somewhat from dominant society in order to create a space for themselves within society. In asserting and appropriating dominant ideology for their own purposes, they will take it as an object for investigation, debate, ridicule, and skepticism.

This disciplining process, which takes place in peer groups and on the streets rather than within the family and in schools, comes with a great deal of humor when it is done in the ritual-like situation of a public party meeting. An important feature of these happenings is the collective joy they generate. This makes these public meetings attractive and worthwhile to attend and take part in. This enjoyment should not be interpreted primarily in relation to a lack of other opportunities for leisure and recreation in Pakistan. That would be an explanation of political mobilization in terms of boredom and, ultimately, unemployment—an explanation that is popular in the right-wing press and the established elite. At the risk of being accused of romanticizing the early MQM, I rather take *fun* as an expression of joy generated by a self-conscious awareness of the impurity and ambiguousness of identity. The public ritual-like atmosphere enabled the young partakers to be more than one person, to act in a self-contradictory manner, and to play out an ambiguous identity.

Through these public events, the young MQM recuperated a public image for Muhajirs that had been denied to them during a process of nation building and the construction of ethnic identities. The new Muhajir identity promoted by the MQM was a rich and paradoxical reconciliation of complementary but contradictory discourses on Muslim nationalism and ethnic solidarity, Islamic modernism and Sufism, the *hijra* and grave worship, reason and passion, the cold and the hot. The MQM, for instance, appropriated many symbols, passions, and moods that had been defined as rural and Sindhi. Although generally speaking not partaking in the youthful events, many of the older generation also appreciated the humor and irreverence and spoke sympathetically of the MQM as initially and essentially a cheerful party.

The humor of these happenings points to yet another dimension of the new public Muhajir identity. *Fun* did not merely make it possible to recuperate a lost set of discourses for Muhajirs and to use them as a counterbalance for the set of discourses already available to them. More than that, fun and humor articulated an ambivalent, and often downright provocative attitude toward ideology as such. The self-contradictory character of Muhajir identity did not bother young MQM supporters much as the distinction between the nation and ethnicity was of little importance to them. If they indulged in anything at all, it was in provocation and transgression rather than a desire for primordial purity and discursive coherence.

The word *fun* may be misunderstood. It may be taken as just cheerful and therefore quite unimportant. That, however, would underestimate the creative power of the youthful, ludic, collective gatherings. I believe that the effervescent and euphoric atmosphere of public activities and manifestations not only enabled MQM supporters to distance themselves from the dominant discourses of society, conveyed to them by their parents, teachers, religious leaders, politicians, etc., but also formed the kernel of their collective identity. I have argued that the shared enjoyment experienced in collective provocation and irreverence serves as an identity marker separating generations, classes, and ethnic groups. In this way, the MQM supporters set themselves apart from the older generation, from the Muhajir elite, and from the former Muhajir-dominated "Islamic" parties like the Jam'iat-i Islami, as well as from the Sindhis, the Pakhtun, and the Punjabis. To a large extent, *fun*, as defined by the MQM youth, was an urban, cosmopolitan, modern asset, enabling them to give a new meaning to the notion of Muhajirs as urban modernists.

Finally, I have also used *fun* as a starting point for explaining a particular form of violence—a form that may be called "dangerous play." Many aspects of violence, such as euphoria, transgression, role reversal, and cruel humor, characterize this form of violence. I have not explained these phenomena with the help of theories that ascribe to the perpetrator of such acts of violence a distorted or perverse relationship with his victim. I have rather interpreted these cases of euphoria in relation to the escalating potential in a competitive masculine subculture within peer groups. These groups, like any social group, are as much characterized by a sense of solidarity as by an internal competition for power and recognition. Already standing somewhat outside mainstream society and often lacking formal leadership, such groups may put pressure on members to show their wit and courage by going beyond the limits of what is generally deemed morally acceptable. Transgression may become a virtue through which one can win social status within the group. Internally, such acts will be shared as good jokes and remembered as stories that elicit laughter.

However brutal such practical jokes may be for their victims, on the basis of the material presented in this book I am inclined to think that there is a limit to their cruelty. In most of the cases I have described, groups of young men indulged in arson, looting, and the public humiliation of their victims. Large-scale killing, however, seemed to require a different kind of mood. However difficult it is to reconstruct such incidents, I have focused extensively on the weeks of ongoing ethnic cleansing in Hyderabad in the summer of 1990. I have tried to demonstrate that for the residents of Pakka Qila this episode constituted a clear break from the excitement and euphoria of their earlier MQM experiences. A major difference was that they found themselves under the attack of hostile state forces. That, including the acute presence of life-threatening violence, made people turn to transhistoric models of crisis in an effort to make sense of the situation, to mobilize potential allies, and to legitimize their actions. As I have shown, two such models were especially important. The story of Karbala, as a story of tyranny and martyrdom, played an important role in mobilizing resistance, while the partition of 1947, already interpreted as a repetition of the *hijra*, shaped the imagination of national purity and the vision of a final solution.

Turned into a moment of extreme antagonism, May 1990 has been important in the renewal of a diasporic Muhajir identity, fostered also by public disillusion with the state and the political process. To end on a more positive note, however, it must also be said that as time passed, it became again possible to resist the ethnic polarization between Muhajirs and Sindhis with reference to the ideal of Muslim unity. Acknowledging the simultaneous existence of the two contradictory discourses on religious solidarity and ethnic exclusivity, and therewith also of the relativity of both, Muhajirs in Hyderabad have been living alongside their Sindhi neighbors since 1990. While disappointed by the fact that the future looks less grand and heroic than it did in the 1980s, most residents of Pakka Qila have also learned to appreciate the delicate quiet of everyday life in Hyderabad. Arguments of nationalist or religious purity are today mostly met with skepticism.

Calendar of Events

14 August 1947	Independence of Pakistan.
December 1970	First democratic elections, won by Pakistan People's Party (PPP).
January 1971	Language riots in Karachi and Hyderabad between Urdu and Sindhi speakers.
July 1972	New round of language riots in Karachi and Hyderabad after the presentation of the language bill in the Sindh Provincial Assembly.
March 1977	National elections, won by PPP; military coup led by Zia-ul Haq.
11 June 1978	Founding of the All Pakistan Muhajir Student Organization.
August 1983	Armed uprising in rural areas of Sindh against the military regime of General Zia-ul Haq.
18 March 1984	Founding of the Muhajir Qaumi Movement.
April 1985	Large-scale riots between Pakhtun and Biharis in Orangi Township and Liaqatabad in Karachi.
8 August 1986	First public meeting of the MQM in Karachi.
31 October 1986	First public meeting of the MQM in Hyderabad, resulting in large-scale anti-Pakhtun violence by MQM supporters in Karachi and Hyderabad.
December 1986	Anti-drug operations by state forces in Sohrab Goth and Orangi Township in Karachi, leading to ethnic riots between Pakhtun and Muhajirs in Karachi.
Winter 1986–87	Pakka Qila youth loots the Archeological Department inside the citadel. The employees of the department do not return.
November 1987	Local elections, won by the MQM in Karachi and Hyderabad.
March 1988	First incident of tension between MQM supporters and Sindhi nationalists in Hyderabad when the former restyle the centrally located Hyder Chowk by replacing Sindhi symbols with posters of Muhajir heroes.
17 August 1988	President Zia-ul Haq dies when his aircraft crashes.
30 September 1988	"Black Friday" in Hyderabad: militants of Sindhi Taraqqi Pasand Party kill dozens of Muhajirs in Hyderabad. MQM militants take revenge in Karachi the following day.
November 1988	National elections, won by PPP and MQM. Both parties form a coalition in both the provincial and national assemblies.

April 1989	MQM leadership visits Hyderabad to persuade the local party supporters to follow party policy.
October 1989	MQM leaves the coalition and joins the opposition led by the Pakistan Muslim League (PML) of Nawaz Sharif.
April 1990	Altaf Hussain holds a hunger strike to protest state persecution of MQM supporters.
May 1990	Police operation against illegally held weapons in Pakka Qila leads to siege of the area, police violence against demonstrating civilians, and weeks of ethnic cleansing in Hyderabad and other towns and villages in Sindh.
6 August 1990	Prime Minister Benazir Bhutto is dismissed by the president.
October 1990	National elections are won by the Pakistan Muslim League. The MQM wins more votes than ever in Karachi, Hyderabad, and smaller Sindhi towns.
June 1991	The MQM-Haqiqi is founded.
1 January 1992	Altaf Hussain leaves for London "for medical treatment."
28 May 1992	Operation Clean-up launched. The military takes over Sindh to fight urban "terrorism" and rural "banditry."
May 1993	MQM chairman Azim Ahmad Tariq is killed in his house.
October 1993	New national elections are held after the dismissal of the PML–run administration. The MQM boycotts the national elections but takes part in the provincial elections. The PPP wins the elections and Benazir Bhutto again becomes prime minister
1994–95	Increasing violence in Karachi among MQM-Altaf, MQM-Haqiqi, and state forces.
February 1997	Landslide victory for the PML in new national elections, which became necessary after the dismissal of the PPP–led government several months earlier. The MQM wins most seats in Karachi and Hyderabad, albeit with smaller margins. The party joins the PML–dominated government in Sindh. Several party workers return from exile, are freed from jail, or join public life again after having lived underground.
October 1998	The MQM leaves the coalition in Sindh. Several MQM workers again go into hiding.
October 1999	Military coup led by General Musharraf; Nawaz Sharif's second government is dismissed.
Autumn 2001	Anti–U.S. demonstrations in large cities after the Al Qaeda attacks on New York and Washington and the military actions against the Taliban government in Afghanistan. The MQM stages an anti-Taliban demonstration in Karachi.
October 2002	National elections won by the PML, followed by PPP and the Muttehida Majlis-e-Amal (MMA), a coalition of "Islamic" parties. The MQM wins in Karachi and Hyderabad.

Glossary

ajlaf — Lower-caste Muslim groups; plural of *jilf.*
akhara — Club; gymnasium.
amir — Leader; commander.
am log — Common people.
ʿaql — Reason; intelligence, etc.
ashraf — Higher-caste Muslim groups; plural of *sharif.*
ʿashura — Tenth day of Muharram.
awam — People.

baiʿat — Oath of allegiance given to Sufi saints.
bania — Hindu moneylender or trader.
baqr ʿid — The feast of the sacrifice commemorating Abraham's offering of his son Ishmael.
barakat — Blessing; spiritual power.
bayan — Left.
bhai — Brother.
bhukhartal — Hunger strike.
biradari — Brotherhood; kin-group.
buzdil — Weak of heart.

chadar — Decorative sheet; cover.
chalak — Schemer.
chowk — Square in center of city or neighborhood.

dacoit — Bandit; brigand.
dahshatgard — Terrorist.
dar al-harb — Lands of war.
dar al-islam — Lands under Muslim rule or lands in which Muslim institutions are maintained.
dargah — Shrine or tomb.
dayan — Right.
desh — Country; region; territory.
dil — Heart.
din ki qurbani — Religious sacrifice.
dunya ki qurbani — Worldly sacrifice.

ehtasab — Accountability.

gharib log — Poor people.
goonda — Rake; gang leader.
gunah — Wrong deed; sin.
gunahgar — Sinner.

hadis — The sayings of the Prophet Muhammad.
hafiz — A person who has memorized the Qur'an.
hajj — Annual pilgrimage to Mecca.
halfnama — A declaration of oath.
haq — Just; true; righteous.
haqiqi — Eternal; real; true.
haq parast — Truth loving.
hari — Peasant.
hijra — Exodus.
hosla — Will power; ambition; courage.

'id ul-fitr — Great feast following the fast of Ramzaan.
ijtihad — Individual inquiry to establish the ruling of the shari'at by a person
   qualified for the inquiry.
'ilm — Knowledge.
iman — Faith.
insaf — Justice; fairness.
'ishq — Passionate, passive love.
ittehad — Unity.
'izzat — Honor.

jalal — Hot; powerful; terrible.
jamal — Cool; passive; beautiful.
jang — War.

kacca — Made of mud or clay.
kalima — Confession of faith.
kaliya — "Black."
Karbala — Battlefield where Imam Hussain was martyred.
khak — Dust.
khairat — Charity.
khalifa — One who receives successorship from a saint.
khidmat — Service; charity.

majlis — Mourning assembly.
majzub — One who is absorbed in the love of God; madman.
makha — Locust.
markaz — Center.
masjid — Mosque.
mast — Intoxication; "hot" passion.
mastan — He who is absorbed in *mast.*
matam — Physical acts of mourning.
matamdars — Performer of *matam.*
mazar — Tomb of martyr or saint.
mazlum — Oppressed people.
mela — Fair.

millat — "Nation"; in the Ottoman Empire, one of the recognized autonomous religious communities.

mochi — Cobbler caste.

mohallah — Neighborhood.

muhajir — Partakers in the Prophet's exodus; migrants from India now living in Pakistan.

mujahid — Soldier in a war against non-Muslims.

mulk — Country.

munafiq — Hypocrite; one who sows discord among Muslims.

musawat — Social justice; principle of equality of believers.

nafs — Bio-psychological powers; breath.

nazm — Discipline.

nazrana — Tributary gifts for a saint.

nur — Light.

pak — Pure.

pardah — Practice of segregation of women.

pir — Saint.

qaʿid — Leader.

qaʿid-i awam — Leader of the people. Title claimed by Zulfiqar Ali Bhutto.

qaʿid-i azam — Supreme leader; Jinnah's title.

qaʿid-i tehreek — Leader of the movement; Altaf Hussain's title.

qalandar — Sufi order; holy man; beggar.

qasai — Butcher caste.

qaum — People; tribe; family; caste.

qawwali — Musical style as part of devotional exercises inducing ecstasy.

qila — Citadel; fortress; castle.

qurbani dena — To sacrifice.

Ramzaan — The month of fasting.

ruh — Spirit.

sadaqa — Voluntary charity.

sajjada nishin — Descendant of a Sufi saint.

shab-i-barat — The night of the fourteenth of Shaʿban when Muslims make offerings in the name of deceased ancestors.

shaheed — Martyr.

shakhs — Personhood.

shariʿat — Islamic law.

shirk — Idol worship.

shuhada — Plural of *shaheed* (martyr).

silsilah — "Chain" of Sufis who share spiritual descent from a common founder.

siyasat — Politics.

sufi — An exponent of Sufism.

syed — Group or caste of the ritually pure claiming direct descent of the Prophet.

tehreek — Movement.
tamasha — Spectacle; show.
tasawwuf — Sufism.
tawiz — Amulet.
taziya — Effigies of tombs, etc., used in Muharram processions.

ᶜulama — Learned men; plural of *ᶜalim*.
ᶜumma — Community of Muslims.

wahdat ul-wujud — Unity of being.
wuzu — Ritual ablution.

zaban — Language.
zakat — Canonical tithe; religious tax.
zalim — Tyrant.
zat — Caste.
zulm — Tyranny.

Notes

INTRODUCTION

1. See also Tambiah (1996: ch. 11).

CHAPTER ONE
ETHNICIZING ISLAM

1. *Dawn Newspaper*, 17 August 1947.

2. See Barth (1969) for a critique on primordialist approaches to ethnicity.

3. See Cohen (1985) for the symbolic construction of community.

4. Aligarh is primarily associated with the Muhammadan Anglo-Oriental College and the Aligarh movement established by Syed Ahmad Khan. These institutions were shaped by both religious reform and exposure to British colonial institutions and culture. The Aligarh college opened in 1875 to provide English education to the sons of well-born Muslim families in order to protect the interests of those Muslim families who had had important positions within the government. The Aligarh movement represents a form of accommodation to the changed political situation of the late nineteenth century that sought to enhance the self-consciousness of the Muslim urban elite and bring Islam in accordance with Western ideas.

5. In a personal conversation with me, Professor Nabi Bakhsh Baloch mentioned the important role the Khaksar Movement may have played in the 1930s to promote a Muslim Sindhi political identity among young Sindhi students and intellectuals (compare Talbot 1996: 62–63). Most historians writing about the rise of Muslim nationalism in Sindh, however, focus on the role of the Muslim League. There is therefore very little known about the impact of other organizations.

6. *Dawn Newspaper*, 28 January 1974.

7. The quote is from the brochure of the committee organizing a cultural program on the occasion of the World Cup Cricket.

8. Kurin's analysis is influenced by cognitive structuralism and resembles E. Valentine Daniel's book (1984) on South-Indian Tamils in which he argues that an ontology of difference and balance underlies thinking on all levels: cosmic, psychological, and social.

9. See I. Ahmad (1976, 1978), Barth (1960), Donnan (1988), Dumont (1972), Fischer (1991), Leach (1960), Lindholm (1986), and Werbner (1989, 1990).

10. *Dawn Newspaper*, 17 September 1947.

11. These include the Deobandi Movement, the Aligarh school, and the Ahl-i Hadis. The leaders of the Deobandi Movement, established in 1867, sought to renew Islamic spiritual life by teaching early Islamic principles in a context of colo-

nial rule that had deprived the Muslims of state power. The Muhammadan Anglo-Oriental College and the Aligarh Movement, opened in 1875, also contributed to an increased religious self-consciousness among Muslims as a separate community in India, fostering the use of Urdu as a language of distinction among Indian Muslims but, in contrast to the Deobandi Movement, seeking an active political role in relation to the colonial government. The Ahl-i Hadis, finally, was a late nineteenth-century Muslim intellectual movement with an avowedly sectarian, Sunni character. See Metcalf (1982).

CHAPTER TWO
THE MUHAJIR QAUMI MOVEMENT

1. *Dawn Newspaper*, 19 November 1988.
2. Haq Parast means "truth-loving."
3. These brochures include: *Karachi Kept on Burning (Karachi Jalta Rahaa)* by Safdar Shaheen (Multan: Book Land, n.d.); *The Rule of the Poor: A Historic Press Conference of MQM's Leader, Altaf Hussain (Ghariboon ki Hukmaraani: MQM ke Qaʿ id Altaf Hussain ki ek Tarikhi Press Conference)* by the MQM Information and Publicity Department (1991); *What Is the MQM's Policy? An Important Policy Statement of Movement's Leader Altaf Hussain (MQM ki policy kiya hai? Qaʿ id-i-tahreek Altaf Hussain ka aham policy bayan)*, author unknown (Karachi: Muhajir Academy, n.d.); *Objective Resolution: What Does Muhajir Qaumi Movement Aspire For? (Qarardad-e Maqasid: Muhajir Qaumi Movement Kiya Chahti hai?)* MQM Publicity Department (1988); *MQM Demands Fundamental and Constitutional Rights for Mohajirs*, by MQM (Karachi, 1994); *Nothing But the Whole Truth*, by Research and Information Cell MQM (London, n.d.), *A Brief History of the Mohajir Qaumi Movement* (probably published by London head office of the MQM; place and date of publication unmentioned).
4. The Chishtiyya order is one of the larger Sufi orders among Muhajirs. Originally established in the Afghan town of Chisht, it is now essentially an Indian order, which has its center in Ajmer in Rajasthan at the shrine of its founder, Khwaja Muinuddin Chishti. Holy men or *pirs* within this or other lineages, such as the Qadriyya or the Nasqbandiyya order, play a considerable role in religious practices such as sessions of meditation (*zikr*) or religious education.
5. *Dawn Newspaper*, 11 June 1978.
6. *Dawn Newspaper*, 12 June 1992.
7. Translated from the original Urdu study by Munir Ahmad, titled *MQM*.
8. *Dawn Newspaper*, 17 March 1984.
9. Both quotes are from *Dawn Newspaper*, 30 September 1989.
10. *Dawn Newspaper*, 29 December 1986.
11. *Dawn Newspaper*, 7 November 1986.
12. *The Muslim*, 1 November 1986.
13. *The News*, 14 June 1987.
14. *Daily News*, 25 June 1989.
15. See Nasr (1994: 47–80) for the party structure of the JI.
16. *Dawn Newspaper*, 22 August 1988.

17. Sindhudesh was the name adopted by Sindhi separatists for a future independent state of Sindh. It was modeled on the name Bangladesh, *desh* meaning land or country.

18. *Star*, 18 August 1986.

19. *Morning News*, 12 March 1988.

20. *Dawn Newspaper*, 10 October 1988.

21. *Frontier Post*, 10 May 1989.

22. *Dawn Newspaper*, 26 April 1989.

23. *Star*, 30 April 1989.

24. *The Muslim*, 23 May 1989.

25. *Daily News*, 8 April 1990.

26. *Morning News*, 10 April 1990.

27. *Daily News*, 9 April 1990.

28. *Morning News*, 14 April 1990.

29. *Frontier Post*, 27 April 1990.

30. *The Muslim*, 11 November 1988.

31. *Frontier Post*, 15 July 1991.

32. *Dawn Newspaper*, 26 July 1991.

33. The controversy about Ahmad Tariq's murder continues. In December 1998, four former MQM workers were arrested in Peshawar. They declared to have murdered Azim Ahmad Tariq on orders of the MQM-Altaf leadership. The allegations were, however, denied by spokesmen of the MQM-Altaf (*Dawn Newspaper*, 5 and 6 December 1998).

34. *Herald Magazine*, February 1997.

CHAPTER THREE
PAKKA QILA

1. From an unpublished and undated document titled *Report on the Use/Encroachment of Archaeological Area of Pucca Fort, Hyderabad*, by the Government of Pakistan Department of Archaeology.

2. See also Karim and Robinson (1986) for figures on independence-related migration.

3. Khoja stands for a high-status group or caste of South Asian Muslims.

CHAPTER FOUR
FUN AND VIOLENCE

1. The original Urdu poem reads as follows: "Apne ke but ko dha sako, to mere sath calo / Khud apne apko mita sako, to mere sath calo / Purana ghar par nazar hai, to lot jao abhi / Khud apna ghar jala sako, to mere sath calo."

2. This information comes from an unpublished and undated report of the department's staff titled *Report on the Use/Encroachment of Archaeological Area of Pucca Fort, Hyderabad*.

CHAPTER FIVE
MAKING MARTYRS

1. The notion of "condensation" is borrowed from Victor Turner's discussion on ritual. Turner uses Edward Sapir's distinction between "referential" and "condensation" symbols to explain why ritual turns the obligatory into the desirable. Referential symbols are "economical devices for purposes of reference" and lack the emotional tension of condensation symbols, which are defined as "highly condensed forms of substitutive behavior for direct expression." According to Turner, ritual symbols are at once referential and condensation symbols, but shifting the emphasis to the latter capacity, ritual action can transform predominantly cognitive symbols into strong emotional stimuli (1967: 28–30).

2. From the monthly magazine *The Herald*, June 1990, p. 33.

3. Ibid., 34.

4. Ibid., 40.

5. *Frontier Post*, 25 July 1990.

6. *Star*, 19 June 1990.

7. Junagadh used to be a semi-independent state within British India and is now a town in the Indian province of Gujerat. It had a large Muslim population as well as several educational institutions that attracted Muslim students from various places in northwest India, including present-day Pakistan. Ajmer is an important place of pilgrimage for Indian Muslims, located in present-day Rajasthan.

8. *Dawn Newspaper*, 20 July 1990.

9. *Dawn Newspaper*, 11 June 1990.

10. *Dawn Newspaper*, 20 July 1990.

11. *Daily News*, 23 August 1990.

12. *Daily News*, 30 August 1990.

13. Ibid.

CHAPTER SIX
TERRORISM AND THE STATE

1. The distinction made by Philip Abrams between the state apparatus and the state idea has informed recent thinking about the state. See Steinmetz (1999) for a good overview of social theorizing on processes of state formation and state power. See also Mitchell (1991, 1999) for an elaboration of the distinction made by Abrams. See Hansen and Stepputat (2001) for ethnographical explorations and elaborations of the notion that the state is as much a product of the imagination as it is a practice of coercion.

2. This theme has been beautifully captured in a recent feature film by director Hasan Zaidi, titled *Raat Chali Hai Jhoom Ke* (The Long Night), which shows the affluent living increasingly hermetic lives, untouched by the chaos, language, and violence of other parts of the city, resulting in a lack of a common ground where the privileged and underprivileged can come together.

3. See Verkaaik (2001) for an elaboration of this argument.

4. See for instance Bhabha (1994). See Van der Veer (1997) for a critique of Bhabha's defense of cosmopolitanism.

Bibliography

Abou Zahab, Mariam. 2002. "The Regional Dimension of Sectarian Conflicts in Pakistan." *Pakistan: Nationalism without a Nation?* ed. C. Jaffrelot, 115–28. New Delhi: Manohar.

Abrams, Philip. 1988. "Notes on the Difficulty of Studying the State." *Journal of Historical Sociology* 1(1): 58–89.

Ahmad, Imtiaz, ed. 1976. *Family, Kinship and Marriage among Muslims in India.* New Delhi: Manohar.

———. 1978. *Caste and Social Stratification among the Muslims.* Delhi: Manohar.

Ahmad, Mujeeb. 1993. *Jamʿiyyat ʿUlama-i-Pakistan, 1948–1979.* Islamabad: National Institute of Historical and Cultural Research.

Ahmad, Muneer. 1964. *The Civil Servant in Pakistan: A Study of the Background and Attitudes of Public Servants in Lahore.* Karachi: Oxford University Press.

Ahmad, Riaz. 1987. *Foundations of Pakistan II.* Islamabad: Quaid-e-Azam University.

Ahmed, Akbar S. 1988. *Discovering Islam: Making Sense of Muslim History and Society.* London: Routledge.

Ahmed, Feroz. 1998. *Ethnicity and Politics in Pakistan.* Karachi: Oxford University Press.

Ahsan, Aitzaz. 1996. *The Indus Saga and the Making of Pakistan.* Karachi: Oxford University Press.

Aitken, E. H. 1986. *Gazetteer of the Province of Sind.* Reprint of 1907. Karachi: Indus.

Ajwani, L. H. 1991. *History of Sindhi Literature.* Lahore: Vanguard.

Alavi, Hamza. 1988. "Pakistan and Islam: Ethnicity and Ideology." In *State and ideology in the Middle East and Pakistan,* ed. Fred Halliday and Hamza Alavi, 64–111. London: MacMillan.

———. 1989. "Politics of Ethnicity in India and Pakistan." In *South Asia: Sociology of "Developing Societies,"* ed. Hamza Alavi and John Harris, 222–46. London: MacMillan.

———. 1991. "Nationhood and the Nationalities in Pakistan." In *Economy and Culture in Pakistan: Migrants and Cities in a Muslim Society,* ed. H. Donnan and P. Werbner, 163–87. London: MacMillan.

Alter, Joseph S. 1992. *The Wrestler's Body: Identity and Ideology in North India.* Berkeley: University of California Press.

———. 1994. "Somatic Nationalism: Indian Wrestling and Militant Hinduism." *Modern Asian Studies* 28(3): 557–88.

Anderson, Benedict. 1991. *Imagined Communities.* Reprint, London: Verso.

———. 1992. *Long Distance Nationalism: World Capitalism and the Rise of Identity Politics.* Amsterdam: Casa.

———. 1994. "Exodus." *Critical Inquiry.* 20(2):314–27.

Ansari, Sarah F. D. 1992. *Sufi Saints and State Power: The Pirs of Sind, 1843–1947.* Lahore: Vanguard.

Anwar, Raja. 1997. *The Terrorist Prince: The Life and Death of Murtaza Bhutto.* London: Verso.

Appadurai, Arjun. 1990. "Disjuncture and Difference in the Global Cultural Economy." In *Global Culture: Nationalism, Globalization and Modernity*, ed. Mike Featherstone. London: Sage, 295–310.

———. 1996. *Modernity at Large: Cultural Dimensions of Globalization.* Minneapolis: University of Minnesota Press.

———. 1999. "Dead Certainty: Ethnic Violence in the Era of Globalization." In *Globalization and Identity: Dialectics of Flow and Closure*, ed. Birgit Meyer and Peter Geschiere, 305–324. Oxford: Blackwell.

Appadurai, Arjun, and Carol A. Breckenridge. 1988. "Why Public Culture?" *Public Culture* 1(1): 5–10.

Apter, David. 1997. "Political Violence in Analytical Perspective." In *The Legitimization of Violence*, ed. Apter, 1–32. London: MacMillan.

Aziz, K. K. 1987. *Rahmat Ali: A Biography.* Lahore: Vanguard.

Bakhtin, Mikhail. 1984. *Rabelais and His World.* Bloomington: Indiana University Press.

Barth, Fredrik. 1960. "The System of Social Stratification in Swat, North Pakistan." In *Aspects of Caste in South India, Ceylon and North-West Pakistan*, ed. E. R. Leach, 113–46. Cambridge: Cambridge University Press.

———. 1969. *Ethnic Groups and Boundaries: The Social Organization of Culture Difference.* Oslo: Universitets Forlaget.

Bauman, Zygmunt. 1997. *Postmodernity and Its Discontents.* Cambridge: Polity Press.

Berland, Joseph. 1982. *No Five Fingers Are Alike.* Cambridge, MA: Harvard University Press.

Bhabha, Homi K. 1994. *The Location of Culture.* London: Routledge.

Bhutto, Benazir. 1988. *Daughter of the East.* London: Mandarin.

Bloch, Maurice. 1974. "Symbols, Song, Dance and Features of Articulation." *Archives Européeennes de Sociologie* 15: 55–81.

Bose, Sugata, and Ayesha Jalal. 1998. *Modern South Asia: History, Culture, Political Economy.* New York: Routledge.

Bourdieu, Pierre. 1999. "Rethinking the State: Genesis and Structure of the Bureaucratic Field." In *State/Culture: State-Formation after the Cultural Turn*, ed. G. Steinmetz, 53–76. Ithaca: Cornell University Press.

Bourdillon, M.F.C. 1978. "Knowing the World or Hiding It: A Response to Maurice Bloch." *Man* 13:591–99.

Bourgois, Philippe. 1995. *In Search of Respect: Selling Crack in El Barrio.* Cambridge: Cambridge University Press.

Brass, Paul. 1997. *Theft of an Idol: Text and Context in the Representation of Collective Violence.* Princeton: Princeton University Press.

Breckenridge, Carol A., and Peter Van der Veer. 1993. *Orientalism and the Postcolonial Predicament.* Philadelphia: University of Pennsylvania Press.

Brohi, A. K. 1981. "The Soul of Sind." In *Sind through the Centuries*, ed. Hamida Khuhro, 17–31. Karachi: Oxford University Press.

Buford, Bill. 1990. *Among the Thugs: The Experience and the Seduction of Crowd Violence*. New York: Norton.

Burton, Richard F. 1988. *Sindh and the Races That Inhabit the Valley of the Indus*. Reprint, Karachi: Indus.

———. 1993. *Sind Revisited*. Reprint, Karachi: Department of Culture and Tourism, Government of Sindh.

Canetti, Elias. 1960. *Masse und macht*. Hamburg: Claassen.

Chatterjee, Partha. 1986. *Nationalist Discourse and the Colonial World: A Derivative Discourse*. London: Zed Press.

———. 1993. *The Nation and Its Fragments*. Princeton: Princeton University Press.

Chaudri, Muhammad Ashraf. 1994. *The Muslim Ummah and Iqbal*. Islamabad: National Institute of Historical and Cultural Research.

Cohen, Anthony. 1985. *The Symbolic Construction of Community*. Chicester: Ellis Horwood.

Cohn, Bernard. 1987. *An Anthropologist among the Historians and Other Essays*. New York: Oxford University Press.

Crenshaw, Martha. 1988. "Theories of Terrorism: Instrumental and Organizational Approaches." In *Inside Terrorist Organizations*, ed. David Rapoport, 13–31. London: Frank Cass.

Dale, Stephen Frederic. 1994. *Indian Merchants and Eurasian Trade, 1600–1750*. Cambridge: Cambridge University Press.

Daniel, E. Valentine. 1984. *Fluid Signs: Being a Person the Tamil Way*. Berkeley: University of California Press.

———. 1996. *Charred Lullabies: Chapters in an Anthropography of Violence*. Princeton: Princeton University Press.

Davis, Natalie Zemon. 1973. "The Rites of Violence: Religious Riot in Sixteenth-Century France." *Past and Present* 59:51–91.

Donnan, Hastings. 1988. *Marriage among Muslims: Preference and Choice in Northern Pakistan*. Delhi: Hindustan Publishing Corporation.

Douglas, Mary. 1966. *Purity and Danger: An Analysis of the Concepts of Pollution and Taboo*. London: Routledge and Kegan Paul.

Dumont, Louis. 1972. *Homo Hierarchicus*. London: Paladin.

Durkheim, Emile. 1995. *The Elementary Forms of Religious Life*. Reprint, New York: Free Press.

Eastwick, E. B. 1849. *A Glance at Sind before Napier, or Dry Leaves from Young Egypt*. Karachi: Indus Publications.

Eickelman, Dale F. and James Piscatori. 1996. *Muslim Politics*. Princeton: Princeton University Press.

Ewing, Katherine Pratt. 1983. "The Politics of Sufism: Redefining the Saints of Pakistan," *Journal of Asian Studies* 42(2):251–68.

———. 1997. *Arguing Sainthood: Modernity, Psychoanalysis, and Islam*. Durham: Duke University Press.

Featherstone, M., ed. 1990. *Global Culture: Nationalism, Globalization and Identity*. London: Sage.

Feldman, Allen. 1991. *Formations of Violence: The Narrative of the Body and Political Terror in Northern Ireland*. Chicago: University of Chicago Press.

Fischer, Michael D. 1991. "Marriage and Power: Tradition and Transition in an Urban Punjabi Community." In *Economy and Culture in Pakistan: Migrants and Cities in a Muslim Society,* ed. H. Donnan and P. Werbner, 97–123. London: Macmillan.

Flaubert, Gustave. 1978. *Dictionaire des idées reçues suivi du Catalogue des idées chic.* Paris: Aubier Montaigne.

Freitag, Sandria. 1989. *Collective Action and Community: Public Arenas and the Emergence of Communalism in North India.* Berkeley: University of California Press.

Freud, Sigmund. 1923. *Massenpsychology und Ich-Analyse.* Leipzig: Internationaler Psychoanalytischer Verlag.

Fuller, C. J. and John Harriss. 2001. "For an Anthropology of the Modern Indian State." In *The Everyday State and Society in Modern India,* ed. C. J. Fuller and V. Bénéï, 1–30. London: Hurst.

Gardner, Katy. 1993. "Desh-Bidesh: Sylheti Images of Home and Away." *Man* 28(1): 1–15.

Geertz, Clifford. 1983. "Centers, Kings, and Charisma: Reflections on the Symbolics of Power." In *Local Knowledge: Further Essays in Interpretive Anthropology,* 121–46. New York: Basic Books.

———. 1993. *The Interpretation of Cultures.* Reprint, London: Fontana Press.

Gellner, Ernest. 1983. *Nations and Nationalisms.* Oxford: Blackwell.

Ghayur, Mohammad Arif, and J. Henry Korson. 1980. "The Effects of Population and Urbanization Growth Rates on the Ethnic Tensions in Pakistan." In *Contemporary Pakistan: Politics, Economy, and Society,* ed. Manzooruddin Ahmed, 204–27. Durham, NC: Carolina Academic Press.

Gilmartin, David. 1989. *Empire and Islam: Punjab and the Making of Pakistan.* Berkeley: University of California Press.

Gupta, Akhil. 1995. "Blurred Boundaries: The Discourse of Corruption, the Culture of Politics, and the Imagined State." *American Ethnologist* 22(2): 375–402.

Hakim, Khalifa Abdul. 1991. "Rumi, Nietzsche, and Iqbal." In *Iqbal as a Thinker,* 119–86. Lahore: Muhammad Ashraf.

Handelman, Don. 1990. *Models and Mirrors: Towards an Anthropology of Public Events.* Cambridge: Cambridge University Press.

Hanif, Muhammad. 1994. "Soldiers of Misfortune." *The News,* 2 December 1994.

Hansen, Thomas Blom. 1996a. "The Saffron Wave: Democratic Revolution and the Growth of Hindu Nationalism in India." Ph.D. diss., Roskilde University.

———. 1996b. "Recuperating Masculinity: Hindu Nationalism, Violence and the Exorcism of the Muslim 'Other.' " *Critique of Anthropology* 16(2): 137–72.

———. 1999. *The Saffron Wave: Democracy and Hindu Nationalism in Modern India.* Princeton: Princeton University Press.

———. 2001. *Wages of Violence: Naming and Identity in Postcolonial Bombay.* Princeton: Princeton University Press.

Hansen, Thomas Blom, and Finn Stepputat, eds. 2001. *States of Imagination: Ethnographic Explorations of the Postcolonial State.* Durham: Duke University Press.

Hasan, Arif. 1997. "The Growth of a Metropolis." In *Karachi: Megacity of Our Times*, ed. Hamida Khuhro and Anwer Mooraj, 171–96. Karachi: Oxford University Press.

Hassan, Ali. 1990. " 'You Can't Shoot me.' " *The Herald*, June 1990, pp. 34–35.

Hayden, Robert M. 1996. "Imagined Communities and Real Victims: Self-determination and Ethnic Cleansing in Yugoslavia." *American Ethnologist.* 23(4): 783–801.

Herzfeld, Michael. 1997. *Cultural Intimacy: Social Poetics in the Nation-State.* New York: Routledge.

Huizinga, Johan. 1938. *Homo ludens: Proeve ener bepaling van het spel-element der cultuur.* Haarlem: H. D. Tjeenk Willink.

Hussain, Akmal. 1990. "The Karachi Riots of December 1986: Crisis of State and Civil Society in Pakistan." In *Mirrors of Violence: Communities, Riots and Survivors in South Asia*, ed. Veena Das, 185–93. Delhi: Oxford University Press.

Hussain, Intizar. 1995. *Basti.* New Delhi: Indus.

Hussain, Syed Rashid. 1991. "In the Making." *The News.* 15 March 1991.

Hussain, Zahid. 1989. "Sindh: A Province Held at Ransom." *Herald Magazine.* August 1989, pp. 14–19.

Inden, Ronald. 1986. "Orientalist Constructions of India." *Modern Asian Studies* 20(3): 401–46.

Iqbal, Muhammad. 1954. *The Reconstruction of Religious Thought in Islam.* Reprint, Lahore: Javid Iqbal.

Ismail, Aquila, and Parveen Rahman. n.d. *Repair and Rehabilitation Aftermath of the December 1986 Riots: A Monograph.* Karachi: Orangi Pilot Project.

Ivianski, Zeev. 1988. "The Terrorist Revolution: Roots of Modern Terrorism." In *Inside Terrorist Organizations*, ed. David Rapoport, 129–49. Londen: Frank Cass.

Jaffrelot, Christophe. 1996. *The Hindu Nationalist Movement and Indian Politics, 1925 to the 1990s.* London: Hurst.

Jafri, A.B.S. 1996. *Behind the Killings Fields of Karachi: A City Refuses to Surrender.* Karachi: Royal Book Company.

Jalal, Ayesha. 1995. *Democracy and Authoritarianism in South Asia: A Comparative and Historical Perspective.* Cambridge: Cambridge University Press.

———. 1997. "Exploding Communalism: The Politics of Muslim Identity in South Asia." In *Nationalism, Democracy, and Development: State and Politics in India*, ed. Sugata Bose and Ayesha Jalal, 76–103. Delhi: Oxford University Press.

Jatoi, Hatim. 1995. *Baba-e-Sindh Hyder Bakhsh Jatoi, 1901–1970: Introduction and Excerpts from His Writings.* Hyderabad: Hatim Jatoi.

Jenkins, Richard. 1997. *Rethinking Ethnicity: Arguments and Explanations.* London: Sage.

Joyo, Muhammad Ibrahim. 1947. *Save Sind, Save the Continent (from Feudal Lords, Capitalists and Their Communalisms).* Karachi: Sind Renaissance Association.

Juergensmeyer, Mark. 1988. "The Logic of Religious Violence: The Case of the Punjab." *Contributions of Indian Sociology.* 22(1):65–88.

Karim, Mehtab S. and Warren C. Robinson. 1986. "The Migration Situation in Pakistan: An Analytical Review." In *Migration in Pakistan: Theories and Facts*, ed. F. Selier and M. S. Karim, 21–39. Lahore: Vanguard.

Kaviraj, Sudipta. 1997. "The Modern State in India." In *Dynamics of State Formation: India and Europe Compared*, ed. Martin Dornboos and Sudipta Kaviraj, 225–50. New Delhi: Sage Publications.

Khan, Aliya Azam. 1991. "The Muhajir Qaumi Movement." M.A. thesis, University of Pennsylvania.

Khan, Muhammad Ayub. 1967. *Friends Not Masters: A Political Autobiography.* Lahore: Oxford University Press.

Khan, Shafique Ali. 1973. *Two Nation Theory as a Concept, Strategy and Ideology.* Karachi: Royal Book Company.

Khuhro, Hamida. 1978. *The Making of Modern Sind: British Policy and Social Change in the Nineteenth Century.* Karachi: Indus.

———. 1981. "Muslim Political Organization in Sind, 1843–1938." In *Sind through the Centuries*, ed. Hamida Khuhro, 170–79. Karachi: Oxford University Press.

———. 1982. Introduction to *Documents on Separation of Sind from the Bombay Presidency*, ed. Hamida Khuhro. Islamabad: Islamic University.

Khuhro, Hamida, and Mooraj Anwer. 1997. *Karachi: Megacity of Our Times.* Karachi: Oxford University Press.

Khuhro, Muhammad Ayub. 1982. "A Story of the Sufferings of Sind: A Case for the Separation of Sind from the Bombay Presidency." In *Documents on Separation of Sind from the Bombay Presidency*, ed. Hamida Khuhro, 196–254. Islamabad: Islamic University.

Kumar, Nita. 1988. *The Artisans of Benares: Popular Culture and Identity, 1880–1986.* Princeton: Princeton University Press.

Kurin, Richard. 1984. "Morality, Personhood, and the Exemplary Life: Popular Conceptions of Muslims in Paradise." In *Moral Conduct and Authority: The Place of Adab in South Asian Islam*, ed. Barbara D. Metcalf. Berkeley: University of California Press: 196–220.

———. 1988. "The Culture of Ethnicity in Pakistan." In *Shari'at and Ambiguity in South Asian Islam*, ed. K. P. Ewing, 220–47. Berkeley: University of California Press.

Lambrick, H. T. 1995. *The Terrorist.* Reprint, Karachi: Oxford University Press.

Lapidus, Ira M. 1984. "Knowledge, Virtue, and Action: The Classical Muslim Conception of Adab and the Nature of Religious Fulfillment in Islam." In *Moral Conduct and Authority: The Place of Adab in South Asian Islam*, ed. B. D. Metcalf, 38–61. Berkeley: University of California Press.

Lari, Suhail Zaheer. 1994. *A History of Sindh.* Karachi: Oxford University Press.

Leach, Edmund. 1960. "Introduction: What Should We Mean by Caste?" In *Aspects of Caste in South India, Ceylon and North-West Pakistan*, 1–10. Cambridge: Cambridge University Press.

———. 1977. *Custom, Law, and Terrorist Violence.* Edinburgh: Edinburgh University Press.

Le Bon, Gustave. 1897. *La psychologie des foules.* Paris: Félix Alcan.

Lelyveld, David. 1978. *Aligarh's First Generation: Muslim Solidarity in British India*. Princeton: Princeton University Press.

Lindholm, Charles. 1986. "Caste in Islam and the Problem of Deviant Systems: A Critique of Recent Theory." *Contributions of Indian Sociology*, 20(1):61–73.

Lukas, Steven. 1973. *Emile Durkheim: His Life and Work*. London: Penguin.

MacClancy, Jeremy. 1996. *Sport, Identity and Ethnicity*. Oxford: Berg.

Malik, Iftikhar H. 1997. *State and Civil Society in Authority, Ideology and Ethnicity*. London: MacMillan.

Malik, Jamal. 1998. "The Literary Critique of Islamic Popular Religion in the Guise of Traditional Mysticism, or the Abused Woman." In *Embodied Charisma: Modernity, Locality and the Performance of Emotion in Sufi Cults*, ed. Pnina Werbner and Helene Basu. London: Routledge: 187–208.

Malkki, Liisa H. 1995. *Purity and Exile: Violence, Memory, and National Cosmology among Hutu Refugees in Tanzania*. Chicago: University of Chicago Press.

Masud, Muhammad Khalid. 1990. "The Obligation to Migrate: The Doctrine of Hijra in Islamic Law." In *Muslim Travellers: Pilgrimage, Migration, and the Religious Imagination*, ed. Dale F. Eickelman and James Piscatori: 29–49. London: Routledge.

———. 2002. "Rethinking Islamic Fundamentalism in Pakistan." Paper presented at the Institute of India-Pakistan Relations, Leicester University.

Metcalf, Barbara Daly. 1982. *Islamic Revival in British India: Deoband, 1860–1900*. Princeton: Princeton University Press.

———. 1984. *Moral Conduct and Authority: The Place of Adab in South Asian Islam*. Berkeley: University of California Press.

Meyer, Birgit and Peter Geschiere. 1999. *Globalization and Identity: Dialectics of Flow and Closure*. Oxford: Blackwell.

Mitchell, Timothy. 1991. "The Limits of the State: Beyond Statist Approaches and Their Critics." *American Political Science Review*. 85(1):77–96.

———. 1999. "Society, Economy, and the State Effect." In *State/Culture: State-Formation after the Cultural Turn*, ed. G. Steinmetz, 76–97. Ithaca: Cornell University Press.

Mujtaba, Hasan. 1993. "Murder in Uniform." *Newsline*, August 1993, pp. 45–47.

———. 1996. "Altered Scenario." *Newsline*. December 1996, pp. 75–78.

Nandy, Ashis. 1983. *The Intimate Enemy: Loss and Recovery of Self under Colonialism*. Delhi: Oxford University Press.

Nasr, Seyyed Vali Reza. 1992a. Students, Islam, and Politics: Islami Jami'at-i Tulaba in Pakistan." *Middle East Journal* 46(1):59–76.

———. 1992b. "Democracy and the Crisis of Governability in Pakistan." *Asian Survey* 32(6):521–37.

———. 1994. *The Vanguard of the Islamic Revolution: The Jama'at-i Islami of Pakistan*. London: Taurus.

———. 2002. "Islam, the State and the Rise of Sectarian Militancy in Pakistan." In *Pakistan: Nationalism without a Nation?* ed. C. Jaffrelot. New Delhi: Manohar: 85–114.

Nordstrom, C. and A. Robben. 1995. *Fieldwork under Fire: Contemporary Studies of Violence and Survival*. Berkeley: University of California Press.

Obeyesekere, Gananath. 1990. *The Work of Culture: Symbolic Transformation in Psychoanalysis and Anthropology.* Chicago: University of Chicago Press.

Pandey, Gyanendra. 1990. *The Construction of Communalism in Colonial North India.* New Delhi: Oxford University Press.

Parry, J. P. 2000. " 'The Crisis of Corruption' and 'the Idea of India': A Worm's Eye View." In *The Morals of Legitimacy,* ed. I. Pardo. Oxford: Berghahn: 27–55.

Pinch, William R. 1996. "Soldier Monks and Militant Sadhus." In *Contesting the Nation: Religion, Community, and the Politics of Democracy in India,* ed. David Ludden, 140–61. Philadelphia: University of Pennsylvania Press.

Pinney, Christopher. 2001. "Introduction: Public, Popular and Other Cultures." In *Pleasure and the Nation: The History, Politics and Consumption of Public Culture in India,* ed. R. Dwyer and C. Pinney, 1–34. Oxford: Oxford University Press.

Pirzada, D. A. 1995. *Growth of Muslim Nationalism in Sindh.* Karachi: Mehran.

Rahman, Tariq. 1996. *Language and Politics in Pakistan.* Karachi: Oxford University Press.

———. 1997. "The Literary Scene." In *Karachi: Megacity of Our Times,* ed. Hamida Khuhro and Anwer Mooraj, 219–30. Karachi: Oxford University Press.

Rehman, J. 1994. "Self-Determination, State-Building and the Muhajirs: An International Legal Perspective of the Role of Indian Muslim Refugees in the Constitutional Development of Pakistan." *Contemporary South Asia* 3(2):111–29.

Rehman, Yusuf. 1989. "Moharram: Changing Patterns." *The Herald.* September 1989, pp. 27–28.

Rizvi, Saiyid Athar Abbas. 1975. *A History of Sufism in India, Volume One.* New Delhi: Munshiram Manoharlal.

Rosen, Lawrence. 1984. *Bargaining for Reality: The Construction of Social Relations in a Muslim Community.* Chicago: University of Chicago Press.

Rosenzweig, Roy. 1983. *Eight Hours for What We Will.* New York: Cambridge University Press.

Roy, Asim. 1983. *The Islamic Syncretistic Tradition in Bengal.* Princeton: Princeton University Press.

Sakata, Hiromi Lorraine. 1997. "Spiritual Music and Dance in Pakistan." *Etnofoor.* 10(1/2):165–73.

Sarwar, Beena. 1990. "The 'Pir' of Azizabad." *Frontier Post.* 27 April 1990.

Sassen, Saskia. 1999. *Guests and Aliens.* New York: The New Press.

Schimmel, Annemarie. 1981. "Shah Abdul Latif's Sur Sarang." In *Sind through the Centuries,* ed. Hamida Khuhro, 245–51. Karachi: Oxford University Press.

———. 1986. "In Memorian Ernst Trumpp." In *Pearls from the Indus: Studies in Sindhi Culture,* ed. A. Schimmel, 19–53. Jamshoro: Sindhi Adabi Board.

Schlesinger, Philip. 1991. *Media, State and Nation: Political Violence and Collective Identities.* London: Sage.

Schubel, Vernon James. 1993. *Religious Performances in Contemporary Islam: Shi'i Devotional Rituals in South Asia.* Columbia: University of South Carolina Press.

Shaheed, Farida. 1990. "The Pathan-Muhajir Conflicts, 1985–6: A National Perspective." In *Mirrors of Violence: Communities, Riots and Survivors in South Asia,* ed. V. Das, 194–214. Delhi: Oxford University Press.

Sharar, Abdul Halim. 1975. *Lucknow: The Last Phase of an Oriental Culture.* Transl. and ed. E. S. Harcourt and Fakhir Hussain, Delhi: Oxford University Press.

Sherani, Saifur Rahman. 1991. "*Ulema* and *Pir* in the Politics of Pakistan." In *Economy and Culture in Pakistan: Migrants and Cities in a Muslim Society,* ed. H. Donnan and P. Werbner. London: MacMillan, 216–46.

Siddiqi, Shaukat. 1991. *Khuda ki Basti.* New Delhi: Rupa and Co.

Soomro, A. D. 1988. "The Manzilgah Masjid Agitation 1939." In *Studies on Sind,* ed. M. Y. Mughul, 123–30. Jamshoro: University of Sind.

Sorley, H. T. 1940. *Shah Abdul Latif of Bhit: His Poetry, Life and Times.* Karachi: Sindh Kitab Ghar.

———. 1968. *The Gazetteer of West Pakistan: The Former Province of Sind (Including Khairpur State).* Lahore: Government of West Pakistan.

Stallybrass, Peter and Allon White. 1986. *The Politics and Poetics of Transgression.* Ithaca: Cornell University Press.

Steinmetz, George. 1999. *State/Culture: State-Formation after the Cultural Turn.* Ithaca: Cornell University Press.

Stepanyants, M. T. 1971. *Pakistan: Philosophy and Sociology.* Moscow: Nauka.

Syed, Anwar. 1992. *The Discourse and Politics of Zulkikar Ali Bhutto.* London: MacMillan.

Syed, Durreshahwar. 1988. *The Poetry of Shah Abd al-Latif.* Hyderabad: Sindhi Adabi Board.

Syed, G. M. 1986. *Religion and Reality.* Karachi: Syed and Syed.

———. 1996. *Shah Latif and His Message.* Sehwan: Sain.

Talbot, Ian. 1996. *Freedom's Cry: The Popular Dimension in the Pakistan Movement and Partition Experience in North-West India.* Karachi: Oxford University Press.

———. 1998. *Pakistan: A Modern History.* London: Hurst.

Tambiah, Stanley. 1986. *Sri Lanka: Ethnic Fratricide and the Dismantling of Democracy.* Chicago: University of Chicago Press.

———. 1996. *Leveling Crowds: Ethnonationalist Conflicts and Collective Violence in South Asia.* Berkeley: University of California Press.

Taussig, Michael. 1987. *Shamanism, Colonialism, and the Wild Man: A Study in Terror and Healing.* Chicago: University of Chicago Press.

Thompson, E. P. 1964. *The Making of the English Working Class.* London: Victor Gollancz.

———. 1973. "The Moral Economy of the English Crowd in the Eighteenth Century." *Past and Present* 50:76–136.

Tilly, Charles. 1978. *From Mobilization to Revolution.* New York: Random House.

Turner, Victor. 1967. *The Forest of Symbols: Aspects of Ndembu Ritual.* Ithaca: Cornell University Press.

———. 1969. *The Ritual Process: Structure and Anti-structure.* London: Routledge and Kegan Paul.

———. 1974. *Dramas, Fields, and Metaphors: Symbolic Action in Human Society.* Ithaca: Cornell University Press.

Van der Veer, Peter. 1994. *Religious Nationalism: Hindus and Muslims in India.* Berkeley: University of California Press.

Van der Veer, Peter. 1995. *Nation and Migration: The Politics of Space in the South Asian Diaspora*. Philadelphia: University of Pennsylvania Press.

———. 1997. " 'The Enigma of Arrival': Hybridity and Authenticity in the Global Space." In *Debating Cultural Hybridity: Multi-Cultural Identities and the Politics of Anti-racism*, ed. P. Werbner and T. Modood, 90–105. London: Zed Books.

Varma, P. K. 1999. *The Great Indian Middle Class*. New Delhi: Penguin.

Verdery, Katherine. 1996. *What Was Socialism, and What Comes Next?* Princeton: Princeton University Press.

Verkaaik, Oskar. 1994. *A People of Migrants*. Amsterdam: VU University Press.

———. 2001. "The Captive State: Corruption, Intelligence Agencies, and Ethnicity in Pakistan." In *States of Imagination: Ethnographic Explorations of the Postcolonial State*, ed. T. B. Hansen and F. Stepputat, 345–64. Durham: Duke University Press.

Werbner, Pnina. 1989. "The Ranking of Brotherhoods: The Dialectics of Muslim Caste among Overseas Pakistanis." *Contributions to Indian Sociology.* 23(2):285–315.

———. 1990. *The Migration Process: Capital, Gifts and Offerings among British Pakistanis*. New York: Berg.

———. 1996. "'Our Blood Is Green': Cricket, Identity and Social Empowerment among British Pakistanis." In *Sport, Identity and Ethnicity*, ed. Jeremy MacClancy, 87–112. Oxford: Berg.

———. 1997. "Essentialising Essentialism, Essentialising Silence: Ambivalence and Multiplicity in the Constructions of Racism and Ethnicity." In *Debating Cultural Hybridity: Multi-cultural Identities and the Politics of Anti-racism*, ed. P. Werbner and T. Modood, 226–54. New Jersey: Zed Books.

———. 1998. "*Langar*: Pilgrimage, Sacred Exchange and Perpetual Sacrifice in a Sufi Saint's Lodge." In *Embodying Charisma: Modernity, Locality and the Performance of Emotion in Sufi Cults*, ed. P. Werbner and H. Basu, 95–116. London: Routledge.

Werbner, P. and H. Basu, eds. 1998. *Embodying Charisma: Modernity, Locality and the Performance of Emotion in Sufi Cults*. London: Routledge.

Westwood, Sallie. 1995. "Gendering Diaspora: Space, Politics, and South Asian Masculinities in Britain." In *Nation and Migration: The Politics of Space in the South Asian Diaspora*, ed. Peter van der Veer, 197–221. Philadelphia: University of Pennsylvania Press.

Wheeler, Richard S. 1970. *The Politics of Pakistan: A Constitutional Quest*. Ithaca: Cornell University Press.

Whyte, William Foote. 1940. *Street Corner Society. The Social Structure of an Italian Slum*. Chicago: University of Chicago Press.

Wolpert, Stanley. 1993. *Zulfi Bhutto of Pakistan: His Life and Times*. New York: Oxford University Press.

Zaidi, S. Akbar. 1992. "The Economic Bases of the National Question in Pakistan: An Indication." In *Regional Imbalances and the National Question in Pakistan*, ed. Zaidi, 90–138. Lahore: Vanguard.

Zaman, Muhammad Qasim. 1998. "Sectarianism in Pakistan: The Radicalization of Shiʿi and Sunni Identities." *Modern Asian Studies* 32(3): 689–716.

Ziring, Lawrence. 1971. *The Ayub Khan Era: Politics in Pakistan, 1958–1969.* Syracuse: Syracuse University Press.

Žižek, Slavoj. 1989. *The Sublime Object of Ideology.* London: Verso.

Zulaika, Joseba. 1988. *Basque Violence: Metaphor and Sacrament.* Reno: University of Nevada Press.

Zulaika, Joseba, and William A. Douglass. 1996. *Terror and Taboo: The Follies, Fables, and Faces of Terrorism.* New York: Routledge.

Texts in Urdu

Ahmad, Munir. 1996. *MQM.* Lahore: Gora Publishers.

Shaheen, Safdar. n.d. *Karachi Jalta Rahaa* (Karachi kept on burning). Multan: Book Land.

Government Publications

Government of Pakistan Department of Archaeology. n.d. *Report on the Use/Encroachment of Archeological Area of Pucca Fort, Hyderabad.*

Government of Sind, Home Department. 1950. *Report of the Court of Inquiry on the Rioting and Firing at Hyderabad (Sind) on 23rd October 1950.*

MQM Publications

1988. *Qarardad-e maqasid: Muhajir Qaumi Movement kiya chahti hai?* (Objective resolution: What does the Muhajir Qaumi Movement aspire to?) MQM Information and Publicity Department.

———. 1991. *Ghariboon ki hukmaraani: MQM ke Qaʿid Altaf Hussain ki ek tarikhi press conference* (The rule of the poor: A historic press conference of MQM's leader Altaf Hussain). MQM Information and Publicity Department.

———. 1994. *MQM Demands Fundamental and Constitutional Rights for Muhajirs.* Karachi.

n.d. *MQM ki palicy kiya hai? Qaʿid-i-tehreek Altaf Hussain ka aham palicy bayan* (What is the policy of the MQM? An important policy statement of Movement's leader Altaf Hussain). Karachi: Muhajir Academy.

n.d. *Nothing But the Whole Truth.* London: Research and Information Cell MQM.

n.d. *A Brief History of the Muhajir Qaumi Movement.*

Index